HISTORY
of
EDUCATION

BARRON'S COLLEGE REVIEWS
WORLD LITERATURE SERIES

An inexpensive paperbound series of expertly written books designed to clarify the great literary works for study or general reading. Each volume contains detailed summaries, interpretations and criticisms of all major and many minor works, historical backgrounds, and biographical data.

CANTERBURY TALES (AN INTERLINEAR TRANSLATION), Hopper 1.50

CLASSICS, Greek and Roman, Reinhold *REVISED*   1.95

CONTEMPORARY LITERATURE, Heiney   1.95

ENGLISH LITERATURE, Grebanier   Vol. I, *REVISED*, 1.75; Vol. II 1.75

ENGLISH ROMANTIC WRITERS, Battenhouse   1.95

EUROPEAN LITERATURE, Hopper-Grebanier Vol. I, 1.50; Vol. II 1.75

BIBLIOGRAPHY OF EUROPEAN LITERATURE,
Hopper-Grebanier   cloth 2.95

RECENT AMERICAN LITERATURE, Heiney   1.95

BARRON'S EDUCATIONAL SERIES, INC.
343 Great Neck Road, Great Neck, N. Y.

ESSENTIALS OF

HISTORY

of

EDUCATION

S. E. Frost, Jr., Ph.D.

Assistant Professor of Education

Brooklyn College

Barron's Educational Series Inc.

343 Great Neck Road, Great Neck, New York

Copyright, 1947

By BARRON'S EDUCATIONAL SERIES, INC.

No part of the material covered by this copyright
may be reproduced in any form without
permission in writing from
the publisher.

Printed in United States of America

Preface

The best thinking in the area of teacher preparation recognizes the strategic position of the History of Education. Techniques of curriculum construction, methods of teaching specific subject material, and the principles of education are important but without the history of education they all lack perspective and teaching is little more than a trade. Only when the teacher is well grounded in the history of education does he have that perspective which raises his occupation into a profession.

Essentials of the History of Education is a contribution to the creating of this perspective. It is in no way intended as a textbook in the field and should be used only as a companion to the text best suited to the purposes of the instructor. *Essentials of the History of Education* is a study guide. In it are combined the best features of a number of standard texts. It contains, in outline and summary fashion, much material not usually included in a text but necessary as supplementary to a good course.

The instructor can make use of this volume to direct his students' thinking into background materials upon which additional work in terms of papers and reports can be prepared. He can also use it to point up discussions and summarize the material of each unit of his course, fixing in the minds of his pupils the salient points of the work. The bibliographical sections will enable him to direct the students' reading beyond the text he is using and into areas of special interest and significance.

The pupil can use this book to bring into focus large bodies of material usually presented by the text and the instructor. In a few sections he will find concentrated the material which he and his instructor have gathered relative to the unit. Further, the book is invaluable for review purposes since the major points are arranged in order of importance and concise statements of important facts are made available to him.

As with all such works, *Essentials of the History of Education* owes much to unnamed individuals. My instructors in the field at Texas Christian University, Southern Methodist University, the University of Texas, and Columbia University have all left their imprint upon my thinking. The numerous texts and other books in the area of the history of education used in preparing this volume have made their contribution. Then there are the hundreds of pupils who have sat in my classes during the many years I have been teaching the course. In their efforts to master the material of the course they have impressed upon me the need for a book of this type. They have also suggested to me from time to time the arrangement of the material, an arrangement which would meet their needs. In addition, I want to express my appreciation to Mr. Charles Smith, Instructor in Education at Brooklyn College, who urged me to undertake the preparation of this book and made many valuable suggestions during the time it was in preparation. Although I owe much to all of these sources, the responsibility for the final form of the book and for whatever errors it may contain is my own.

Brooklyn College
Brooklyn, New York
September, 1947

S. E. FROST, JR., PH.D.
Assistant Professor of Education

Table Of Contents

CHAPTER I

Education In Primitive Communities

Primitive Cultures. Distinguish between prehistoric cultures and primitive cultures:

PREHISTORIC - before written records. Many relics of prehistoric cultures remain. We may infer from these something of the social patterns and practices of prehistoric people.

PRIMITIVE - simple society, crude, "culturally arrested," intellectual infancy, "nature people." Many primitive people are living today. A study of present-day primitive communities may reveal parallels with prehistoric communities, but there is danger in considering prehistoric and primitive synonymous.

Why Study the Education of Primitive Communities? To discover the simple forms out of which modern education has developed and to contrast the simple with the complex.

Primitive people deal, in a simpler setting, with the essential problems of all education.

To understand present-day primitive communities and deal with their educational problems more wisely.

Primitive Cultural Patterns

CHARACTERISTICS. Primitive culture is relatively simple; its arts are not highly specialized or differentiated; it has narrow social and cultural contacts; its organization is tribal; it lacks the methods and content of exact scholarship; there is an absence of reading and writing; it is conservative, superstitious.

EDUCATIONAL AIMS

1. *Practical Education:* To enable the individual to satisfy his immediate wants: economic - to make the most of his environment; social - to live with his fellow men; leisure time - to express his impulse to create.

2. *Theoretical Education:* To enable the individual to deal with the unseen: philosophical and religious - to feel at home in the world and at peace with himself.

3. *General Aim of Both Practical and Theoretical: Conservative:* to transmit unchanging practices that have proved successful and to subordinate the individual to the group.

EDUCATIONAL AGENCIES AND METHODS. Primitive educational agencies include the family, community life, and initiatory ceremonies. The

1

methods employed are observation, participation, trial and error, instruction by parents and old men of the community.

Initiatory Ceremonies

PUBERTY RITES. The only formal education among primitive people. A boy, at adolescence, is instructed by the elders and admitted to full membership in the community. "A short course in tribal lore." These rites aim to stamp out any tendency toward individualism and to impress upon the youth his social status and responsibilities. They are severe tests of endurance, obedience, and self-control.

MEMBERSHIP IN SECRET FRATERNITIES. Similar to modern lodges or fraternities. There are values and dangers to the social group in these organizations. They give the initiate a special status in the community and may become socially oppressive. They cut across customs and laws.

OCCUPATIONAL GROUP MEMBERSHIP. Similar to medieval guilds or some modern labor unions. Controlled by members and tend to monopolize the occupation. Members initiate those especially chosen and instruct them in the secrets of the occupation. Often they entrench groups in an occupation and narrow the opportunities of others.

Religious Education

CONTENT: belief in animism, totemism, ancestor worship.

METHODS: observation of and participation in religious ceremonies - dances, processions, dramas, prayers, making of sacrifices and offerings. Instruction by parents and during initiatory rites.

Education of Girls and Women.
Much like that of men, but the emphasis is upon home duties. The girl learns from her mother by observation and participation. At adolescence there are initiatory ceremonies for membership in special groups, puberty rites for girls, and instruction by the elders in duties and responsibilities.

Meaning for Students of Education.
The educational practices and institutions of every group are conditioned by their culture.

The necessity for logical sciences. All primitive communities lack these and cannot progress to a higher civilized status.

Rites, customs, and traditions are valuable educative forces.

Ordinary life situations and incidental instruction are important teachers in any society.

The family, as an educative institution, is found in all cultures.

The forms of education are intimately related to the forms of social organization.

BIBLIOGRAPHY

Adams, John, *Evolution of Educational Theory*, pp. 104-127. London, Macmillan & Co., Ltd., 1912.

Barnes, Harry Elmer, *An Intellectual and Cultural History of the Western World*, pp. 27-61. New York, Random House, 1937.

Eby, Frederick and Arrowood, Charles F., *The History and Philosophy of Education, Ancient and Medieval*, pp. 1-35. New York, Prentice-Hall, Inc., 1940.

Frazer, James George, *The Golden Bough*. New York, The Macmillan Company, 1935.

Graves, Frank P., *A History of Education, Before the Middle Ages*, pp. 8-19, New York, The Macmillan Company, 1925.

Graves, Frank P., *A Student's History of Education*, pp. 10-12. New York, The Macmillan Company, 1936.

Hambly, W. D., *Origins of Education Among Primitive Peoples*, Chapters II-IV. London, Macmillan & Co., Ltd., 1926.

Miller, Nathan, *The Child in Primitive Society*, Chapters VIII-X. New York, Brentano's, 1928.

Monroe, Paul, *A Text-Book in the History of Education*, pp. 1-16. New York, The Macmillan Company, 1907.

Monroe, Paul, *A Brief Course in the History of Education*, pp. 1-10. New York, The Macmillan Company, 1909.

Monroe, Paul (Editor), *Cyclopedia of Education*, Vol. V, pp. 31-35. New York, The Macmillan Company, 1911.

Mulhern, James, *A History of Education*, pp. 24-58. Ronald Press Co., New York, 1946.

Webster, Hutton, *Primitive Secret Societies*, Chapters I-V. New York, The Macmillan Company, 1932.

Wilds, Elmer H., *The Foundations of Modern Education*, pp. 15-34. New York, Rinehart & Company, Inc., 1942.

CHAPTER II

Education Among Transition People

Transition People. The ethnological term for primitive culture is savagery. Many people, in the development of their culture, pass beyond most of the characteristics of savagery but have not as yet reached the stage of civilization. This intermediate stage is referred to by ethnologists and historians as barbarism. People at this state are often called transition people.

Most important of transition people are: Babylonian and Assyrian, Chinese, Egyptian, Hindu, Persian, and Phoenician. Some of these moved gradually into the stage of civilization while others did not.*

BABYLONIAN AND ASSYRIAN EDUCATION

1. *History* (c. 4000 to 539 B.C.)

   Growth of the Babylonian Empire - it extended over the Tigris-Euphrates district and Syria, 2300-1600 B.C.; importance of Hammurabi - law code. **Revolt** of the city of Assur from Babylonia and growth of the kingdom of Assyria; Babylonia and Assyria equal. **Assyrian Supremacy** - rise began in the 10th century B.C. and extended sway over Babylonia; height of the empire reached by 670 B.C. **Assyrian Collapse** - Medes and Babylonians destroyed Assyria at the end of the 7th century B.C.; return of Babylonian magnificence. **Babylonia Crushed** - by the Medes allied with the Persians in 539 B.C.

2. *Social Pattern*

   Classes: King, nobility and priests, soldiers, common people; rise of the commercial and trade classes. Society was never a caste system. **Women** were treated with some consideration but subordinated to men.

3. *Religion and Ethics.* Religion began as nature worship - polytheism - organized into henotheism (various gods held as supreme at different times). There was little understanding of ethical principles and fear was the motive for morals.

4. *Cultural Pattern*

   Science: Some progress was made in engineering, arithmetic, geometry, mechanics, astronomy, and medicine. There was no real science, merely empirical knowledge mixed with superstition. **Architecture:** This was comparatively advanced but inclined to conventionality. **Literature:** There

* While each of these transition people is important educationally and illustrates some particular phase of development, if limited by time one may consider only the Egyptian as typical.

4

were many large libraries of clay books on religious and scientific subjects, history, and official documents; there were reading books, grammars, and lexicons. Assurbanipal's library at Nineveh contained many thousand volumes.

5. *Education*

Aim: practical; education was preparation for professions; often called priestly. **Organization and Content:** some elementary education; above this was training given in temple schools and in libraries; some technical subjects were taught. **Method:** memorization and imitation; individual instruction rather than class work; many teachers of elementary work; priests taught the advanced work. **Influence upon Progress:** held to the conventional; individuality was disregarded; influenced the Phoenicians, Greeks, and Jews.

CHINESE EDUCATION IN TRANSITION STAGE

1. *The Chinese Nation.* The country is almost twice the size of the United States with a population five times as great today. Accurate knowledge of its history dates from the 7th century B.C. Its educational system was established in 617 B.C. and remained comparatively unchanged until the early part of the 20th century. Since the Revolution there has been much copying of western educational procedures.

Confucius (551-478 B.C.) saved China from a growing degeneracy and civil disorder. His doctrines are contained in the *Five Classics* and the *Four Books*. Mencius (372-289), a disciple, wrote the second of the *Four Books*.

2. *Chinese Religion and Ethics.* In early Chinese religion Heaven, the Ultimate Principle, sanctioned the tradition which everyone had to follow blindly - no individualism was permitted. This was expressed in family relationships: the father was endowed with absolute power. The state was .a development of the family with the Emperor as absolute ruler. Religious observances were formal and based upon ancestor worship.

Confucianism was the state religion professed by the educated people; the masses followed an idolatrous form of Buddhism and a degenerate Taoism.

3. *Chinese Culture.* The language was monosyllabic, analytic, and juxtapositive. The literature was dry, formal, and written in a language so different from the colloquial that only the highly educated could read.

Devotion to the past blocked the advance of science, arts, and crafts. There was some beauty and delicacy of production in art materials, but largely cramped and imitative.

4. *Chinese Education*

Aim of Education: To conserve the past and maintain things as tradition dictated; to produce uniformity. Thus, education "was static, ancestor, family, or formal," trained one to pass examinations. **Means of Education:** There was no national system of schools, but the state encouraged private schools designed to train boys to pass the state examinations. Women were excluded from the examinations and only girls of wealthy families had any education beyond that of family duties and deportment. a) Elementary schools - met in the teacher's home or that of a wealthy patron; much ceremony attached; the work was severe and the hours long; practice of backing the book (turning back to teacher who holds the book and reciting the lesson loudly). Teachers were highly revered. b) Academies - a few existed for higher training for passing state examinations. c) Examinations - there were two preliminary examinations and three tests for degrees. The fourth examination, open to those who had the doctor's degree, led to the Imperial Academy (the Emperor's cabinet). Examinations led to state offices. Those who failed became teachers. Examinations were rigorous and formal. **Course of Study:** a) Elementary period - children learned important language characters, committed nine sacred books to memory, learned to write, and learned some arithmetic. This lasted five or six years and was all the education most boys received. b) Second period - the nine sacred books were translated into modern Chinese; commentaries were studied and meanings made clear, c) Third period - essays and poems were written in the style of the *Five Classics*. A student could continue until he passed the government examination. **Teaching Methods:** Extreme formalism, memorization, exact imitation; instruction was individual; much shouting when reciting; writing learned by tracing a model set by the instructor. More advanced education sought imitation of the classical style, no originality. The student had to memorize classical works and practice writing prose and verse. Discipline was harsh and artificial stimulation was used to overcome the deadliness of the material employed. All methods sought to bind the individual to the past and suppress all individuality, initiative, or originality. **Results:** This education secured the stability of society, the perpetuity of the empire, and conservation of the past. It gave thorough training in retentiveness, the application to mastery of details, ability to recognize fine distinctions of form, ability to imitate; but no initiative, inventiveness, adaptability, creativity.

ANCIENT EGYPTIAN EDUCATION

1. *Significance for Students of Education.* Here we have a culture dating back to approximately 5000 B.C. Here are the roots of conceptions basic to western civilization: righteousness, truth, justice, the moral distinction between right and wrong, the operation of conscience, and

the conception of one god. The dry, mild climate has helped preserve a great mass of historical material: pictures, sculpture, tombs, buildings, and mummies. Egyptian culture is in the direct line, through the Jews and the Greeks, to modern western cultures.

2. *The Egyptian Cultural Pattern*

Development of the Arts and Crafts: Egyptian craftsmen attained great proficiency in a) building: producing the pyramids, obelisks, and temples; b) irrigation, growing out of the need for control of the Nile river and use of its waters, and c) embalming. **Development of Institutions and Ethical Concepts:** a) The family was the source of the deeper feelings of social relationships. It became the basis for religion, the training of children, transmitting the secrets of trades and arts, and private property. b) Society grew from primitive uniformity to a vast bureaucratic organization, then became decentralized as individualism increased. It was not a caste system though classes were clearly marked. There were the ruling class or landowners, freemen, and slaves. The upper classes were well educated. c) The government had its beginning when the Lord of Heliopolis organized the principalities of Egypt into a unified pattern before 4000 B.C. This was followed by the growth of a strong autocratic rule between 3500 and 2500 B.C. This was in the hands of despots and the priesthood. The despot had absolute power, in theory, but was limited actually by the priestly class, powerful nobles, and written law. The population was under bureaucratic control. d) The religion transcended primitive nature worship and animism.. There were many gods, including the sun, the earth, and the Nile river. This religion had no relation to the moral life of the people for a long time. Gradually, however, the moral order found in the family was transferred to the universe as a whole. This led to monotheism. Central in the religion was preparation for life after death. Death was a happy thing, as one might prepare to retire and enjoy himself. The *Book of the Dead* was the official handbook of the after life. **Development of the Sciences and Higher Arts:** These evolved in vital connection with the growth of practical skills in the arts and crafts. They were empirical: wholly the result of experience; action preceded thought, and practical experience reconditioned thought. a) Arithmetic grew out of a need for counting, but the Egyptian never understood clearly the fundamental arithmetic operations. b) Geometry grew out of a need for measuring the earth. It was not a science, but merely the art of measuring. The Egyptian did not think abstractly. c) Astronomy grew out of a need for control of the Nile river. The Egyptians devised a calendar in 4241 B.C. They also made some maps of the heavens. d) Mechanics was an area in which the Egyptians excelled. Their buildings were mechanically perfect. e) Geography consisted in making some maps and learning about the lands and their characteristics. f) Medical knowledge was written down by Imhotep in 3000 B.C. and no one was allowed to deviate from his prescriptions. The Egyptians had little knowledge of anatomy since the body was preserved for its future life. Knowledge in this area was empirical, not scientific. **Development of the Language Arts:** a) Symbolism, drawing, and writing were stages in a development. Writing developed from drawing. The circumstances that encouraged advance in writing were the availability of quantities of papyrus and other writing materials, the need for writing in government and business, and the use of writing in religion, making inscriptions on tombs, and conduct of temple business. b) The alphabet evolved from picture writing, from pictogram to phonogram.

3. *The Egyptian Educational Pattern*

Elementary Education: During the Old Kingdom (3000 to 2000 B.C.) education was largely in the hands of the father. There were no public schools. Though accurate data is lacking, it appears that three types of elementary schools developed during the Middle Kingdom (2000 to 1600 B.C.) and the New Kingdom (1600 to 1000 B.C.): a) Temple schools in every temple, taught by the priests, in which boys learned to write; b) Court schools established in the courts to train the heir to the throne and some companions in the duties of royalty, and c) Department schools conducted in each government department to prepare boys for official careers. All this education was vocational. The boys learned to write the vocabulary of specific careers and engaged in apprentice duties. The school day ended at noon. Among the subjects taught were writing, arithmetic, fairy tales, swimming, sacred songs, dancing, manners, and morals. **Secondary Education:** At this level the teachers used copybooks to teach writing along with morals. The emphasis was upon style in schools for higher officials after 2000 B.C. Works studied were largely from the Middle Kingdom. Among these was *The Speeches of the Eloquent Peasant*. **Educational Principles:** a) Motivation: the boy was motivated to learn to write by ambition to become a scribe and enjoy his lot, to gain promotion to high office, and to avoid harsh punishment. b) Moral aim: morals were practical and prudential. The basic qualities sought were bravery, good character, social and personal responsibilities. The literature was didactic. It taught piety toward the gods, a sense of absolute submission to the supreme and overshadowing will of these gods, abject loyalty to the king, slavish deference to officials, honor to parents, neighborliness especially toward the poor and needy, and self control. Moral action was motivated largely by the law of reward and favor and aimed at happiness in a purely worldly life. **Professional Education:** a) Higher liberal education was centered in the temples. The subjects taught included ancient forms of writing, geography, cosmography, astronomy, chronology, sculpture, painting, ritual dancing, theory of music, law, medicine, morals, arithmetic, mensuration, hydrostatics, and architecture. b) Education for professional careers emphasized practice rather than theory. Secrets of each profession were handed down within a family and transmitted through apprenticeship. The areas of professional training included medicine, the priesthood, the military, architecture, and skills of the scribe.

4. *Causes of the Decline of Egyptian Culture.* The priests gained a monopoly of higher learning, were conservative, slaves to traditional practices, feared change, and held learning in slavery to the past.

Formalism came to dominate all art.

The Egyptian became mentally lazy. He lost his early mental and physical energy.

All practices came under the domination of the older men who had lost the spur of desire and the power to adjust to new conditions.

Egyptian education was an apprenticeship.

The incapacity of the Egyptian mind to ascend from the level of the practical and the empirical to that of the scientific and the universal. The Egyptian thought on the level of individual cases, in terms of concrete situations, rather than on that of general principles. Having exhausted the stimulus and growth that springs from practical needs, his thinking was spent. He used science for practical needs and had no conception of the search for truth as an end. He showed no genuine intellectual curiosity.

PERSIAN EDUCATION

1. *Social Pattern.* The Persians lived in a physical environment which made them rugged and warlike so that they tended to prey upon their more wealthy neighbors. *Cyrus* (d. 528 B.C.) added much to the Persian empire. *Darius* (d. 485 B.C.) completed the empire, which was the largest the world had ever known. This empire was made up of many "provinces" with great autonomy and independence. Conquered people were permitted to have freedom in customs and religion. At home administration was wise and the laws were just and humane. The religion was militant. At its base was a dualism of Ormazd and Ahriman formulated about 600 B.C. by Zoroaster. The Magi were the priests of this belief. The masses had another religion, a

worship of natural forces. There was no idolatry. Belief persisted in
bodily resurrection and a final trial of the soul. There was no caste
system. The religious beliefs are stated fully in the *Zend-Avesta*.

   2. *Educational Pattern*

   Aim was to produce a nation of soldiers, thus people who were strong
physically, brave, resourceful. **Organization and Content:** a) From birth
to 5 years the boys were trained at home by the women to obey and the
girls were given domestic training. b) From 5 to 15 years was the period
of formal training when the boy was introduced into the national religion. The more wealthy and aristocratic boys were given some military
training and ethical instruction and were indoctrinated with the national
tradition. There was no literary or intellectual training. c) From 15 to
manhood the boy was given more military training with service to the
state and attendance upon the important religious ceremonies. At the
conclusion of this he was made a citizen. (See Xenaphon's *Cyropaedia*).
d) Higher education was for the Magi only and consisted of study of the
sacred scriptures, philosophy, astrology, medicine, law, and finance. The
aim at this level was to prepare advisers to the Great King. **The method**
was informal, imitation, precepts and examples. Constant practice was
stressed. **The results** included a high regard for personality (individualism). The unity which existed during the rise of the empire disappeared
with completion of the empire. Education made good soldiers but failed
to train for peace and leisure. There was a lack of moral strength.

   PHOENICIAN EDUCATION

   1. *Social Pattern.* Phoenicia was a small area, about 2000 square
miles, but with an extensive empire. The people were engaged in commerce
and manufacture. They borrowed much from others but made some improvements
in what was borrowed. They reached a high development in the science of
navigation, weights, measures, and money. They gave us the phonetic
alphabet. They were a materialistic people absorbed in money-getting,
were cruel, crafty, hypocritical, and treacherous. Their religious
conceptions were crude and often disgusting.

   2. *Educational Pattern.* The aim of education was industrial and
commercial. Reading, writing, and knowledge of the arts and sciences
were taught in the schools. Their ethical teachings were depraved and
individual initiative was repressed. The Phoenicians are a good example
of the destructive effect of a purely industrial education and absorption
in commercial success.

   ANCIENT HINDU EDUCATION

   1. *Social Pattern.* **The people** were Aryan. Aboriginal tribes, overcome
by the enervating climate, were invaded by Aryans about 2000 B.C. The

early Hindus were nature worshippers. **Their religion** grew from nature worship to Brahmanism. The latter was a mystical religion of unity in Brahma. It taught metempsychosis. Brahmanism was for the priestly class; the masses had only a polytheistic religion. Buddhism arose around 500 B.C. as a reform movement teaching disregard of the caste system and complete self-annihilation in Nirvanna. The Brahmans crushed Buddhism around 500 A.D. and drove it out of India. **The caste sysyem** was the dominant force in social life. The castes were: *Brahmanas* - the priestly caste and those skilled in law, medicine, architecture, music, legislation, and other learning; *Kshatriyas* - the warriors and administrators of the country; *Vaisyas* - merchants, farmers, and others employing laborers; *Sudras* the serving class and all menials; *Pariahs* - the outcasts. One might fall in caste but could never rise. With few notable exceptions, women were held in low esteem and charged with serving the men and bearing children.

2. *Educational Pattern*

The aim was to prepare for the future life and final absorption in the infinite and to preserve the caste system. Each caste was to learn its place and duties. No education was allowed the Sudras or women. **The Means and Content:** The family trained the boys in laws, traditions, and customs. In more modern times some schools arose in which children were taught fables, parables, and allegories. Higher education was confined to the Brahmanic colleges called *Parishads.* Here the pupil committed to memory material from the sacred books, the *Vedas* and commentaries, and was given much general learning. **Methods:** Texts were memorized with explanations later. Writing was learned by following the teacher's copy. The teachers were Brahmans and were treated with great respect. They received no pay but many " presents". Discipline was mild. **Results:** Emphasizing despair and escape from life, the people made little progress. They cultivated the negative virtues and became a passive people.

GENERAL CHARACTERISTICS OF TRANSITION PEOPLE. Here we see a growing ability to analyze experience and make generalizations that were impossible for the primitive mind. Transition people were learning to control nature to some extent.

Here are class distinctions and opposition to the development of the individual. Education aimed to maintain conditions as they existed in the past.

Education consisted largely in training for occupations.

The method of education was largely memorization of material from the past, not merely imitation.

While transition people had largely overcome primitive enslavement to the past, they were in bondage to the past, fearful of freedom for the individual, and non-progressive.

BIBLIOGRAPHY

Barnes, Harry Elmer, *An Intellectual and Cultural History of the Western World,* pp. 63-112, New York, Random House, 1937.

Davidson, Thomas, *A History of Education,* pp. 24-74. New York, Charles Scribner's Sons, 1900.

Eby, Frederick and Arrowood, Charles F., *The History and Philosophy of Education, Ancient and Medieval,* pp. 36-105. New York, Prentice-Hall, Inc.; 1940.

Emerson, Mabel I., *Evolution of the Educational Ideal,* pp. 5-14. Boston, Houghton Mifflin Co., 1914.

Graves, Frank P., *A History of Education, Before the Middle Ages,* pp. 20-109. New York, The Macmillan Company, 1925.

Graves, Frank P., *A Student's History of Education,* pp. 12-18. New York, The Macmillan Company, 1936.

Knight, Edgar W., *Twenty Centuries of Education,* pp. 33-40. Boston, Ginn and Company, 1940.

Laurie, Simon S., *Historical Survey of Pre-Christian Education,* pp. 104-195. New York, Longmans, Green & Co.; 1915.

Messenger, James F., *An Interpretative History of Education,* pp. 17-28. New York, Thomas Y. Crowell Company, 1931.

Monroe, Paul, *A Brief Course in the History of Education,* pp. 11-26. New York, The Macmillan Company, 1909.

Monroe, Paul, *A Text-Book in the History of Education,* pp. 17-49. New York, The Macmillan Company, 1907.

Mulhern, James, *A History of Education,* pp. 60-61. Ronald Press Co., New York, 1946.

Painter, Franklin, *A History of Education,* pp. 11-27. New York, D. Appleton-Century Company, 1904.

Wilds, Elmer H., *The Foundations of Modern Education,* pp. 35-57. New York, Rinehart & Company, Inc., 1942.

CHAPTER III

Education Among The Early Hebrews

The Hebrew Character

THE FUNDAMENTAL PRINCIPLE: Everything in the universe had its origin in one eternal principle which was vividly experienced or apprehended as a living deity, *Yahweh.* This early deity was a sort of universal Patriarch, a creator and ruler. This idea was so all-pervasive that Hebrew social life, education, and government were theocratic.

THE EFFECT OF THIS PRINCIPLE: The tradition was limited to that which was congruent with this understanding of Yahweh and His law. Much was borrowed from other people, but was fitted into this theocratic pattern. The early Hebrew confined creative genius to the spiritual. The art impulse was repressed lest it lead to idolatry. The result was emphasis upon the spiritual and upon conceptual thinking.

HEBREW LITERATURE varied as to form, but was religious in tone. Its purpose was didactic, aiming to teach about Yahweh and man's duty to obey His laws. The periods of this literature were: 1. *Pre-Biblical* - many writings, such as the J (Jahweh) and the E (Elohim) documents and other works mentioned or quoted in later books, have been lost; 2. *Biblical* - the Old Testament canon consisting of writings from the 9th century on, and 3. *Extra-Biblical* - the *Apochryphal* books and the *Talmud* containing valuable information about Hebrew education. In all this literature historical truth is secondary. The writings are intended primarily as instruments for teaching and inspiration.

Pre-Exilic Education

EDUCATION IN THE PATRISTIC AGE (before the Exodus, about 2300 to 1300 B.C.) We have little certain knowledge of this period. What evidence there is indicates that there were no schools, that the family and family life were the sources of all education, that learning came through participation in the practical activities of the community and in the religious rituals of the common life.

EDUCATION FROM THE EXODUS TO THE EXILE (about 1300 to 586 B.C.)

1. *Moses' Educational Program:* Moses faced the task of weaving the various tribes of Israelites into a people with a national character and spirit. This required: A powerful **tradition** that would be the common possession of all social elements. Moses made the deliverance of Israel from Egypt basic to the national tradition. A common **aim** for future realization. Moses gave the people a sense of destiny, charging them to

realize justice and righteousness throughout the world. This became the "concept of the chosen people." Both of these made necessary a national education adequate to initiate the young into the tradition and inspire them with a sense of group destiny.

2. *How the Program was Implemented:* The family was made the chief educational institution. Parental instruction was made compulsory. Other educational means were: **Monuments** of stones were erected to mark historical spots and point the young to the sites of memorable events; **Sacred feasts** commemorating national happenings and in which the children participated, and the **priests** and **Levites** were commanded to teach the law to all the people, women and children as well as men.

3. *The Content of Mosaic Education:*

Religion was the one inclusive subject; **music** was taught as religious expression of the emotions; everyone learned the **law and obedience to the law** was stressed as the way to material prosperity, and **writing** was not widely taught since the early Hebrew placed great emphasis upon memory.

Education and the Growing Conception of God

THE IDEA OF YAHWEH. Yahweh was not a nature god, but was fashioned after the ruler of a patriarchial government. He was conceived as the ruler or Patriarch of the entire family of Israel, a defender, father, and ruler. He was just, but demanded obedience.

FROM YAHWEH TO GOD. Yahweh was a tribal god, one among many, to be worshipped by his people and in specified places. From this conception the Hebrews came, through the experiences of their history, to conceive of a god who: **is** the one and only deity; created the earth and all people; can be worshipped anywhere; is the ethical principle in an ethical universe; manipulates history to his ends, toward the ultimate triumph of righteousness, truth, mercy, and love, and is the father of all men.

THE FATHERHOOD OF GOD. As the idea of the fatherhood of God developed, two opposing views took form: 1. The *prophetic* - religion is a warm spiritual communion with a loving and understanding father; 2. The *legalistic* - religion is a ritualistic and legalistic performance and God is a lawgiver who punishes those who disobey.

Post- Exilic Education

THE CULTURAL EFFECTS OF THE EXILE. In 722 B.C. Israel (the northern kingdom) was conquered by the Assyrians and the people were absorbed by Assyria. These were known as the "lost tribes." In 566 B.C. Judah (southern kingdom) was conquered by the Babylonians and the people carried into exile. They remained in exile until 536 B.C. when Cyrus permitted many to return and rebuild Jerusalem. The effects of this exile upon the Hebrews were: contact with a civilization superior to their own made them aware of the importance of schools and literature; they turned from agriculture and sheepherding to fishing, trading, and craft activities in towns, and the priests and scribes rose to prominence while the prophetic forces were weakened. The priests became the educators of the Hebrews, the first professional teachers. They were lawyer, copyist, and interpreter in one. They formed a literary guild and advocated the establishment of an aristocracy of the intellectual. Their legalistic position gained dominance.

THE SYNAGOGUE, SEAT OF ELEMENTARY EDUCATION

1. *The synagogue* grew during the exile as a place for instruction, meditation, and prayer. Later it became the center for religious service and a place where the law was taught. The synagogue existed from the time of the return from exile, and each synagogue had a school for the teaching of the law and primary arts.

2. *The Elementary School:* This grew as a function of the synagogue. Reasons for its inception were: the family was no longer capable of functioning as the sole educational agency; the experience of the Hebrews with Babylonian culture during the exile; the growing demand for an institution to instruct youth in the primary arts. This was based on an increase in the mass of general knowledge and culture, a major expansion of Hebrew literature, and the increasing need for writing as commercial life expanded, and the demand for training in the written law increased the need for reading and writing.

EARLY HEBREW EDUCATORS

1. *Simon ben Shetach.* His reforms, instituted about 75 B.C., included a demand that parents send their children to school.

2. *Joshua ben Gamala.* His decree of 64 A.D. made education compulsory for young boys and required that schools be established throughout Palestine.

BASIC EDUCATIONAL PRINCIPLES. The child is naturally evil and needs strict discipline just as a wild animal needs to be tamed. Thus, education must be a rigorous discipline.

Education is moral and religious training leading to reverence and respect for the best.

LEVELS OF HEBREW EDUCATION

1. *Pre-school* (from birth to 6 years): Began teaching as early as possible. The child learned the Shema, prayers, proverbs, Psalms, parts of the scriptures, and participated in feasts and rituals. Some children

learned to read.

2. *Elementary* (from 6 to 10 years): this work was connected with the synagogue. The boy was taught by the scribe or his assistant. The textbook was the *Penteteuch*. The boy memorized *Levitical* and *Deuteronomic* laws and learned reading, writing, and arithmetic.

3. *Higher Education* (from 10 to 15 years): the boy attended the school of the Midrash and learned the oral law. At 12 or 13 the boy became a "son of the law."

4. *Incidental Advanced Learning:* Beyond 15 years of age wealthier boys became attached to some great teacher of the law: Hillel, Shammai, Gamaliel are examples. Jerusalem was the center of this advanced learning, though other large cities boasted of their noted teachers.

THE CURRICULUM. The law was basic. In addition there was trade training and some sacred music.

METHODS OF TEACHING. "Learn the letter of the law." No variation was permitted. The fixed statement of the law was sacred.

Memory was developed and stressed. The boy repeated the law until he knew it letter perfect. Many mnemonic devices were employed.

Practical exercises were combined with instruction.

Severe punishment was employed to "tame" the child and impress learning upon him. The rod was used freely and more severe punishments were used if necessary.

THE EFFECT OF GREEK INFLUENCE. Greek influence came with the Macedonian conquests. This resulted in the formation of a Hellenistic party aiming to make over Jerusalem into a Greek city. Greek training was introduced and Greek language taught in Palestine. This Hellenizing was opposed by the orthodox. The results of this Greek penetration were: a) skepticism in doctrine; b) licentiousness and debauchery in conduct; c) bitter divisions among the Hebrews with the rise of the Pietistic party, and d) translation of the Hebrew Bible into Greek (the *Septuagint*), completed about 150 B.C.

THE EDUCATION OF GIRLS AND WOMEN. There was no discrimination among the sexes. Young women were highly respected in ancient times. After the exile, however, women were placed below men (the oriental attitude). Women were permitted to attend the synagogue services and worship in the temple. Otherwise their education was domestic. Some girls of wealthy families learned to read and write.

ATTITUDE TOWARD TEACHERS AND TEACHING. Teaching was held in great reverence and teachers were highly esteemed. The teacher was looked upon as a spiritual father and teaching as a divine task.

BIBLIOGRAPHY

I. Primary Sources:

Apocrypha, edited by Henry Wace. 2 volumes. London, John Murray, 1888.

Babylonian Talmud, edited by M.L. Rodkinson. 11 volumes. New York, New Talmud Publishing Company, 1900.

Old and New Testaments.

The Works of Flavius Josephus, translated by William Whiston. London, Ward, Lock & Company.

2. Secondary Materials:

Barnes, Harry Elmer, *An Intellectual and Cultural History of the Western World,* pp. 78-102. New York, Random House, 1937.

Cornill, Carl H., "The Education of Children" in *The Culture of Ancient Israel* (trans.). Chicago, Open Court Publishing Company, 1914.

Davidson, Thomas, *A History of Education,* pp. 77-86. New York, Charles Scribner's Sons, 1900.

Duggan, Stephen, *A Student's Textbook in the History of Education,* pp. 7-13. New York, D. Appleton-Century Company, 1936.

Eby, Frederick and Arrowood, Charles Flinn, *The History and Philosophy of Education, Ancient and Medieval,* pp. 108-158. New York, Prentice-Hall, Inc., 1940.

Ellis, G. Harold, "Origin and Development of Jewish Education," in *Pedagogical Seminary,* Vol. IX, pp. 50-62. Worcester, Mass., 1902.

Ginzberg, Louis, *Students, Scholars, and Saints,* Chapters I, II, and III. Philadelphia, Jewish Publication Society, 1928.

Graves, Frank P., *A History of Education, Before the Middle Ages,* pp. 110-136. New York, The Macmillan Company, 1925.

Graves, Frank P., *A Student's History of Education,* pp. 20-27. New York, The Macmillan Company, 1936.

Jewish Encyclopedia, The, edited by Cyrus Adler and others, articles on "Education" (Vol. V), "Pedagogics" (Vol. IX), "Talmud Torah" (Vol. XII), and "Yeshibah" (Vol. XIV). New York, Funk & Wagnalls Company, 1912.

Laurie, Simon S., *Historical Survey of Pre-Christian Education,* pp. 65-100. New York, Longmans, Green & Company, 1915.

Monroe's Cyclopedia of Education, edited by Paul Monroe, article by I.L. Kandel and I. Grossmann, "Jewish Education, Ancient, Medieval, and Modern," Vol. III. New York, The Macmillan Company, 1911.

Painter, Franklin, *A History of Education,* pp. 27-33. New York, D. Appleton-Century Company, 1904.

Swift, Fletcher H., *Education in Ancient Israel.* Chicago, Open Court Publishing Company, 1919.

Wilds, Elmer H., *The Foundations of Modern Education,* pp. 60-74. New York, Rinehart & Company, Inc., 1942.

CHAPTER IV

Education Among The Greeks

The Early Greeks: Who and What They Were

THEIR VALUE FOR MODERNS. The early Greeks were "the European genius in its first and brightest bloom." They show us the highest culture and enlightenment of the race. They became the pioneers in personal liberty and thus made possible the finest products of the human race. They revealed the strengths and weaknesses of democracy. Among them freedom made possible great genius. At the same time free rule of the masses led to chaos and a kind of individualism that resulted in social disintegration and dictatorship. In the Greeks we see a culture and education purely humanistic in origin.

WHO AND WHAT WERE THE GREEKS?

1. *As a Race:* The early Greeks were a mixture of a native stock (dark-haired and with considerable artistic ability) and invaders from the steppes of Western Asia (light-haired, blue-eyed, with much athletic ability and military strength).

2. *Their Home:* the northeastern shores of the Mediterranean Sea and the Agean Sea and the islands in this area. The rugged country with many natural barriers made for isolation, defense, differentiation, and the growth of many independent city-states. The closeness to the sea made for travel and contact with other people and their ideas, thus change and versatility.

3. *The Climate:* the equitable temperature favored physical vigor and much life in the open air. It was not too cold nor was it so warm as to be devitalizing.

4. *Attitude Toward Work and Leisure:* the aristocratic class engaged in agriculture. There were also manufacturing, fishing, tanning, commerce. But the Greek did not measure one by his wealth. In his thinking, man needed moderate wealth to give him the leisure necessary for creative growth and study of the problems of human existence. There were sufficient slaves to do the menial work and leave the Greek citizen free to develop his creative genius.

5. *A Restless People:* The Greeks traveled widely and made contacts with many people and ideas. They were free to examine critically all they saw and heard. This made for intellectual stimulation.

THE GREEK AS A SPORTSMAN. The early Greeks were superb sportsmen. The characteristics of their sports were: 1. in early days the contests were purely spontaneous; 2. only mature men engaged in their contests and participation was confined to the aristocracy; 3. sports had religious significance. This spontaneous outpouring of youthful energy was a living sacrifice to the gods.

Out of this the great Greek games developed: 1. *Olympic games* - celebrated every fourth year at Olympia in honor of Zeus and other deities. All states declared a truce for the duration of the games. Women were excluded. There were no musical or literary contests during the best years of these games. All classes of society came to watch and each city had its contestants. 2. *Isthmian games* - celebrated in Corinth during the 2nd and 4th years of the Olympiad in honor of Poseidon. The contests included athletics, riding horses, music, boating. Considerable attention was given to competition among boys. 3. *Pythian games* - celebrated near Delphi every four years in honor of Apollo. They consisted of physical contests and musical competition as well as drama, poetry, and painting. 4. *Nemean games* - celebrated every two years in honor of Zeus. The contests were almost wholly athletic with some musical competition. 5. *Panathenic games* - celebrated at Athens every fourth year in honor of Pallas Athena. The competitions were athletic, literary, and musical.

Awards in all these games were garlands and the adulation of the winner's fellows. There were no material awards.

GREEK CHARACTERISTICS

1. *Intense Rivalry:* rivalry was the master passion of the Greeks. They sought to excel in everything.

2. *Sensitivity:* the senses of the Greeks were keen and highly discriminating. This was basic to the development of art, literature, and science. Their intelligence was related to this keen sensitivity.

3. *The Secret of Their Genius:* they attained a perfect coordination of the psychological and the physical. Their conception of music is illustrative: music was an intimate union of melody, verse, and dancing.

4. *Highly Intelligent:* the Greek intelligence was revealed in a) desire for clearness of ideas; b) freedom from prejudice; c) readiness to adopt the new; d) passion for the dissimilar; e) open-mindedness, and f) comparative attitude of mind. Here is found for the first time in history pure intellectual curiosity, learning for its own sake without any utilitarian motive. Thus, here is seen the highest development of human intelligence.

5. *Love of Beauty:* the beautiful and the good formed a single idea and word for the Greeks. The Greek mind was captivated by the order found in the world and believed that this was evidence of an inner order in the universe. It combined beauty and utility. In art the Greek projected

beautiful ends which he sought to attain. His art was not an imitation
of nature, but the perfection of the idea which existed before the
creation and was worked into creation. This is the basis of Greek
idealism.

GREEK RELIGION. Religion was basic to all Greek life. The earth, for
the Greek, was peopled with exalted beings, the causes of all things.
These were like the Greeks, but idealized - a royal family of superior
beings. These were not nature deities nor were their images worshipped. The
Greeks worshipped living, energizing personalities. The gods were like
men, with the good and bad qualities of men. The Greeks lacked both an
authoritative statement of moral law (a Ten Commandments) and a divine
personality to motivate obedience of that law (a Jesus).

The influence of Greek religion was pervasive of all Greek life. The
religion did not make the Greek purer, truer, or more genuine. He was
not interested in these qualities. His religion made him courageous,
physically and mentally alert, independent, appreciative of beauty.

The significant facts of Greek religion were: 1. It had no organized
priesthood; thus progress was possible. There was no entrenched group to
demand uniformity and conservatism. 2. Its gods hated the proud and the
haughty and set bounds over which no one dared go. Thus, it set modesty
and shame over against the great weakness of the Greeks, pride. 3. It
influenced a great deal of Greek education. 4. It stimulated the imagination and the idealization of human qualities. 5. It was favorable to
the highest physical development. 6. Its weakness lay in the fact that
it lacked any mysticism. It was predominantly aesthetic and realistic. It
had no ideal of infinite spiritual perfection.

After the 5th century B.C., Greek religion was challenged by philosophic
skepticism and radical living. Excessive mystical cults developed, such
as the Dionysian, Orphic, and the Eleusinian.

THE PROBLEM OF THE INDIVIDUAL AND INSTITUTIONS. The Greek faced the
problem of effecting a balance between freedom of thought, feeling, and
action and unification under institutional forms. Individualism gradually
emerged from the conventionality of mass life. This posed the problem of
the relation of the individual and the state. The Greek answer was: The
state must be small enough for each citizen to participate directly in
its affairs. The citizen must subordinate his interests and will to the
state. Virtue is civic efficiency. The state is the expression of the
will of the people and must dominate the life of all. Thus, the Greek
found freedom in regimentation. Education is the supreme function of the
state for the creation of the free citizen who finds his highest freedom
in service to the will of the group.

UNIFYING AND DIVIDING FACTORS

1. *Factors unifying all the Greeks were:* a) a common language; b) a common literature, and c) a common religion.

2. *Factors tending to divide the Greeks were:* a) the rugged terrain; b) their initiative and spontaneity; c) the Greek games which led to an exaggeration of the individual ego by stressing individual effort rather than teamwork and cooperation; d) the intellectual basis of life which emphasized discrimination and difference of opinion, and e) local worship.

EDUCATION AMONG THE EARLY GREEKS

1. *In Homeric Times* (before the 8th century B.C.): Education of this period is pictured in the Homeric poems. There was no systematic education; there were no schools. There might have been some private tutoring. Emphasis was upon the physical and the military. The method was largely participation.

2. *After the 9th Century B.C.:* The early development of poetry and music among the Aeolian Greeks produced wandering rhapsodists who taught informally. The Dorian Greeks developed so that learning to write became necessary and schools for the teaching of writing arose before 500 B.C. There was some public support of the education of poor boys. By 400 B.C. the teaching of reading and writing was general.

Spartan Education

WHO WERE THE SPARTANS?

1. *Their City:* Near the 8th century B.C. a Dorian tribe of Greeks pushed into Laconia and conquered the original inhabitants of the area. They settled in a fertile plane, 5 by 18 miles and isolated by high mountains. Here they established small villages which were little more than military barracks.

2. *Their Society and Government:* Lycurgus (c. 800 B.C.) is the legendary author of the Spartan constitution and code of laws. The Spartans did not mix with the conquered, but became their masters. Thus, a constant danger of uprising made the Spartan citizens little more than a standing army ever on the offensive. In the Spartan social pattern were: **Spartan citizens** (never more than 9,000 to 10,000 families) ruled by military power; The **Perioeci** (about 120,000 individuals) were the former masters of Laconia who retained their land, tilled the soil, engaged in commerce. They were of Greek blood and had some freedom. They furnished troops for the Spartan armies, paid taxes, but had no rights of citizenship, and the **Helots** (about 250,000 individuals) were serfs bound to the soil and constantly menaced by the Spartans. Only Spartan citizens were permitted to share in the government, but among these there was a pure democracy. Citizenship depended upon Spartan training, not on birth or

blood. The Spartan spent his full time in the art of war and in training the soldier citizen. He was so thoroughly relieved of all cares of support that he could devote his full time and interest to public affairs.

3. *The Family in Sparta:* The Spartans feared the family as a menace to complete devotion to group interests. Thus, family functions were reduced to a minimum. Every man was father and schoolmaster to every Spartan boy.

THE SPARTAN EDUCATIONAL STRUCTURE

1. *The Aim and Purpose:* Education was the first concern of the Spartan state. Its purpose was to perpetuate the state. It was education for war and only the virtues of the soldier were cultivated. The authority for education was in the hands of the *Ephors* or chief rulers of the city. A *Paidonomus* was chosen each year from the chief magistrates to supervise the training of the young. Hè had absolute authority. He was assisted by *bidioi* and "whip-bearers." There were no professional teachers or trainers. The boy was given no freedom. Each citizen was responsible for teaching the young.

2. *The Educational Pattern:*

Infancy (from birth to 7 years): The elders selected those who were to live and the rest were exposed as unfit. Fit children were turned back to their mothers who functioned as state nurses. Children were taught early to endure hunger and pain. Boys were taken very early to the men's club houses by the fathers to play in the presence of the men. **Elementary** (from 7 to 18 years): Education was in the hands of the *paidonomus*. Boys were placed in state boarding schools and divided into bands of 64 each with the bravest serving as "herd leader" and each band under an *eiren* (a young man over 20). The aim here was to build the feeling of equality, comradship, *esprit de corps.* Boys were trained to endure hardships. Their living and clothing were scant. They were taught to forage and to hunt, to learn to take care of themselves and know the country. There was much flogging as punishment and as a test of endurance. Fighting was encouraged as a form of exercise and hardening but the *pancratium* was forbidden. *Gymnastic training* was an organized system of physical culture for the sole purpose of military strength. Exercises were graded to build strength and endurance gradually. The system was brutalizing. *The dance and choral work* were used for the training of soldiers. Here military maneuvers were simulated to train boys to be clever on their feet. Training in *music* was given as a means of social and moral education of the citizen-soldier. The solemn Doric rhythms were used to inspire courage, obedience, respect for law, and self-control. There was no interest in intellectual training. Neither reading nor writing was taught though some learned these privately. The Spartans disliked oratory as a sign of intemperance. They preferred Laconic brevity. They gave some attention to poetry, Homer, laws, war songs, ballads. Memory was emphasized. **Advanced** (from 18 to 30 years): Military training became more severe. Bands were sent out on maneuvers, ambushed the *helots*. War was declared annually on the *helots* to make this legal. At 20 the Spartan youth took the oath of allegiance. At 30 he became a citizen and was obligated to sit in public assembly, attend public barracks, and serve as teacher of the boys. **Education of Girls and Women:** Women were considered equals and assistants to men. They were trained to be mothers of soldiers. Girls lived at home rather than in the barracks, but their training was very similar to that of the men. They had strong physical exercise aimed at hardening their bodies. They exercised and wrestled with the boys without a sense of immodesty. At marriage a woman wore a veil and was no longer required to take physical exercise. The Spartan women were not good housekeepers but were fine physical specimens. They had high moral standards. There was no prostitution or adultery and jealousy was extremely rare.

RESULTS OF THE SPARTAN SYSTEM. In terms of the Spartan aim - the training of superior soldiers - the system was a phenomenal success. Efficient soldiers were trained and long after other Greek communities had lost their independence, Sparta was unconquered. Sparta was able to maintain group unity amid a general wave of individualism that inundated Greece.

In terms of human welfare the Spartan system was a complete failure. When Sparta became mistress of Greece she was incapable of leadership. She built for war and could not lead in times of peace.

Sparta was the ideal realization of primitive communism and of the effective education of a military state. She subordinated the individual to the welfare of the state, but each citizen was so identified with the state that there was no feeling of repression.

Education in Early Athens
WHO WERE THE ATHENIANS?

1. *Their City:* Athens was a city built on the Acropolis, four miles from the sea, surrounded by a fertile plane triangular in shape, about 25 to 40 miles by the longest measurements, and connected with the sea by a high wall extending to Piraeus. The land was owned by old aristocratic families who farmed the soil. Later these families moved into the city and slaves worked the farms. The population varied from 90,000 to 125,000 *free citizens,* 60,000 to 70,000 adult *slaves,* and about 45,000 *metics* - foreigners permitted to settle in Athens and engage in commerce and manufacture. The citizens ruled the state while the slaves and metics

supported it.

2. *Their Government:* In the earliest times the landed aristocracy ruled. After the Persian Wars (500 to 479 B.C.) Athens became a pure democracy with all the citizens ruling. They were freed of all other obligations and devoted themselves wholly to civic duty.

3. *The People:* They possessed in the highest degree all those qualities that made Greece immortal - initiative, inventiveness, versatility, enterprise, adventurousness, volatility, and self-confidence. They were the "adolescence of the race." Compared with the Spartans, "to pass from Sparta to Athens, is to pass from a barracks to a playing-field."* But they had all the weaknesses of the artistic and temperamental - vanity, shallowness, incapacity for a deep sense of obligation to any supreme moral law, a deficiency of reverence and loyalty.

THE ATHENIAN EDUCATIONAL STRUCTURE

1. *The State's Attitude toward Education:* The first duty of the citizen was service to the state. He could best serve the state who had developed most fully and completely all his capacities. Therefore, the state permitted all human capacities to develop to their fullest. This was possible only where freedom was guarded. Thus, education was held to be a family prerogative. The state's concern with education was expressed in a few general provisions: Public gymnasiums, temples, and theaters were provided. The Athenian *Areopagus* supervised, in a superficial fashion, all civic affairs including education. The city paid for the education of boys whose fathers had died fighting for the state. The few educational laws required that every boy be taught his letters and swimming, parents provide elementary education in music and gymnastics for their sons, fathers give their boys vocational training, schools be kept small, and boys be protected from immoral influences during school hours. Beyond this the state did not go, but left education in the hands of the parents and private teachers.

2. *The Ideal of Athenian Education:* Athenian education aimed to produce a young man who would combine beauty of body with beauty of soul, a perfect harmony of the mental and the physical. This meant that: The young man must develop beauty of figure, grace of movement, and refinement of behavior. The young man must develop a personality without exaggeration of any part, the "Golden Mean," "nothing in excess," no specialization or professionalism. The young man must be educated for positive service to the state so that he can function equally well in war and in peace and will be eager for civic service. The young man must develop good

---

* Dickinson, G. Lowes, *The Greek View of Life*, p. 111. Garden City, Doubleday, Page & Co., 1927.

manners and morals, reverence for the gods, respect for parents, polite-
ness, and good form. Through the cultivation of all aspects of the boy's
nature, Athens sought to fashion its citizens into integrated wholes,
equally efficient in all human functions.

Weaknesses in the ideal were: Women were not considered as worthy of
the same rich education as men. No education was provided for the masses
and for the slaves. There was no genuine ethical motivation behind this
·ideal. Intelligence without deep ethical direction tended to expression
in hair-splitting and disputation. There was little development of
sympathy. The ideal was local and institutional, never personal and
universal.

3. *The Process of Athenian Education:* The Athenian thought of education
as *paideia* (guiding the spontaneous activity of the child into artistic
and graceful forms). This involved: Leisure - work "done for the love of
it;" freedom for development with no forcing of the child into a predetermined mold; supervision for moral restraint and cultivation by the
pedagogue whose chief function was training in manners, morals, and
deportment; inculcation of the proper behavior by habituation, and
education aimed at training and developing the whole nature, not a
one-sided intellectual process.

THE PATTERN OF ATHENIAN EDUCATION

1. *General Facts:* The first establishment of schools is not known. Solon's
educational laws reach back to the 6th century B.C. The training of the
child before 6 years was in the home by his parents, nurse, or governess.
The child played a great deal, was told fairy tales and traditional
stories, and learned childhood songs and nursery rhymes. The boy entered
school at 6 or 7 years of age. There was little stress upon grading since
education was private and often each subject was taught by individual
instruction.

2. *The curriculum* consisted of: **Gymnastics:** largely for enjoyment of
physical exercise, but the value as preparation for military service was
recognized. It was also valued for mental health and a balanced personality. It served to develop the moral life and a sense of sportsmanship. The
work was graded in terms of the boy's capacity. Rivalry governed by
self-control was stressed. Boys under 16 exercised in private *palaestra.*
The state provided gymnasiums for all ages - the *Academy,* the *Lyceum,* and
the *Cynosarges.* At first these were simple exercise spaces. Later rooms
for conferences and lectures were added. The *gymnasiarch* was in charge.
After 16 a more formal and strenuous training was given. This included
the *pentathlon* - running, jumping, throwing the discus, hurling the
spear or javelin, and wrestling. There was no teamwork and all training

and play were wholly individual. **Music:** This included all the arts. In early times music meant melody, rhythm, poetry, dancing, and gesture. Later the meaning was widened to include reading, writing, arithmetic, poetry, learning the laws, the sciences, philosophy, and moral and aesthetic development. The first teachers of the Greeks were their poets, not priests. Thus, Greek culture arose from the poets and was emotional and creative rather than conservative. Music, in the more restricted sense, had a seductive power over the Greeks, an intoxication that was interpreted as participation in the divine. The effect was often therapeutic. Music was used to cultivate the moral nature and to engender patriotism. The lyre and cithera were the most popular musical instruments. No attempt was made to reach perfection of performance. The purpose was participation in the chorus, religious festivals, patriotic and social singing, and enjoyment. Dancing was used as a means of coordinating the sensory and motor elements of the growing child and producing a social and artistic individual. The essential facts about Greek dancing were that it was a religious ceremonial or act of worship including movement of the entire body; in it the body and soul united to represent or dramatize life; and it was accompanied by song. Festivals and other occasions for dancing were many. Dancing was not taught as such in the schools since all the necessary movements were learned in the *palaestra* and the school of music.

3. *Literary Instruction:* Instruction in reading and writing was given in private schools by a *grammatist*. Every Athenian citizen learned these arts as they became necessary. Children learned the alphabet by games and play devices. Reading was difficult to learn because of the Greek pattern of writing. The child learned to read with his mind since he could get little help from his eyes. Much stress was placed on perfect pronounciation. The child wrote on wax at first and later used papyrus. He learned a great deal of poetry. Instruction in arithmetic was practical and concrete. Teachers of these subjects on the elementary level were poor and despised and were held responsible for the results of their teaching.

4. *The Organization of Athenian Education:* The school day was long, usually divided into gymnastic, instrumental music, and literary studies. There were many breaks in the day and many holidays, festival occasions, and religious events. Both class work and individual instruction were practiced.

THE EDUCATION OF ATHENIAN WOMEN. Girls were trained to domestic life. Their education aimed at beauty and grace. They were taught home management, sewing, cooking, supervision of slaves. They received some instruction in reading, writing, singing, and playing the lyre. The emphasis of their education was upon piety, religion, self-control, and manners. However, mistresses were on a different level and often became highly cultured and powerful.

EPHEBIC EDUCATION IN EARLY ATHENS. Before 335 B.C. Ephebic education consisted in a ceremony recognizing the 18 year old boy as coming of age. He took the oath of citizenship and became subject to call for military or police duty. There was no elaborate training or education of the boy.

VOCATIONAL TRAINING IN ATHENS. Vocational training was not considered worthy of the Athenian gentleman. The mechanical arts were despised by the Athenians because: 1. they deprive one of leisure which was so important for doing the really valuable things of life; 2. most crafts distort the body, and 3. vocations narrow one's vision. Socrates was one of the few Athenian citizens who believed in "the dignity of labor."

Education in the Athens of the Periclean Age

THE SOCIAL AND INTELLECTUAL SETTING OF NEW ATHENS

1. *Historical Factors:* The Persian Wars ended in 479 B.C. with Athens as the leader of Greek resistance. In 477 B.C. the Delian League was formed with Athens as the treasury. Thus, Athens became the center of a wealthy empire. Pericles ruled Athens from 469 to 429 B.C. This was the "age of the common man" in Athens. The lower-middle class was enfranchised as were many foreigners and slaves. These came to monopolize political power. Athens turned from agriculture to manufacturing and commerce. Leisure and wealth were increasing and the people were becoming soft. The older aristocratic classes knew how to use their leisure and wealth to realize the highest self in service to the state. The newly enfranchised masses put selfish interests above the welfare of the state. They turned away from rigorous discipline and specialization arose.

2. *Intellectual Factors:* **Art** was at its highest - Phidias was producing and many imposing buildings were being erected. In **literature** Aeschylus, Sophocles, Euripides, and Aristophanes were writing. In **philosophy** were Socrates, Plato, and Aristotle. **Other geniuses** producing at this time were Xenophon, Isocrates, Herodotus, Thucydides, and Aesop. **Oratory** began to flourish as never before. Each one had to defend himself in court and the decision went to him who could sway the emotions of the jury. Promotion and leadership depended upon one's ability to sway the masses. **Philosophy** reached great heights. First, it became critical, then constructive. Greek philosophy began in Asia Minor with the work of Thales (640-556 B.C.) who substituted natural causes for mythological and personal causation. He held all things to come from water. He was interested in geometry, physics, astronomy, and cosmology and directed

later Greek thought to nature. **Science** developed because a mass of factual material was being accumulated; the Athenians were psychologically ready to attempt careful analysis of sense experiences; the Athenians had unusual ability to integrate; the Athenian mind was unconcerned with the practical or utilitarian since he had ample leisure; Athenian society was open-minded and tolerated differences; the Athenians had unusual creative imagination; and they had a sense of causal relations. All this resulted in remarkable advances in geography, history (Herodotus and Thucydides), and mathematics (Thales and Pythagoras).

Gradually the Greek mind turned from interest in nature to interest in knowledge for its own sake: insight, logical connections, systematic explanations. Also it turned to interest in ethics and human problems.

3. *The Moral Collapse of the Athenians:* The old morality of custom and tradition was challenged by new insights and values and a new morality was in the making. This came about because: Traditional theology, with base acts of the gods, was contradicted by the ethics taught in Athenian homes. Observation of other people and their moral codes led to a doctrine of the relativity of all morals. This led to skepticism and the belief that there was no universal right or wrong. The ideas of development (evolution) pointed to slow progress from the simple and less good to the complex and more good. Thus, there was no "golden age" in the past and no absolute authority from the past. Atheism and agnosticism grew and religious sanctions of morality were weakened. Social unity disintegrated under pressure from growing individualism. Patriotism was at a low ebb and many traitors were abroad in the land. Athenian education contributed to this. The newly enfranchised masses were dominated by self-interest.

COLLAPSE OF THE OLD ATHENIAN EDUCATION. Old Athenian education was based on the state as the supreme interest and upon the religious pattern of Homeric literature. With the growth of individualism and the fall of the Homeric gods, Athens had to find a new basis in education for building moral character. Changes that took place were: 1. Gymnastics for the training of the whole man gave way to athletics for training to win by developing muscle and brawn. This led to brutality. Most citizens abandoned physical training so universal before the Persian Wars. The reasons for this were the growing love of ease and luxury, the degrading practices of older men at the *palaestra,* professionalism, bribery, no physical education for military fitness, and youths were turning to new interests. 2. Youths turned from the gods and national heroes to extravagances, debauchery, and sporting events. There was no respect for parents and elders. 3. There were changes in music - the flute rivaled the cithera, words became subordinated to melody, and pantomimicry developed. 4. The old education could not meet the needs of the new times. The old education was good for a small city-state and the simple life. New needs developed - for training in the higher fields of general culture, for information and higher skills in science and language, for a more inclusive philosophy, including a philosophy of education, for more specialization, for vocational training, and for training in oratory. Thus a new education was necessary to meet these new demands of a new society and build good moral character and efficient citizens for the New Athens.

The Sophists

WHO WERE THE SOPHISTS? Gomperz says that the sophists were "half-professor and half-journalist." They were teachers of rhetoric and ethics who wandered from place to place and accepted money for their teaching.

SOME FAMOUS SOPHISTS

1. *Protagoras* (c. 481-411 B.C.): Came from Thrace. He professed to teach young men to become good citizens, successful both in public and private affairs. He wrote in the field of education, expressing many ideas that sound very modern. He is called "the father of secondary education." He also wrote on grammar.

2. *Prodicus* (465-399 B.C.): Came from Ceos. He aimed to teach good citizenship, virtue and good character. He also taught morals, nature philosophy, history of religions, and language.

3. *Hippias* (born c. middle of 5th cent. B.C.): Came from Elis. He sought universal learning. He was a popularizer of knowledge, a superficial thinker. He aimed to train young men to speak equally well on both sides of any question. He wrote in many fields of learning.

4. *Gorgias* (c. 483-375 B.C.): Came from Leontini. He was interested in rhetoric. He employed prose instead of poetry to convey his ideas and introduced at Athens the study of rhetoric.

THE SOPHISTS' GENERAL PRINCIPLES

1. Happiness is the goal of man's life. One should experience as many pleasurable sensations as possible.

2. The interests of the state are subordinate to the interests of the individual.

3. Traditional morals as motivation for conduct should give way to spontaneous impulse (nature as over against conventions).

4. The individual man is the criterion of the ethical world. Right and wrong are relative to him. This is the climax of individualism.

5. One's sensations are the measure of truth. This is a doctrine of the relativity of truth.

CONTRIBUTIONS OF THE SOPHISTS. The sophists met the need of the times for investigation and the massing of a body of accurate knowledge. They became the first research professors. Their work led to more clearness and definiteness in thinking and thus to careful study of expression or language. Grammar became a scientific subject and its study led to greater accuracy of meaning. Rhetoric and oratory grew in interest and soon entered the curriculum.

The sophists taught the young men of Athens, and other Greek cities, the techniques and thought patterns necessary for success in the new age. They made secondary and higher education popular.

Socrates (469-399 B.C.)

HIS PERSONALITY. Socrates was physically ugly. He had great physical endurance and was capable of sustained thinking. He was friendly but hated all pretense.

HIS LIFE. Socrates was born at Athens of poor parents. His father was a stone mason. Socrates became a stone mason and later a sculptor. He married Xantippe who bore him three sons. Later he gave up sculpturing and became a teacher. He taught informally by talking to people. Some followed him to learn, others out of curiosity or for thrills. Among his pupils were Plato, Xenaphon, Euclid of Megara, Isocrates, and Alcibiades.

WHAT DID SOCRATES BELIEVE?

1. *Area of Interest:* Man and human relations. He was not interested in science and religion. He was above all an educational philosopher.

2. *Ideas About the Curriculum:* Areas of the curriculum should include gymnastics, dancing, music, poetry, practical religion, geometry, astronomy, arithmetic, psychology, and ethics. Socrates was interested only in matters which touched on practical living; he was not a theorist. He was an advocate of the "pragmatic theory of education."

3. *Clear Thinking Was Most Important.* Ethics based on clear concepts, not on vague and confused ideas.

4. *Knowledge and Virtue Equated:* To know the good is to do it. The only reason one does evil is ignorance. Teach one what is good and he will do it. Socrates' reasoning: Pleasure is the only good; all men seek pleasure (happiness); all men seek to do that which will bring them pleasure; those acts which produce pleasure are good; man chooses evil only when he is ignorant of the consequences of such an act. Socrates arrived at this position through his own ideal and temperament. He thought of other men like himself, as seeking to live a happy life. The means for attaining this, for him, was insight into consequences. Thus, the moral life was dependent upon intelligence. On the basis of this he

sought to develop a philosophy of the ethical life.

SOCRATES' METHOD OF TEACHING. He challenged his hearers to think. He did not offer solutions of problems but constantly conducted investigations. His method of questioning was known as "Socratic irony."

SOCRATES' DEATH. This was an educational event. Athens had been defeated by Sparta in 404 B.C. Many Athenians attributed this to anger of the gods because of the prevailing atheism of the era, an atheism growing out of the skepticism engendered by the critical teaching of men like Socrates. Further, Socrates' pupils often turned from Athenian democracy either as traitors or totalitarians. The Athenians felt that the new teaching of the sophists and Socrates was the cause of Athens' degradation and defeat. Thus, they demanded Socrates' exile or death.

New Educational Problems in the New Age. The great minds of the Periclean Age and later dealt with certain basic social problems: Is it possible by teaching to produce good citizens? This led to the question, What is virtue? Is education a concern of the family or of the larger group? What should be included in the secondary curriculum? Should the emphasis here be on general education or specialization? Should higher education emphasize philosophy, rhetoric, and oratory, or military training? What should be the aim of the new education?

Xenophon (430-355 B.C.)

WHO WAS HE? A shallow writer and thinker who represents the conservative element of his day. He wanted to solve social problems by returning to the "good old days." He wrote *Memorabilia* (tells about Socrates), *Oeconomicus* (his ideas on the education of women), *Cyropaedia* (gives his ideas on the education of boys and youths). He was a pupil of Socrates.

HIS IDEAS ABOUT THE STATE. He had little use for Athenian democracy, but held Sparta in great respect.

HIS IDEAS ABOUT EDUCATION. Education is the concern of the state, for the preservation and development of the state. The individual is subordinate to the interests of the state. Thus, education should consist of military training, physical exercise, and training in manners. He wished no literary training beyond, perhaps, some early reading and writing. He believed that the education of women should be limited to training in care of children, handling of servants, and supervision of the household.

Isocrates (436-338 B.C.)

WHO WAS HE? He was born at Athens of a wealthy family and had the best of education. He was a pupil of Socrates. He did not engage in public life, but taught.

HIS SCHOOL. He established a school near the Lyceum in 392 B.C. Here he taught rhetoric and wrote widely. He drew pupils from all parts of the world and trained many of the most brilliant orators of his times.

HIS IDEAS ON EDUCATION

1. A good speaker must be grounded in knowledge and clear thinking, not merely platform skill.

2. Knowledge is a tool and not an end in itself. Thus, education must be practical.

3. Rhetoric and oratory have their artistic side as well as their practical side.

4. Education should effect a unity of all Hellas, a unity that is cultural and spiritual. He sought a unity of the Hellenistic mind.

Plato (427 or 429-349 or 347 B.C.)

WHO WAS HE? He was born at the height of Athens' glory, of wealthy parents from the aristocracy, a descendant of Codrus and Solon. He was given every educational and cultural advantage. He had the best possible education, studying with the best minds of his age; a pupil of Socrates.

The stages in his career were: 1. *The Socratic Period* (c. 409-399 B.C.) - This period, spent with Socrates, shows the Socratic influence. His dialogues written during this period discuss ethical questions, hold that virtue is the result of knowledge and that accurate knowledge, especially of ethical matters, is most essential. During this period his idea of virtue changed and he came to feel that a prior question to be answered was, What is virtue? As he became skeptical of Socrates' doctrine that "virtue is teachable," he turned to a study of the nature of virtue. 2. *The Period of Exile* (399-389 B.C.) - Socrates died in 399 B.C. and Plato fled Athens and traveled and studied for 10 years, observed, and became acquainted with many points of view. He visited Megara, Egypt, Italy. 3. *The Period of Teaching at Athens* (389-349 or 347 B.C.) - He returned to Athens as a reformer with fundamental interest in education. All his thinking moved about this central theme. He sought a system of state education which would make the citizen good and solve the social and political problems of Athens. This led him to his philosophy and social theory. He founded the Academy.

HIS PHILOSOPHY. Plato is in the tradition of ethical philosophers. He began with Socrates' problem of the teachableness of virtue. This was basically an educational problem. He soon saw that the solution of this problem depended upon an understanding of man and the world. This led to the construction of his entire philosophy.

1. *The Theory of Knowledge:* Knowledge is inherent in the soul at birth. The soul existed before birth and during this prenatal state

learned all that it can ever know in life. There are three kinds of knowledge: **Sense Knowledge:** This is not innate nor is it true knowledge since sensed things are not real. **Opinions About Things:** These are hypotheses and are not innate nor are they real knowledge. **Knowledge That Cannot Be Doubted:** This knowledge is innate and thus is real knowledge.

At birth the soul forgets temporarily all that it learned in its prenatal existence. The soul can be made to recall this forgotten knowledge by reminiscence.

2. *Doctrine of Two Worlds:* There are two worlds - **The Real World:** Perfect ideas exist in a supersensible world as ideal forms. These are real, eternally unchanging, abstract. These unite into an organic whole, the "world of ideas." Each perfect idea unites with all others to form the "idea of the Good." Perfect ideas are the thoughts of God. **The World of Things:** Its objects exist but are copies or shadows of the real world.

HIS PSYCHOLOGY. Man consists of soul and body. Body is of the material world (sense world) and the soul is of the spiritual. There are three levels of the soul: 1. *Appetites* - the drives and strivings of man; 2. *Spirit* - the source of courage, aggressiveness; 3. *Reason* - intelligence and rationality. The first two are of the body, are born when it is born and die when it dies. The third is divine. It is imprisoned in the body and is immortal, surviving the death of the body. It lived in the real world before birth and there experienced all true reality. It is part of the divine reason.

HIS THEORY OF ETHICS. Each level of the soul has its own virtue or good: 1. *Appetites* - temperance and self control; 2. *Spirit* - courage; 3. *Reason* - wisdom. When each level is in right relationship with the others justice reigns - appetites are controlled, courage is active, and reason rules. Pleasure is the highest good. Each level of the soul has its peculiar pleasure. The highest pleasure comes through the exercise of reason in knowing the good. The material world is the source of all evil.

HIS THEORY OF GOVERNMENT. The state is an organism - the "individual writ large." In it there are three classes: 1. *The Rulers* - a small group with reason predominating. These make the laws and determine education. They have the deepest insight and form a ruling oligarchy. They are the "philosophers." 2. *The Guardians* - the police and army. In these courage predominates. 3. *The Masses* - These are the workers, artisans, manufacturers, in whom the appetites are predominant. Individuals are placed in the class for which they are best fitted by nature. A child of a man in one class may be put in another class, either lower or higher depending upon his nature. Justice reigns in the state when each class is performing its proper function. The best interests of the individual and those of the state are the same. No private property.

HIS ATTITUDE TOWARD THE FAMILY. He feared the family as a danger to group unity and solidarity. In Athens the family had failed to teach the young. Thus, he held that the good of the state demanded public control of breeding, nursing, and training of children. Only slaves were permitted to have family life.

Women have the same qualities as men but to a lesser degree. Thus, he would admit them to all work of the state. He would have all marriages regulated by the state and children the property of the state to be reared and educated by the state.

HIS THEORY OF EDUCATION

1. *Introduction:* Plato wrote against a background of a decadent and defeated Athens. His aim was to reform Athenian society; thus he held that the prime business of the state was to make its citizens better. His ideas on education changed from the days of his early study with Socrates to the days when he wrote the *Laws*.

2. *What is Education?* Education is "the particular training in respect of pleasure and pain which leads you always to hate that which you ought to hate and love that which you ought to love, from the beginning of life to the end."* This training must be in complete harmony with the rational life when it appears.

3. *Can Virtue Be Taught?* Socrates held that "to know the good is to do the good." In the *Protagoras,* written under Socrates' influence, Plato agrees with Socrates. By the time of the *Meno* he is doubtful. He wants to know first what virtue is. In the *Republic* he discusses the nature of virtue and concludes: The virtues of the appetites and the spirit, temperance and courage, are due to habituation and strict discipline; the virtues of reason, wisdom and justice, are due to intelligence and can be taught since they depend upon the awakening of the rational nature.

4. *The Aims of Education Are:* **Unity of the Whole** - the Athenian state was being undermined by individualism. For Plato the state was superior to the individual and education was to produce social unity. **Develop Virtue** - Plato made virtue and civic efficiency synonymous. Education was to produce the good citizen. **Set the Rule of Reason Over the Other Elements of the Individual** - to awaken the rational faculty. **Develop One's Aesthetic Nature** - stimulate love of the beautiful. **Produce a harmony** of all phases of the individual's nature. Bring the individual

* Laws, par. 653. Translated by R. G. Bury.

to that point when intelligence rules conduct and laws are not needed - makes one self-governing. Socialize the individual.

5. *The State and Education:* The state must control all education and each citizen must have the same education. This will produce state solidarity. Only the citizens to be educated.

6. *How Shall the State Educate?* There were, for Plato, two kinds of education: **Education for Practical Affairs** - This was for the artisans and aimed at wealth and bodily strength. Actually, it is "training." **Education for Service to the State** - On the lower level this consists of habit formation through discipline and music-poetry. On the higher level this consists of conformity with the rational nature. The movement from the lower to the higher comes through a study of arithmetic which makes a bridge from the concrete to the abstract.

Compulsion should be used in physical training and building habits, but no compulsion in the "learning" of young children. As regards older persons, Plato was a formal disciplinarian.

Creativity in poetry is a form of madness. There is actually no creativity since all knowledge is merely recall.

No change is to be made from the simple ways of the past in games, music, poetry, lest the spirit of change produce disrespect and lawlessness. Plato would allow no innovations, no individualism.

Women were to have the same education as men.

7. *The Curriculum:* Plato's curriculum included gymnastics and music in right proportions so as to produce a harmony of the personality and spiritual depths. He thinks of music as including poetry, rhythm, and dancing. The child should learn much poetry. He would include mathematics for understanding of certainty and as a stepping stone to higher understanding. Also, he held, it makes one quicker, more retentive, shrews.

ORGANIZATION AND ADMINISTRATION OF EDUCATION

1. *How Organize Education:* All children of the citizens must be compelled to attend schools provided and staffed by the state. There could be no family education.

2. *How Administer Education:* At the head is a superintendent elected for a 5 year period. He is to be assisted by a director of gymnastics and a director of music and other aides. All assistants are to be in pairs, one for the boys and one for the girls.

He would have each level of society educated for its work in the state with no true education for the artisans.

For Plato the levels of development were: **Infancy** (from birth to 3 years) - the child to be fed and cared for; he should develop no fears;

he should experience little pain or pleasure. **Nursery** (from 3 to 6 years) - the child may be punished but not so as to bring disgrace; he should play much and hear fairy tales and mother goose stories. **Elementary** (from 6 to 13 years) - boys and girls should be placed in separate living quarters. They should learn music, religion, morals, letters, mathematics. Some military training should be given the boys. **Middle** (from 13 to 16 years) - study instrumental music, theory of arithmetic, and memorize poetry. **Gymnastic** (from 16 to 20 years) - boys should receive more strenuous gymnastic training and formal military training. **Higher** (20 to 30 years) - only the better pupils to receive this higher education in which they study science to discover the inner relationships of facts and to integrate thinking. **Officers** (30 to 35 years) - education for those who are to hold the higher offices consists of dialectics, philosophy, education. Officers serve the state from 35 to 50 years of age. **Philosophers** (after 50 years) - at 50 the man is relieved of further service to the state to devote himself to the study of higher philosophy.

Aristotle (384-322 B.C.)

WHO WAS HE? He was born of a family of physicians, thus interested in science. He came to Athens from Stagira at 17 and studied with Plato for 20 years. At the death of Plato he left Athens for 12 years, traveled in Asia Minor and Macedonia, tutored Alexander from his 12th to his 16th year. He returned to Athens in 335 B.C. and established the Lyceum where he taught until his death.

HIS TYPE OF MIND. He was coldly analytical, was concerned with particulars, encyclopaedic, inductive, interested in knowledge for its own sake.

HIS EDUCATIONAL WRITINGS. He wrote no work devoted exclusively to education, but discussed the subject in his *Ethics, Rhetoric,* and *Politics.*

HIS PHILOSOPHY.

1. *His Theory of the Universe:* The universe is an organism in which are four causes: **The Material Cause** - This is the crude material out of which a thing is constructed. **The Final Cause** - This is the function which the thing is to serve and exists as an idea in the mind of the maker before work on the thing is begun. **The Formal Cause** - This is the exact form of the thing wanted and exists in the mind of the maker. **The Efficient Cause** - This is the active work of constructing the thing. Aristotle combined the last three into the "formal" cause. Thus, he has two causes - the material and the formal or *matter* and *form.* These two are found in everything. Matter is that which is potential and form is that which is realized.

This is progressive. Each state of growth is form of the previous stage and matter for the next stage. Thus all nature is teleological. This is a doctrine of immanence.

God is pure form, the "unmoved mover." The form immanent in matter pulls matter to the realization of its potentiality. Matter looks to God and strives to be like Him. This striving is caused by God's being. God is absolute realization.

2. *His Psychology:* Life and soul are the same. Wherever there is life there is soul. The soul is the form, the body is the matter. They are related just as function and structure. The soul is the life of the body. There are three levels of the soul: **The Vegetative Soul** - This is in all living things and is the cause of growth, decay, nutrition, and generation. In plants it is diffused throughout. **The Animal Soul** - This is in all animals and causes desire, imagination, senses, movement, appetites, perception. Animals have both the vegetative and the animal soul. **The Human Soul** - This is in man only and is his rational or *noetic* part. This last has two parts: a) the practical which makes judgments of good and bad, prudent and imprudent, and is called "wisdom," and b) the theoretical which makes judgments of truth or falsity and is the "higher knowledge." Man has the vegetative, the animal, and the human souls. Each soul is related to the higher as matter is to form. The human soul is both passive and active. The passive is matter and the active is form. The active is divine and immortal.

3. *His Philosophy of Politics:* The state is an organism which furnishes those institutions through which man may realize his reason. Democracy is the best form of government, but may degenerate. The good of the individual and that of the state are identical. Man is a "political animal." Some men lack the deliberative faculty and are born to be slaves. Thus, slavery is in the nature of things. The state should be small and be united by education. The function of the state is to make the good citizen.

4. *His Theory of Ethics:* Ethics is that area of political science dealing with the making of good citizens. Man functions as a knower and a doer. The moral nature belongs to the latter, the practical. Thus ethics is an art and not a science. Its aim is happiness - activity of the soul in accordance with virtue and right reason. The highest happiness comes from intellectual contemplation, but happiness depends upon certain external factors also: **Material Properties** - sufficient wealth, slaves, health, and the like, and **Leisure** - time for living the life of contemplation.

5. *His Theory of Conduct:* To answer the question as to the nature of

moral conduct we must study the psychology of conduct. Nature has endowed man with impulses to action (instincts). They are neither good nor bad. They lead to activities. Whether these activities are good or bad depends upon how they are controlled by reason. When an impulse is associated with an image of an object it becomes a desire. This causes all movements in animals. To understand one's conduct we study his desires. A desire deliberately chosen is an act of volition.

Pleasure and pain on lower life levels and wisdom on the higher control desires. Virtue is impulse and desire directed by reason to what is good.

As there is theoretical and practical reason so there are theoretical judgments (true and false; these are necessary, universally valid) and practical judgments (good and bad; these are relative). There are also intellectual virtues (wisdom, intelligence, prudence) and moral virtues (courage, temperance, liberality, justice). The practical reason chooses the right means to happiness, activities which lead to the establishment of moral virtues. Morally good judgments choose between two vices - too much or too little action.

Thus, ethics is an art since reason can never be certain when deciding what is right and wrong. It has greater certainty when deciding what is true or false.

HIS EDUCATIONAL THEORY

1. *Basic Principles:* Education, being part of politics, is a function of the state. The state must train the young for its welfare. Education should shape the young for the good of the state. Thus, the same education must be given to all. Education is propaganda for state interests. Education is the art of so shaping children that they "love that which they ought to love and hate that which they ought to hate." Education aims at happiness within the state by the harmonious functioning of all its parts.

2. *Educational Positions:* All education should be public and no private education permitted. This is necessary for social stability and unity. It guarantees the same education for all. The curriculum should consist of reading and writing for utility; gymnastics for strength, health, agility, and manly beauty; and music for education (character formation), purgation, and intellectual enjoyment. There must be no professionalism in music. Intellectual education will not make men good. One comes to desire the good through habituation; then he can use knowledge to determine the best means of realizing the good. Moral instruction and theories of virtue are useless without a basis in habit. Only that which does not vulgarize the individual can be admitted into education. A liberal education and not one for toil, common vocations, or trades, is true education. Moral character involves three

factors: a) Nature, which supplies the impulses, the drives which are basic. b) Habits: Children are like animals, but have potentialities for higher development. Since the irrational develops before the rational, habits of right acting must be established early. Virtues are fixed habits or attitudes, "states of character." When they are established, a man will act in accord with them. Character is a disposition, fixed by habit, to act in a certain way. One chooses good acts, does them, and builds a habit of doing good acts. c) Reason. The intellectual life requires instruction. While moral virtues come by habits built upon choice, the intellectual virtues come through teaching.

3. *Methods:* We learn by experience organized by induction. One must start with experience as a base for any future learning and move from the known to the unknown, from the particular to the general, from the concrete to the abstract. Each science must be learned by first having direct experience of the phenomena of that particular science.

This method was ignored by future generations and emphasis was placed upon the elaboration of Aristotle's deductive method.

4. *Organization of Education:* **Infancy** (from birth to 7 years) - the child should be reared in the home and be allowed much play and physical exercise. He should be kept away from servants and all he does should be in terms of his later life. **Elementary** (from 7 years to puberty) - the child should study the ordinary subjects of reading, writing, arithmetic, gymnastics, music, and the like. **Secondary** (from puberty to 16 or 17 years) - the youth should have instruction in mathematics, instrumental music, poetry, grammar, rhetoric, literature, geography. **Higher** (beyond 21 years) - the young man should study psychology, politics, ethics, and education. He should also learn biology, the physical sciences, and philosophy.

THE RESULTS OF ARISTOTLE'S WORK. Little is known of his influence over Alexander. He would most certainly not agree with the dream of military empire which characterized Alexander.

His educational theories had practically no effect upon contemporary Athens, but had considerable influence upon later times (the Schoolmen and the Middle Ages).

He founded the Lyceum, a school located in a garden. This consisted of several buildings and a large endowment. Here Aristotle taught both advanced students and the popular crowds. The Lyceum was a fraternal society for fellowship and study and became part of the University of Athens.

Education during the Hellenistic Era (338 B.C. to 529 A.D.)

INTRODUCTION. Athens was defeated by Philip of Macedonia at the battle of Chaeronea in 338 B.C. and became part of the Macedonian empire. In 146 B.C. it came under the control of Rome and a section of the Roman empire.

Justinian closed all pagan schools in 529 A.D. and thus brought to a close the classical period.

ATHENIAN EDUCATION IN THE 4TH CENTURY B.C. Oratory, including rhetoric and the study of language, became of major interest in Athens as the best preparation for life and the mark of an educated man. In addition, a school system took form in Athens:

1. *Elementary Instruction:* Music became more complicated; grammar, rhetoric, and oratory replaced the old music-poetry pattern; drawing was added to the curriculum.

2. *Secondary Instruction:* The secondary level was differentiated from the elementary and the higher. It grew out of the needs of Athenian youths. Independent teachers arose to meet these needs. This gave rise to the *grammaticus* and special teachers for special subjects, all supported by fees. New subjects introduced for youths included grammar, arithmetic, geometry.

3. *Ephebic Training:* This was established by the Athenian Assembly in 335 B.C. because many authorities in the field of education, such as Xenophon and Plato, advocated it and the Athenians were awakening to their military weakness and felt the need for military training of all youths. This was the first move made by Athens toward state support and control of education. It required that at 18 all boys of Athenian parentage be made citizens and given two years of military training and patriotic indoctrination. The boy also took the Ephebic oath. By 300 B.C. the training was reduced to one year. Later compulsion was abolished, academic studies added, and foreigners admitted.

4. *Higher and Professional Instruction:* Private teachers (sophists and others) were cluttering up the gymnasiums of Athens so that they became a nuisance. Thus, laws were passed excluding them. This led to their establishing themselves in private quarters and setting up schools.

Four of the great schools of Athens were: **The Academy** - a garden and cottage purchased for Plato and where he taught for 40 years. At his death the estate was passed on as a permanent institution for the study of his writings and for fellowship. **The Lyceum** - Aristotle's home and gardens located near the Lyceum. Here Aristotle taught and established a library and laboratory for scientific study. He passed on this institution to his friends and it became a fraternal organization for the study of the master's works and fellowship. **The Epicurean School** - located in the garden of Epicurus where he taught his pupils and others. Epicurus willed the place to friends for meetings to study his philosophy. **The Stoic School** - founded by Zeno, a follower of the Cynics. It was established in a porch of the Agora. It was not an institution but rather an ascetic order.

These schools were brotherhoods established for study and fellowship. Strict regulations for their association were established and great zeal was shown among members of each group.

THE MACEDONIAN ERA (338-30 B.C.). With the conquest of central Greece by the Macedonians, Greek language and literature as well as Greek culture spread throughout the known world. Greek schools became the models for similar institutions on the elementary level in:

1. *Teos:* Polythrus gave an endowment for public education. A *gymnasiarch,* a Superintendent of Youth, and three literary teachers were elected each year by the citizens. One music and two military instructors were appointed by the administrative officers. Girls as well as boys were taught by the literary teachers. All children of free citizens were given instruction. There were three grades of literary instruction.

2. *Miletus:* Eudemus endowed the school. The people elected for the school a superintendent of gymnastics, a superintendent of instruction, four teachers of gymnastics, and four teachers of elementary subjects. Only boys of free citizens were taught in the school.

3. *Rhodes:* King Eumenes of Pergamon gave an endowment for the school.

4. *Delphi:* Attalus I, King of Pergamon, gave an endowment to pay salaries of teachers in the school.

Likewise, schools fashioned after Greek models on the secondary level arose in:

1. *Alexandria:* The city of Alexandria was founded in 332 B.C. by Alexander the Great. The work of establishing a school there was carried on by the successor of Alexander, Ptolomy Soter. With the assistance of Demetrius of Phaleron, he established a library and a museum. Out of this grew a great school, a research center, and a place of productive scholarship. The contributions of the school at Alexandria were: Teachers and research scholars were trained and sent to all parts of the world. Much research and formulation of the sciences were undertaken. Considerable editorial work was done and literary criticism flourished. The city was a melting pot for scholars and ideas from all parts of the world.

2. *Pergamon:* A royal library was established by King Eumenes II. This attracted many scholars interested in art, travel, topography, chronology, literary and grammatical studies, and medicine.

3. *Rhodes:* Here rhetoric and philosophy were the foremost interests and many of the era's greatest orators studied and taught in the school.

4. *Tarsus:* This city devoted itself largely to the training of its own residents in philosophy and other subjects. It was the home of Saint Paul.

5. *Antioch:* Here were a library and a museum. The city reached its highest development after the rise of Christianity.

The subject matter taught in these schools was developed by the Greeks and extended and expanded by others under Greek influence. The subjects included:

1. *Language:* Dionysius Thrax (born c. 166 B.C.) wrote the first textbook in Greek grammar. Grammarians of this period made contributions in language and literature. Some of these were: **Aristophanes of Byzantium** (c. 257-180 B.C.) who was librarian at Alexandria, did considerable editorial work on the classics, and made contributions in technical grammar. **Aristarchus of Samothrace** (c. 220-143 B.C.) succeeded Aristophanes at Alexandria and founded a school of philologists. **Apollonius Dyscholus** (2nd century B.C.) helped reduce grammar to a science. Because of this work scholars came to regard grammar as the basis of all education and some even worshipped it. In addition, oratory was taught and studied and a high perfection reached in its use.

2. *Mathematics:* Interest in this area of knowledge was high because: The age had many practical problems that demanded mathematical knowledge for reaching solutions; the solution of mathematical problems gave the Greeks a sense of emotional satisfaction; mathematics was related to philosophy, and mathematics satisfied the puzzle interest of a great many. Geometry flourished especially, producing many great scholars in the field: Hippocrates of Chios, Euclid, and Apollonius.

3. *Physics:* This was given great impetus by Archimedes (287-212 B.C.).

4. *Geography:* The first geography was written by Scylax of Caryanda in the 4th century B.C. (*Periplus*). Eratosthenes of Cyrene (276-194 B.C.) made geography a science. Strabo and Ptolemy wrote the most authentic work in the field.

5. *Astronomy:* Early advances in the science were made by the Egyptians, Thales, Pythagoras, Heracleides, and Ponticus. Eudoxus (middle of the 4th century B.C.) gave mathematical proof of a round world and of moving planets. Eratosthenes discovered the method of calculating the circumference of the earth. Aristarchus of Samos held that the earth moves about the sun. Hipparchus (2nd century B.C.) made many important discoveries and calculations in both astronomy and mathematics. Ptolemy (2nd century A.D.) wrote the *Almagest* and set a pattern of astronomy for many centuries.

6. *Social Sciences:* Little was done in this area save in history. Demetrius of Phalerum collected Aesop's fables around 300 B.C. This work

became one of the most popular readers and remained so for many generations.

This systematizing of fields of knowledge was basic to learning, teaching, and advancement in each area. The Greek interest lay in knowledge for its own sake and practical use was discouraged. The Greeks feared that emphasis upon the practical use of knowledge would warp the free study of the sciences.

Although much of the Macedonian period was not creative as past periods had been, it did make a real contribution in critical editorial work and in bringing together and systematizing the growing body of material in the various sciences.

THE ROMAN ERA (30 B.C. to 529 A.D.). This was an era of organization rather than creative advancement. The Roman Emperors used education to train men for official positions; thus public subsidy of schools increased. The early cultural aim gave way to utilitarian aims.

1. *The Growth of Public Subsidy of Education:* This began with the payment of salaries of top educators by the government and led eventually to complete control of education.

2. *The University of Athens:* Athens remained the cultural and educational center of the west. Roman rulers gave money and special privileges to the city. Antonius Pius established a chair of Rhetoric and a chair of Grammar at Athens and paid the salaries of the holders from the government treasury. Marcus Aurelius established another chair of Rhetoric there and appointed Herodes Atticus to the post. He also provided for the appointment of two professors of philosophy to each of the four philosophic schools at Athens - the Academy, the Lyceum, the Epicurean, and the Stoic - with salaries paid from the government treasury. This was the basis for the University of Athens.

3. *The Study of Law:* Roman interest in law led to the establishment of many schools for the study of the subject. Gradually interest in law took the place of interest in Greek philosophy.

4. *The Curriculum:* This consisted of: **Gymnastics -** Professionalism dominated and the older standards of morality and sportsmanship were ignored. Corruption and bribery became so rife that the Olympic games were abolished in 394 A.D. **Oratory -** This became more important with the rise of Roman power. It was a necessary tool for public life. The sophists, teachers of oratory and great orators, were held in high esteem. But the emphasis was upon winning victories over opposition rather than discovery of the truth.

5. *Educational Theory:* Plutarch (45-125 A.D.) wrote *Moralia, On the Education of Children,* and *Lives.* He held that good education depends

upon three essentials: **Memory** - this is a most important natural endowment and must be highly trained; **Correct Habits** - these should be
built by strict discipline, and **Instruction.**

6. *The Decline of Greek Culture:* In 324 A.D. Christianity was
recognized as the state religion of the Roman Empire. In 385 A.D.
Theodosius destroyed the Seraphium of Alexandria, making an end of
Greek religion. In 529 A.D. Justinian closed pagan schools and withdrew
all grants of public funds for pagan education.

The possible causes of this decline are: Christianity; books were
being studied in place of life; formalism took the place of vitality;
the moral weakness of the pagan world, and individualism.

BIBLIOGRAPHY

I. Primary Sources:

Aristotle: *Works of Aristotle,* translated by St. George Stock. Oxford, The Clarendon Press, 1925). Also translation by Benjamin Jowett. (Oxford, The Clarendon Press, 1925.

Cubberley, Ellwood P., *Readings in the History of Education,* pp. 1-22. New York, Houghton Mifflin Company, 1920.

Plato: *Works of Plato,* translated by several scholars in the Loeb Classical Library. London, William Heinemann Ltd..

Monroe, Paul, *Source Book of the History of Education for the Greek and Roman Period.* New York, The Macmillan Company, 1913.

Xenophon: *The Works of Xenophon,* translated by H.G. Dakyns. New York, The Macmillan Company, 1892.

2. Secondary Material:

Adamson, J.E., *The Theory of Education in Plato's Republic.* New York, The Macmillan Company, 1903.

Barnes, Harry Elmer, *An Intellectual and Cultural History of the Western World,* pp. 117-193. New York, Random House, 1937.

Bosanquet, Bernard, *The Education of the Young in the Republic of Plato,* Cambridge, The University Press, 1908.

Burnet, John, *Aristotle on Education.* Cambridge, Harvard University Press, 1928.

Butts, R. Freeman, *A Cultural History of Education,* pp. 24-79. New York, McGraw-Hill Book Company, 1947.

Cubberley, Ellwood P., *A Brief History of Education,* pp. 3-26. New York, Houghton Mifflin Company, 1922.

Cubberley, Ellwood P., *The History of Education,* Chs. I, II. Boston, Houghton Mifflin Company, 1920.

Davidson, Thomas, *A History of Education,* pp. 86-105. New York, Charles Scribner's Sons, 1900.

Davidson, Thomas, *Education of the Greek People,* pp. 103-176. New York, D. Appleton-Century Company, 1904.

Davidson, Thomas, *Aristotle and the Ancient Educational Ideal.* New York, Charles Scribner's Sons, 1904.

Dickinson, G. Lowes, *The Greek View of Life.* New York, Doubleday, Page & Co., 1927.

Dobson, J.F., *Ancient Education,* Chs. I, II, III. New York, Longmans, Green and Company, 1932.

Duggan, Stephen, *A Student's Textbook in the History of Education,* pp. 15-48. New York, D. Appleton-Century Company, 1936.

Eby, Frederick and Arrowood, Charles Flinn, *The History and Philosophy of Education, Ancient and Medieval,* pp. 160-513. New York, Prentice-Hall, Inc., 1940.

Encyclopaedia Britannica: Articles on *Sparta, Sophists, Socrates, Isocrates, Plato, Aristotle, Athens.*

Freeman, K.L., *Schools of Hellas from 600 to 300 B.C.* London, Macmillan and Co., 1912.

Graves, Frank P., *A History of Education Before the Middle Ages,* pp. 138-338. New York, The Macmillan Co., 1925.

Graves, Frank P., *A Student's History of Education,* pp. 29-49. New York, The Macmillan Company, 1936.

Hart, Joseph K., *Creative Moments in Education,* pp. 27-85. New York, Henry Holt and Company, 1931.

Laurie, Simon S., *Historical Survey of Pre-Christian Education,* pp. 197-300. New York, Longmans, Green & Co., 1915.

Messenger, James F., *An Interpretative History of Education,* pp. 29-46. New York, Thomas Y. Crowell Company, 1931.

Melvin, A. Gordon, *Education, A History,* pp. 37-102. New York, The John Day Company, 1946.

Monroe, Paul, *A Brief Course in the History of Education,* pp. 28-78. New York, The Macmillan Company, 1909.

Monroe, Paul (editor), *A Cyclopedia of Education.* New York, The Macmillan Company, 1925.

Monroe, Paul, *A Text-Book in the History of Education,* pp. 52-172. New York, The Macmillan Company, 1907.

Moore, Ernest C., *The Story of Instruction. The Beginnings,* Chs. I-V. New York, The Macmillan Company, 1936.

Mulhern, James, *A History of Education,* pp. 133-160. Ronald Press Co., New York, 1946.

Painter, Franklin, *A History of Education,* pp. 39-77. New York, D. Appleton-Century Company, 1904.

Reisner, Edward H., *Historical Foundations of Modern Education,* pp. 1-104. New York, The Macmillan Co., 1928.

Wilds, Elmer Harrison, *The Foundations of Modern Education,* pp. 78-113. New York, Rinehart & Company, Inc., 1942.

CHAPTER V

Education Among The Early Romans

Introduction

DIVISIONS OF ROMAN HISTORY AND EDUCATION

1. *Ancient Period* (753-275 B.C.): According to tradition, Rome was founded in 753 B.C. During this period education was largely in the homes. There were a few elementary schools. There was only slight literary culture. Rome was an Italian state with a culture dominantly Latin and Etruscan.

2. *Transition Period* (275-132 B.C.): During this period Rome changed from a small Italian state to a world power. It developed schools on the Greek model, schools of Greek grammar and rhetoric. Literary culture increased.

3. *The Golden Age* (132 B.C. to 100 A.D.): During this period the Roman government became that of an empire. The Christian church was established. The Latin Grammar School was perfected. There were the beginnings of public subsidies for education. Latin literature was at its height.

4. *The Silver Age* (100-275 A.D.): Municipal patronage of education was extended. Law became a university subject. Greek medicine was formulated by Galen and others. Christianity was spreading.

5. *The Age of Roman Despotism* (275-529 A.D.): The government monopolized education. Christianity became dominant. Justinian closed all pagan schools.

THE CONTRIBUTIONS OF ROME TO CULTURE

Rome was a transmitter of cultures, but she made her contribution to what she passed on; the concept of delegated authority; institutional organization, as seen in the Roman church; the Latin language; Latin literature; Roman law; the Latin Grammar School; and culture as the possession of the elite and not a part of daily life. This conception of culture has influenced education through the ages even to the present.

Roman Geography and History

THE LAND. Rome was located at the center of the Mediterranean world, but extended her empire from Asia to England and from the Black Sea to the Atlantic Ocean.

THE PEOPLE. The Roman population was not homogeneous. People of Indo-European stock settled in the area in prehistoric times. Etruscans came around 800 B.C. The Greeks settled in southern Italy and Sicily in the 7th and 6th centuries B.C. The Gauls entered northern Italy in the

48

5th century B.C. As Rome conquered other lands it brought their citizens to Rome. Thus the city was a cosmopolitan center in which many stocks fused. In 210 A.D. all freemen in the empire were made Roman citizens.

THE POLITICAL HISTORY OF ROME

1. *Kingdom:* In the 6th century B.C. Etruscan kings ruled Rome as part of an Etruscan federation. The Etruscans were builders, engineers, and were industrious in developing the area. They engaged in extensive commerce.

2. *Aristocratic Republic:* The Etruscan kings were overthrown in 509 B.C. by the noble Roman families and an aristocratic republic established. The struggles between these aristocrats and the plebians - the commoners - resulted in the Laws of the Twelve Tables in about 450 B.C.

The Gauls invaded the area and sacked Rome in 390 B.C. After this Rome began a series of wars with other Italian cities which resulted in her becoming master of all Italy south of the Rubicon by 264 B.C. Her conquests were extended until the empire was built. As this progressed, Rome became a cosmopolitan city with Greek culture as a base. But Rome was unable to rule her empire as a republic. This led to civil wars and the eventual fall of the Republic.

3. *Empire:* Octaviun became Princeps in 27 B.C. Augustus built a bureaucracy able to rule the empire. Gradually the rulers became despotic and the power of Rome declined. Constantinople was established in the 4th century A.D. as a second capitol to ease the strain of administration of the rmpire. Alaric sacked Rome in 410 A.D. and Roman power collapsed, leaving Constantinople the only center of Roman empire rule. During this period the Roman Empire became Christian.

These changes were confined largely to the upper classes of Roman society and did not materially influence the masses of plain people who continued their Latin culture and simple craft society. Only when Christianity came were the masses affected and their culture changed.

The Roman Social Pattern

THE ROMAN TYPE. The Roman was characterized by high respect for constituted authority and skill in governing. These characteristics were built on a foundation of: 1. *Virtus* - manliness, courage, strength; and 2. *Pietas* - reverence for ancestors, divine power, and sacred customs. The Roman had a high sense of responsibility to duty.

THE ROMAN STATE. The magistrate had unquestioned authority and everyone was trained to recognize and respect this fact.

THE ROMAN FAMILY. The father had unquestioned authority in the family, but his acts were governed by rigid custom. Women had a high position in the family and were held in great respect. The family had the functions of work, worship, and political service.

Roman Education in the Republic

EDUCATION IN THE FAMILY. The family controlled and dominated education during the Republic. Even after 250 B.C., when schools began to assume importance, the family was a significant educational factor. Children were held in high regard. The mother was charged with the responsibility for the care of the children and was concerned with their early training and education. The father was the chief teacher of the boy who learned through observation, participation, and some direct instruction.

The boys learned the Laws of the Twelve Tables, history, governmental practices, war, business, sports, crafts, and skills. The girls learned deportment and the knowledge and skills necessary for running a home and being a mother.

PUBLIC EDUCATION. This supplemented the education of the home and consisted of attending public affairs, ceremonies, funerals, and seeing state functions. In later years the sons of wealthy or important families served an apprenticeship in some public office or at some state duty. Thus, they were prepared to hold office and serve the state. Prominent men usually served as the boys' mentors.

The masses had only education in the home and apprenticeship training for their station in life.

GREEK INFLUENCE IN EDUCATION. Before 300 B.C. schools existed in Rome but were of only slight importance. After 272 B.C. - the fall of Tarentum - many Greek captives and freemen came to Rome. Among these were: 1. *Livius Andronicus* - he was brought to Rome as a captive, was freed, and became a famous teacher and writer. He translated Greek classics into Latin; 2. *Naevius* (about 235 B.C.), and 3. *Plautus* (254-169 B.C.), the father of Roman literature. These men, and many others, introduced Greek literature and language into Roman life and thereby stimulated the development of the Latin language and literature.

Greek captives and freemen became teachers in the homes of wealthy Romans. Slaves often taught the children to read. Later these men began teaching for fees and were permitted to establish schools and earn a living in this manner. In 170 B.C. Crates of Mallus came to Rome and began teaching philosophy and grammar.

Many Romans feared this trend toward things Greek as a threat to Roman tradition and put through the Roman Senate a law, in 161 B.C., to drive Greek teachers out of the city. This attempt failed and Greek philosophers and rhetoricians grew in number. Cato the Censor fought this trend away from the traditions of early Roman life.

In time three levels of schools took form in Rome: 1. *Elementary* - here the *ludi magister* or *litterator* taught reading and writing; 2. *Grammar School* - here the *grammaticus* or *litteratus* taught all the liberal subjects, and 3. *The School of Rhetoric* - this was taught by a *rhetor* and aimed to prepare boys for the profession of the orator.

Roman Education in the Empire

POLITICAL AND SOCIAL EVENTS. Tiberius Gracchus was assassinated in 132 B.C. There followed a period of wars with Rome's Italian allies and of struggles between classes in Rome. The popular party undermined the Roman government. Marius (c. 157-86 B.C.) became the leader of the popular party and built a strong, well-trained army. Gradually the professional military class came to dominate the Roman government.

THE RISE OF THE LATIN GRAMMAR SCHOOL. With the rise of the popular party schools of Latin grammar and rhetoric came into prominence and began to supplant those of Greek grammar and rhetoric. Attempts to stop this development failed. Many books on Latin grammar appeared and research in the Latin language increased. M. Terentius Varro (116-27 B.C.) contributed much to this development. Latin grammar took form and much Latin literature was produced.

As the Roman Empire came into being the Latin language and literature was spread throughout conquered lands and schools of Latin grammar and rhetoric were planted throughout the Empire. Many books were produced by copyists and Latin literature became widely known.

THE FALL OF THE REPUBLIC AND RISE OF DESPOTISM. Caesar conquered Gaul and assumed the power of a dictator. Octavius Princeps took the title of Augustus in 27 B.C. Soon the Empire began decentralization with many self-governing cities in which were schools of Latin grammar and rhetoric.

With the fall of the Republic the orator as leader and shaper of public opinion was no longer necessary since the army was in control. Thus, Latin rhetoric became a matter of the schools with little practical use. Scholars were produced, not statesmen.

CICERO (106-43 B.C.). He was the leading Roman orator and statesman, trained in Greek rhetoric and philosophy. He wrote widely on politics, philosophy, rhetoric, and education. In *The Orator (De Oratore)* he discusses the education of the orator. The orator, he holds, must have a well-rounded education in the liberal arts as well as training in platform skills. This must be supplemented with wide experience upon which the orator will build his philosophy. The orator needs an inventive mind.

THE RISE OF PUBLIC PATRONAGE OF EDUCATION. Early Roman education was in the hands of the family with little state interference. The state's decrees were protective only. State intervention came gradually. Special privileges and protection were given to agriculture, medicine, architects, physicians, and teachers of the liberal arts. Also, the rulers became patrons of the arts and of learning. Augustus established Marcus Varrius Flaccus in the palace to teach his sons and grandsons. This was the first "palace school" under imperial patronage. Vespasian (c. 76 A.D.) paid teachers of Latin and Greek rhetoric from the imperial treasury. This was followed by the founding of schools of rhetoric and grammar in many cities and under municipal support and control. This led eventually to complete government control of education.

VITRUVIUS (Ist century B.C.). He wrote *About Architecture (De Architectura)* and was the authority on the subject for many generations. He influenced greatly Christian and medieval architecture. He discussed the education of the architect, or engineer, holding that he must have a broad education with a clear understanding of the liberal subjects. The architect must also be trained as a skilled craftsman.

QUINTILIAN (c. 35-97 A.D.)

1. *Introduction:* He wrote the *Institutes of Oratory (Institutio Oratoria)* which outlines his ideas concerning the education of the orator. His theories on education set the pattern of the Latin Grammar School and influenced higher education for many centuries. Born at Calagurris, in Spain, he studied at Rome and taught there for some time. He became a public teacher when Vespasian established the principle of paying teachers of rhetoric from the public treasury.

2. *The Education of the Orator:* The good orator must have: above all a good moral character; mastery of the liberal arts; skill in speaking, and a rich memory. The orator of his day was similar to the lawyer of today. He represented his client; thus he should have a code. The code suggested by Quintilian included: accept pay for services only in terms of the client's ability to pay; advise the client for his good; the orator's duty to serve the public is paramount; and the orator must seek justice above all else.

3. *His Principles of Education:* The responsibility of parents is great. Begin education right since early impressions are the most important. Since the young child can endure a heavy schedule, he should be pushed to learn and should carry several subjects at the same time. Play is educationally important. Gymnastic training is good for boys. Education in schools is better than private education by a tutor in the home, but classes in schools must be small enough to make possible an efficient teaching job. The curriculum should be built in terms of the child's ability and interests. The teacher must make learning interesting and provide for

success. There must be no corporal punishment, but praise and emulation must be the incentives used. The educational process must eventuate in a mind stored with factual material.

4. *The Curriculum:* **Elementary** - correct speech, writing, reading, Greek grammar, Latin Grammar. **Grammar School** - correct speaking, wide acquaintance with literature and literary criticism, astronomy, philosophy, geometry, music. **School of Rhetoric** - literary subjects, history, composition, rhetoric, logic, professional ethics.

Roman Education After 100 A.D.

THE CULMINATION OF PUBLIC PATRONAGE. The Roman Emperors extended public subsidies of education and of the arts throughout the Empire so that by the middle of the 3rd century this had become an educational policy. State control of education followed imperial patronage. Teachers had to have the approval of the authorities. Theodosius established a state monopoly of education. Thus, the principle that opinion and teaching should be regulated by the government was firmly established in the Roman Empire and dominated Europe until modern times.

THE RISE OF PROFESSIONAL EDUCATION

1. *Medicine:* This was originally a Greek science which grew slowly in Rome. Wealthy families had private physicians who taught youths by apprenticeship methods. Later schools were established though medical instruction was never standardized in Rome. Both surgery and pharmacy were taught. Dioscorides, who wrote *Materia Medica,* has been called the father of pharmacy.

Rome developed hospitals and municipal medicine. Many cities in the Empire employed public doctors and there was a large medical corps with the military services. Galen (c. 130-200 A.D.) wrote extensively in the field of medicine and influenced medical teaching in the medieval universities.

2. *Philosophy:* Greek philosophy, having become highly utilitarian, entered Rome where special interest was evidenced in Epicureanism and Stoicism. Philosophy was cultivated by literary and public men and by professional practitioners of wisdom and consolation called "philosophers."

3. *Law:* This developed from The Twelve Tables to a great body of legal material for the governing of an empire. The "Perpetual Edict" established the principle of precedent; however, the law could grow by decisions of the Emperor or by opinions of able jurists. Gradually the conception of *jus gentium* or universal law arose.

The first schools of law were private and the teachers collected fees. Theodosius established a professorship of law under public patronage at

Constantinople and made the teaching of law a public monopoly. He was responsible for the *Code of Theodosius* which had considerable influence upon codes of law developed by the "barbarians."

Justinian, Emperor from 527 to 565, had a commission prepare under his supervision: **The Institutes of Justinian**, a basic textbook in law; **The Code**, a collection of imperial ordinances; **The Digest**, or *Pandects,* opinions of jurists, and **The Novels**, imperial decrees issued after the compilation of the *Code.* He also permitted the teaching of law only in Rome, Constantinople, and Beyrout. In these places a five-year course in the subject was established. The *Code* governed in the Exarchate of Ravenna after the barbarians drove the Empire from most of Italy and here the University of Bologna arose later.

LATIN TEXTBOOKS

1. Aelius Donatus (c. 350 A.D.) wrote *Ars Minor* which became the basic grammar text for many centuries.

2. *The Distiches of Cato* was an elementary reader with a moral aim.

3. Capella wrote the *Marriage of Philology and Mercury,* a summary of the liberal arts.

4. Priscian wrote an advanced grammar.

Education in the Roman Empire during the 4th and 5th Centuries. Roman schools - elementary, Latin Grammar, and rhetorical - were popular throughout the Empire. However, they were wholly literary and divorced from the life of the times. Also, schools of practical subjects appeared.

The schools of Gaul were famous. These preserved much early learning and passed it on to the Christian church. The curriculum and methods were much like those of Rome's Golden Age.

Reasons for the decline of Roman scholarship were: The decline of Roman culture; the utilitarian emphasis in learning with less concern for creative work; scholarship was divorced from living; the loss of freedom as Rome became a great empire and developed its imperialism; and the coming of the barbarians.

BIBLIOGRAPHY

I. Primary Sources:

Chase, W.J., *The Distichs of Cato.* Madison, University of Wisconsin, Studies in the Social Sciences and History, #7, 1922.

Chase, W.J., *The Ars Minor of Donatus.* Madison, University of Wisconsin, Studies in the Social Sciences and History, #11, 1926.

Cicero, Marcus Tullius, *De re Publica,* in Loeb Classical Library. New York, G.H. Putnam's Sons, 1928.

Cicero, Marcus Tullius, *On Orators and Oratory,* translated by J.S. Watson. London, George Bell and Son, 1903.

Cubberley, Ellwood P., *Readings in the History of Education,* pp. 23-39. New York, Houghton Mifflin Company, 1920.

Monroe, Paul, *Sourcebook of the History of Education for the Greek and Roman Period.* New York, The Macmillan Company, 1913.

Plutarch, *Lives of Illustrious Men,* translated by John and William Langhorne. Baltimore, William and Joseph Neal.

Quintilian, *Institutes of Oratory,* translated by H.H. Horne. New York, New York University Book Store, 1936.

Suetonius, *On Grammarians.*

Suetonius, *On Rhetoricians.*

Tacitus, *Dialogue Concerning Oratory.* New York, Harper and Brothers, 1858.

Vitruvius, *De Architectura,* in Loeb Classical Library. New York, G.P. Putnam's Sons, 1931.

2. Secondary Material:

Abelson, P., *The Seven Liberal Arts,* New York, Teachers College, Bureau of Publications, 1906.

Barnes, Harry Elmer, *An Intellectual and Cultural History of the Western World,* pp. 195-256. New York, Random House, 1937.

Butts, R. Freeman, *A Cultural History of Education,* pp. 80-132. New York, McGraw-Hill Book Company, Inc., 1947.

Cole, P.R., *Later Roman Education.* New York, Teachers College, Bureau of Publications, 1909.

Cubberley, Ellwood P., *A Brief History of Education,* pp. 28-41. New York, Houghton Mifflin Company, 1922.

Cubberley, Ellwood, P., *The History of Education,* Ch. III. Boston, Houghton Mifflin Company, 1920.

Davidson, Thomas, *A History of Education,* pp. 105-150. New York, Charles Scribner's Sons, 1900.

Duggan, Stephen, *A Student's Textbook in the History of Education*, pp. 51-65. New York, D. Appleton-Century Company, 1927.

Eby, Frederick and Arrowood, Charles F., *A History and Philosophy of Education, Ancient and Medieval*, pp. 515-577. New York, Prentice-Hall Inc., 1940.

Encyclopaedia Britannica: Articles on *Cicero, Livius Andronicus, Quintilian, Vitruvius.*

Graves, Frank P., *A History of Education Before the Middle Ages*, pp. 230-270. New York, The Macmillan Company, 1925.

Graves, Frank P., *A Student's History of Education*, pp. 50-59. New York, The Macmillan Company, 1936.

Gwynn, Aubrey, *Roman Education from Cicero to Quintilian.* New York, Oxford Press, 1926.

Laurie, Simon S., *Historical Survey of Pre-Christian Education*, pp. 301-411. New York, Longmans, Green & Co., 1915.

Melvin, A. Gordon, *Education, A History*, pp. 103-106. New York, The John Day Company, 1946.

Messenger, James F., *An Interpretative History of Education*, pp. 47-53. New York, Thomas Y. Crowell Company, 1931.

Monroe, Paul, *A Brief Course in the History of Education*, pp. 81-99. New York, The Macmillan Company, 1909.

Monroe, Paul, *A Text-Book in the History of Education*, pp. 176-218. New York, The Macmillan Company, 1907.

Moore, Ernest C., *The Story of Instruction: The Beginnings*, pp. 310-375. New York, The Macmillan Company, 1936.

Mulhern, James, *A History of Education*, pp. 160-180. Ronald Press Co., New York, 1946.

Painter, Franklin, *Great Pedagogical Essays*, pp. 83-142. New York, American Book Company, 1905.

Reisner, Edward H., *Historical Foundations of Modern Education*, pp. 105-222. New York, The Macmillan Company, 1928.

Wilds, Elmer Harrison, *The Foundations of Modern Education*, pp. 117-138. New York, Rinehart & Company, Inc., 1942.

Wilkins, A.S., *Roman Education.* Cambridge, The University Press, 1931.

CHAPTER VI

Education Among The Early Christians

Introduction

THE NATURE OF CHRISTIANITY. Christianity grew out of the spiritual genius of the Hebrew people and the personality of Jesus. Jesus built upon the Hebrew tradition, but added:

1. *An Enriched Interpretation of God:* God is universal and can be worshipped anywhere; God is a father who loves all animate nature; and God is an ethical being who can be approached only by the good.

2. *A Widened and Deepened Meaning of the Individual:* The individual soul is of supreme value and can attain perfection through self-sacrifice and absolute subordination of human nature to divine goodness. This goal is motivated by devotion to Jesus, the incarnation of the ideal.

3. *A Divine Society:* The Kingdom of God is the object of supreme loyalty. This is a universal society built on an ethical foundation. Loyalty to this is superior to all local loyalties or patriotisms. Love is the motivating force.

4. *A Spiritual Conception of the Church:* The church is a model of the good society, a spiritual organism. All members are equal.

JESUS AS A TEACHER. Jesus used teaching as the method of spreading his ideas. He was educated, as were the young Jews of his day, in the home and synagogue, and by listening to and questioning learned men. His teaching techniques were: 1. Informal conversation. 2. Use of proverbs. These were vivid, simple statements of truths which he used in place of long and involved reasoning or argument. 3. Use of parables: These were simple stories with a moral. The deeper spiritual meaning was apparent to those able to understand. They appealed to the imagination. 4. Speaking with authority and not as a disputant.

The Development of Christian Culture

BEGINNINGS. The Apostles had the personal experience of Jesus and the Jewish tradition of the Old Testament. Paul had a vision and a mission.

GROWTH OF A LITERATURE. *Mark* (65 to 70 A.D.), *Matthew* (70 to 75 A.D.), *Luke* (about 80 A.D.), *The Acts of the Apostles, John* (about 100 A.D.), *The Epistles, Revelation.* Other early Christian writings were *The Teaching of the Apostles, The Epistle of Barnabas, The Shepherd of Hermas.*

THE GROWTH OF A THEOLOGY. Christianity came into contact with other religions and philosophies and had to construct a systematic theology to justify itself to the inquiring minds of the day.

57

Christianity and the Greek World

RISE OF THE GREEK FATHERS. Many Christians, especially those at Alexandria, Constantinople, and other Eastern centers, were steeped in Greek learning and culture. Among these were:

1. *Saint Paul:* He was influenced by the Stoics and often quotes from the Greek writers.

2. *Clement of Alexandria:* He was a Platonist who believed that Christianity should be interpreted from the point of view of Plato. He held that philosophy is a revelation of the deeper meaning of God.

3. *Origen:* He studied philosophy and the sciences to better understand Christianity.

4. *Gregory of Nazianzen:* He taught that one should cull out the bad from philosophy and use the remainder to understand Christianity.

5. *Basil "the Great":* He greatly admired pagan thought.

But some eastern churchmen feared and even hated Greek philosophy and all " pagan" thought. This is illustrated by the position taken in the *Apostolic Constitution.*

RISE OF THE ROMAN FATHERS. The Roman leaders were practical men who saw Christianity as a way of life rather than a philosophy and thus were hostile to all Greek cultures. Some of these were:

1. *Tertullian:* He held that Satan had perverted human reason so that it could not be trusted, that all pagan thought was dangerous and would lead to contradictions and doubt.

2. *Augustine:* He loved the classics in his early life, but came to see no value in them later.

3. *Jerome:* He admired Cicero in his youth. Later he reached the opinion that one cannot serve both Cicero and Jesus and gave up Cicero.

4. *Fourth Council of Carthage:* In 398 A.D. this body prohibited the reading of secular material.

5. *Gregory the Great:* He held that liberal studies were the cause of schisms in the Greek church and banned them from the Roman Church in the interest of harmony.

Education in the Early Church

INTRODUCTION. Christianity is an educational religion. Jesus was a teacher, the Apostles were teachers, and Christian literature was pedagogical.

THE PROBLEM OF PAGAN LEARNING AND SCHOOLS. The question uppermost in many minds among the early Christians was: Should teachers in pagan schools continue their profession after their conversion to Christianity? Tertullian held that they should quit. A similar question worried Christian parents: Should parents send their children to pagan schools?

Tertullian said that they should send them to these schools but should teach them to separate learning from worship. Many parents feared pagan learning and refused to send their children to these schools.

THE CHRISTIAN HOME. Following Jewish tradition and Christian admonition, the home was the first Christian school. Many early church leaders owed their success to early home training.

Chrysostom (347-407 A.D.) wrote *Concerning the Education of Children.* In this he urged strict training from the cradle, that children be protected from early evil influences, and that they be encouraged to develop new and right interests. He developed a method of sex education, an education that led to marriage.

THE EDUCATIONAL STRUCTURE

1. *The Church and Teaching:* Teaching and preaching were of equal rank in the early church. Early Christians used the synagogue as a place to teach their way of life. The early leaders were basically teachers. Teaching was not an office and teachers were not a separate class. Teaching was a function of the early church.

2. *The Training of Leaders:* Church leaders gathered about themselves young men whom they taught to carry on their work. This was an apprenticeship technique.

3. *Catechumenal Schools:* The catechuminal training was a system of probation and instruction for all who wished to become members of the early church. The procedure consisted of: a preliminary examination and initiatory ceremonies, then two years as a "hearer," then application and instruction for baptism. After baptism the individual was a full member of the church.

These schools were discontinued after the 9th century. Texts used in instruction were: The *Old* and the *New Testaments,* the *Teachings of the Apostles,* and the *Epistle of Barnabas.*

4. *Catechetical Schools:* The reasons for the rise of these schools were: a) The Christians had abandoned hope for an immediate return of Jesus and the end of the world; b) Many from the cultured classes, well versed in pagan thought and highly educated, were entering the church, and c) Attacks were being made on Christianity by learned pagans. Private Schools: a) Justin Martyr (c. 100-163 or 167 A.D.), a philosopher converted to Christianity. He sought to reconcile pagan thought and Christianity and taught Christian thought to pagans. Tatian was his pupil. b) Theodotus (the cobbler) and Theodotus (the banker), sought to reconcile Aristotle's logic and Christianity. They also taught geometry and did some textual criticism. Church Schools: a) Alexandria: The school here grew out of the catechumenal school because of the great number of

learned and inquiring catechumens. Its purpose was to explain Christianity to the learned. Pantaenus, a converted Stoic, gave the first instruction in 179 A.D. Clement, a Platonist and a pupil of Pantaenus, was made assistant teacher and took over the school from about 189 until 202 A.D. Origen followed Clement from 202 to 231. Though Christain doctrine was central, general subjects were taught. These were used as leading to Christianity. b) Caesarea: The school here was established by Origen after he left Alexandria. Pamphilius collected a great library and Eusebius, his pupil, used the library to write his *Ecclesiastical History.* c) Antioch: Melchion founded the school here. He was followed by Lucian (c. 250 to 312 A.D.). John Chrysostom became its head. Here also Nestorius studied. This school opposed the allegorical method and used historical and grammatical methods. d) Edessa: Here was the "School of the Persians" established by Ephraem the Syrian in 363 A.D. Nestorius came to Edessa after 431, bringing Aristotle's works and those of many Greek scientists. This became the seat of Nestorian Christianity under the leadership of Ibas, the Bishop. The school was destroyed in 489 by the Greek Emperor Zeno because of his hatred of the Nestorians. e) Nisibis: Nestorius went to Nisibis to avoid persecution. Here a school was established with Nassai at the head. This school flourished and became highly influential. The school was housed in a monastery and the pupils were under strict rule. Scholars translated the Greek classics in Syrian and from the school many Nestorians went among the Arabians, translated the classics, and manned many of the Mohammedan schools. The Nestorians carried Greek science to the Mohammedans who developed it and passed it on to the Persians, Hindus, Chinese, and Moslems in Spain. **The Values of These Schools:** They were centers of instruction, inquiry, and research. They were centers of Christian literature and theology - the scholarly centers of the early church.

THE EDUCATION OF GIRLS. The early church held women in high respect. The Scriptures were the basis of their education. Saint Jerome wrote on the education of girls and had considerable influence upon this for many years after his death. Girls were trained in handicraft and religion, were permitted no freedom or self-expression, given strict monastic protection, and were to avoid all temptation; so Jerome advocated.

Growth of the Church

THE PERIOD OF THE EVANGELISTS. The apostles and young men trained by them preached and taught the people in the synagogues, private homes, and public places.

THE RISE OF CATHEDRAL CHURCHES. As churches were organized, separate church buildings were erected and leaders employed. The churches in cities became the seats of the bishops or leaders of the areas and were called cathedrals. The bishop and his assistants organized smaller churches in outlying areas. Thus the parish and diocese developed.

CHANGES WITHIN THE CHURCH

1. *The Development of Creeds:* It became necessary to state Christianity in logical and systematic form because: Christianity needed to defend itself in the face of pagan criticism, and it became necessary to separate the orthodox from the heretical. Thus, three creeds developed: the Apostles' Creed, the Nicene Creed, and the Athanasian Creed.

2. *The Development of Worship:* Worship grew out of the synagogue service but became more elaborate and, in time, the celebration of the Last Supper was made central.

3. *Organization of the Clergy:* Early churches were independent and democratic bodies with officers and leaders. As leaders of large churches gained control of outlying or nearby churches and increased their power, the bishop as teacher and ruler of the church developed. Gradually an hierarchy took form consisting of a bishop, priests, deacons, and lower orders of the clergy.

4. *The Results of These Changes:* Beliefs became formal and the regimentation of control built a strong organization but tended to destroy the personal side of religion.

EDUCATION IN THE BISHOP'S HOUSE. The bishop lived in a Cathedral House with his assistants and a few young boys dedicated to the church by their parents. The bishop was the teacher of these. Thus, a school developed and an ordered household for religious service, training of the priesthood, and elementary education eventually took form. Much emphasis was placed upon music in the training of young men for the church choir.

BIBLIOGRAPHY

I. **Primary Sources:**

Augustine, *De Catechizandis Rudibus,* translated by Joseph Patrick Christopher. Washington, Catholic University of America, 1926.

Basil, *Ad Juvenes.*

Chrysostom, John, *Concerning the Education of Children,* translated by John Evelyn. London, Harvy Colburn, 1825.

Jerome, *On Female Education,* in American Journal of Education, Vol. V, pp. 593-598.

2. **Secondary Material:**

Barnes, Harry Elmer, *An Intellectual and Cultural History of the Western World,* pp. 267-325. New York, Random House, 1937.

Cubberley, Ellwood P., *A Brief History of Education,* pp. 44-59. New York, Houghton Mifflin Company, 1922.

Cubberley, Ellwood P., *A History of Education,* pp. 82-105. Boston, Houghton Mifflin Company, 1920.

Duggan, Stephen, *A Student's Textbook in the History of Education,* pp. 67-73. New York, D. Appleton-Century Company, 1936.

Eby, Frederick and Arrowood, Charles F., *The History and Philosophy of Education, Ancient and Medieval,* pp. 578-627. New York, Prentice-Hall, Inc., 1940.

Graves, Frank P., *A History of Education, Before the Middle Ages,* pp. 272-296. New York, The Macmillan Company, 1925.

Graves, Frank P., *A Student's History of Education,* pp. 62-68. New York, The Macmillan Company, 1936.

Hodgson, Geraldine, *Primitive Christian Education,* Chs. II III, IV, and VII. Edinburgh, T. and T. Clark, 1906.

Leis, Sister M. de Chantal, *Christian Utilization of Pagan Educational Facilities.* University of Pittsburgh, Bulletin, Oct. 1, 1934.

Marique, Pierre J., *History of Christian Education.* New York, Fordham University Press, 1924.

Messenger, James F., *An Interpretative History of Education,* pp. 54-62. New York, Thomas Y. Crowell Company, 1931.

Monroe, Paul, *A Brief Course in the History of Education,* pp. 102-110. New York, The Macmillan Company, 1909.

Monroe, Paul, *Cyclopedia of Education,* Articles on *Christian Education, Chrysostom.*

Monroe, Paul, *A Text-Book in the History of Education,* pp. 221-243. New York, The Macmillan Company, 1907.

Moore, Ernest C., *The Story of Instruction: The Church, the Renaissance and the Reformation,* pp. 1-91. New York, The Macmillan Company, 1938.

Mulhern, James, *A History of Education,* pp. 183-189. Ronald Press Co., New York, 1946.

Painter, Franklin, *A History of Education,* pp. 104-114. New York, D. Appleton-Century Company, 1904.

Reisner, Edward H., *Historical Foundations of Modern Education,* pp. 169-194. New York, The Macmillan Company, 1927.

Wilds, Elmer H., *The Foundations of Modern Education,* pp. 142-163. New York, Rinehart & Company, Inc., 1942.

CHAPTER VII

Education In The Middle Ages

Education between 300 and 600 A.D.

INTRODUCTION. This is a period of transition during which the ancient period of European history was passing and the Middle Ages were beginning. The Romans carried over much of the old into the new. During this period we constantly look backward to the past and ahead to the future.

MONASTICISM AND EDUCATION

1. *The Story of Persecutions of the Christians:* Persecution began in 64 A.D. and continued through the reign of Diocletian. While Rome was tolerant of religions, it persecuted the Christians because: Christianity was one sect among the Romans that abandoned the customs and beliefs of their fathers. The secrecy of Christianity led to many stories of evil practices. The Christians refused to take part in state religious observances. This meant disloyalty.

Persecutions strengthened Christianity in the Roman Empire. *Schools of the Martyrs* were founded to train and prepare Christians for the ever-possible persecution. In these Christians were taught self-denial, how to act before judges and in the arena, and methods of hardening the body to withstand suffering. This led to some fanaticism and exhibitionism.

2. *Growth of Asceticism:* Pre-Christian asceticism is to be found in the Greek mysteries, the practices of the Pythagorean Brotherhood, the Essenes, the Therapeutae, the Cynics, and the Neoplatonists. All these sects forsook pleasure and the things of the flesh in order to experience spiritual ecstacy. There was also much asceticism in the Old Testament.

The Christian Hermits: Many Christians practiced self-denial as they lived in society. Others forsook society to practice extreme self-denial. They lived as hermits because: a) The Christians were being persecuted and they wished to escape this danger. b) They desired to flee from the temptations of the Roman world. c) Taxation had become unbearable for many. d) They could not endure the tensions of the period of uncertainty. e) They were disgusted with the degeneracy and vice of the times. Some hermits dramatized the movement and made it popular, first in Syria and Egypt, and later throughout the Roman Empire. Considerable fanaticism and charlatanry resulted so that the church, desirous of using the movement, had to cull out the excesses. In spite of the extremes of some, asceticism had many values for Christianity.

3. *The Rise of Monasticism:* Hermits, who originally lived alone, began

to live in colonies and famous or well-known hermits attracted others
and became leaders of a group. Some of these leaders were: **Anthony,** who
formed a colony of hermits about 350 A.D. The members of the colony lived
as hermits but met on Saturdays and Sundays for worship. **Pachomius,** who,
in 320 A.D., formed a colony and established a "rule" governing the life
of the group. Soon other groups, both for men and for women, were
organized under this "rule." They combined work and worship. Later an
"order" developed under the rule of a Prior and with an Abbot in charge
of each group. Thus, monasticism was born. **Basil,** who founded Greek
monasticism near Pontus about the middle of the 4th century. His organization included an orphanage for both boys and girls and a school for
boys who planned to enter the monastery. Other boys who merely wanted an
education were also enrolled. Several monasteries under Basil's control
were organized in other sections of the country. **Athanasius** introduced
monasticism into Italy about the middle of the 4th century. **Eusebius,**
bishop of Vercelli, organized the staff of his cathedral as a monastery.

LEADERS OF THE ROMAN CHURCH

1. *Ambrose* (c. 340-397 A.D.). He was a famous church administrator, the
Bishop of Milan, who wrote widely on Christian theology. He held that on
matters of religion the Church was supreme. He was a leader of the ascetic
movement and urged perpetual virginity with such force that he had great
influence upon the education of girls during the Middle Ages. He developed
the Ambrosian chant and wrote many hymns.

2. *Augustine* (354-430 A.D.). He was Bishop of Hippo and a Latin
rhetorician who wrote widely on matters of religion. His most important
books for students of education are *Confessions, City of God,* and *Of
Christian Doctrine.* His *City of God* is based on the Neoplatonic conception of an earthly and temporal world over against a heavenly and
eternal city, the seat of all goodness and truth.

His educational theory is: The world of sense is full of error while
truth and goodness are in a Platonic world of ideas. We grasp truth
through intuition. Truth is defined by the church and only the church can
pass on truth or error. Reason is limited by church authority. One may
study secular subjects, but only to glean material for the study and
understanding of the Scriptures. This sets the pattern for mystical
meanings of Scriptures and definitely blocks progress in Biblical
scholarship. He did not trust the human mind and held that it must be
subordinate to the church, the source of true knowledge. Thus he retarded
free scholarship. He also held that the child's nature is evil and must
be curbed by severe punishment and discipline.

3. *Jerome* (331-420 A.D.). He was the translator of the *Vulgate.* A noted

scholar and ascetic, he turned from interest in Cicero and Latin scholarship to Christian asceticism. His letters on the education of girls had wide influence during the Middle Ages. In these he held that girls should be denied all liberty and all their normal life suppressed. He held that sense life is evil. He fixed the list of canonical books and apocryphal books of the Bible.

4. *Benedict* (480-543 A.D.). He fled from the evils of the world and lived as a hermit in a cave near Rome. Later he became abbot of a monastery nearby. In 520 A.D. he moved to Monte Cassino where he ruled for the remainder of his life. While at Monte Cassino he prepared the famous *Rule of Saint Benedict.* This required that each monk be attached to the monastery for life, that each monastery be an independent unit, and emphasized chastity, humility, charity, obedience, and poverty. He held that the monks should devote themselves to work and worship, should spend some time each day in reading, and that none should have private property.

In the 10th century several Benedictine monasteries united under one head and formed the Clunic Benedictines. This Order spread throughout Europe. The Cistercians or Grey Monks organized in the 10th century also. Houses of Benedictine nuns were established as early as the 6th century.

THE STORY OF THE PAPACY

1. *The early church was a loose organization.* Gradually the clergy became a separate class and strong bishops arose at Rome, Alexandria, Antioch, Jerusalem, and Constantinople. Valentinian III gave recognition to the Bishop at Rome as supreme in the west in 445 A.D. He was then called Pope.

2. *Leo I* (Pope from 440 to 461 A.D.) held the church together in the west and built its power in a Roman world overrun by barbarians.

3. *The West and the East grew apart* over bitter theological disputes and differences in language and ideas.

4. *Gregory the Great* (Pope from 590 to 604 A.D.) strengthened the power of the Roman church. He sent Augustine to England in 596. His writings had considerable influence upon the education of the clergy. He held that secular learning must be subordinated to religious learning and that Christian bishops should not read pagan literature.

THE SAVING OF CLASSICAL LITERATURE

1. *Boethius* (c. 480-524 A.D.): He was a bridge between the classical age and the Middle Ages. He translated Aristotle's writings, wrote commentaries on Porphyry's *Isagoge* and on Cicero's *Topics* and *Consolations of Philosophy.* He wrote in the fields of logic, religion, music, and

arithmetic.

2. *Cassiodorus* (c. 480-575 A.D.): He sought to preserve Latin learning and to Romanize the Goths. To accomplish the latter he worked through young Athalaric, but failed. He established two monasteries on his estate in southern Italy, made literary work paramount for his monks, and established a *scriptorium* in which many books were copied and bound. This practice was followed by other monasteries. His chief educational works are: *De Orthographia,* a work on spelling, and *Institutes,* a book containing a summary of the seven liberal arts.

WESTERN EUROPE IN 600 A.D. Western Europe was broken from the Roman Empire with its seat in Constantinople. The Franks, Lombards, Angles, and Saxons were masters of Europe. Teaching and learning were at a low ebb. Pagan schools were closed and pagan scholarship was in disfavor. The Church was in control of learning and the most important schools were in monasteries and cathedrals where the seven liberal arts were taught and the aim of education was dominantly religious.

Education between 600 and 1050 A.D.

INTRODUCTION. Although in many ways this period is a "dark age" of western culture, it is characterized by certain important educational developments and certain social and political factors which laid the foundations for later educational growth.

POLITICAL AND SOCIAL EVENTS OF THE PERIOD

1. *The Rise of Mohammedanism:* Mohammedanism was founded by Mohammed (c. 569-632 A.D.) in Arabia. Its sacred book is the *Koran.* Mohammed claimed absolute authority which he passed on to the Caliph. His followers, the Moslems, overcame Persia, northern Africa, Egypt, India, Spain. The Caliphs became sponsors of learning in these conquered areas so that the people assimilated and developed the arts and sciences.

2. *The Spread of Roman Christianity:* The Mohammedan conquests left Rome master in the west with no rival in Constantinople. Celtic Christianity was brought under Roman control. Britain had become Christian in Roman times but was overrun by the Saxons who wiped out the church everywhere save in Ireland. Here Christianity grew and the churches eventually sent missionaries to England, Scotland, and the continent. When Augustine went to England in 597 A.D. he found this work and was able to effect a union of Roman and Celtic beliefs and customs. Gradually all western Europe was brought under Roman control.

3. *The Rise of the Frankish Empire:* The early Frankish kingdom was weak from the time of Clovis to that of Pippin who founded the Carolingian dynasty in 751 A.D. The church gave its sanction to Pippin and he established a Papal state with the Pope as ruler. He was succeeded by his two

sons, Charles and Carloman. Carloman died and in 771 A.D. Charles, called Charlemagne, became sole king. He extended his kingdom, worked closely with the Pope, and was made Emperor of the Holy Roman Empire in 800 A.D. by Pope Leo III. He encouraged learning and established a "palace school" in his court. The Empire declined after his death.

4. *The Vikings:* These were Scandanavian warriors and explorers who planted colonies in France, England, and at other places along the shores of Europe. They penetrated into the Frankish kingdom and became Christian. These were known as the Norsemen and their area called Normandy. They also conquered Sicily and Italy. The Norsemen also penetrated England and dominated southern England while the Danes were in control of England north of the Thames. Alfred the Great, king of Wessex, stopped the Norsemen and the Danes and organized a strong military government. His successors became kings of England and merged the Saxons and Norsemen under their rule. Canute, in 1016, united England and Denmark and later Norway and the Hebrides into an empire. He made England a nation with distinctive institutions.

5. *Feudalism:* Weakness of Roman rule in Western Europe led to grants being made to strong warriors in return for military help. This eventually created a noble class of powerful lords and marks the breakdown of the large-pattern state. Under Feudalism military skill, loyalty, and courage were stressed in education and the sciences and liberal arts were neglected.

6. *The Growth of the Papacy:* Gradually the papacy fell into disrepute. The office became a prize of rival Italian factions. Later the German Emperors rescued it from the Italians only to become its masters. But forces were at work which laid the foundation of its later power and prestige: Its missionary work among the people of Britain, Ireland, and the Teutonic countries produced vast populations loyal to Rome. The church made alliances with secular rulers which were beneficial to both. The church gave prestige to the rulers and the rulers accepted the authority of the church in many matters. Forged documents were employed to bolster the power of the church: a) The Donation of Constantine - a deed by which Constantine, after the establishment of Constantinople, gave all power in the west to the Bishop at Rome, b) The Pseudo-Isidorean Decretals - falsely dated documents holding that the pope had power at a much earlier date than he actually held such.

The church issued educational decrees of considerable importance at this time: A council called by Eugenius II in 826 ordered the bishops to designate teachers of liberal arts and religion in all diocese and parishes. A council held at Rome in 853 ordered clerics to teach in episcopal schools and required elementary instruction be given in the Bible and in worship in all parishes.

7. *Organization of the Church:* The parish was a community served by a priest and a diocese was many parishes supervised by a bishop. In about 685 Theodore of Tarsus divided England into parishes and diocese. Many parishes were endowed by local civil authorities who sought to control the priests. The Kings gave land to the bishoprics and claimed the right to nominate and control the appointment of bishops. Thus, a struggle developed between the church and the civil authorities for power. This was a factor leading to the Reformation. Further, the clergy - monks or regular clerics, and priests or secular clerics - were often nationalistic and fought the power of Rome. Many monasteries were federated, as the Congregation of Cluny, and came under direct control of the Pope. These turned from secular learning to devotion and good works.

EDUCATION IN WESTERN EUROPE BEFORE CHARLEMAGNE

1. *Isadore of Seville* (c. 570-636): He was bishop of Seville from 600 to 636. A scholar typical of his age, he wrote *Etymologies,* an encyclopedia of the liberal arts and general knowledge. Characteristics of his work are: absolute subservience to authority; the religious dominated the secular; allegory prominent; and the supernatural dominated the natural.

2. *Education in Spain:* There were many schools in monasteries serving as training centers for the clerics. The Council of Toledo, in 531, ordered that boys sent to bishops for training for the priesthood must be educated by masters chosen for the purpose. Another Council of Toledo, held in 633, ordered boys in cathedral schools to live in one room under the supervision of older men and the discipline of the church.

3. *Education in Ireland:* Ireland produced the Bards and a literature that was its own, not Roman. Many Christians fled to Ireland during the barbarian invasions. The Druids had pupils who followed them from place to place and learned. Schools of law, military science, and literature were established early. Bardic schools were organized in time. Also, the practice of fosterage, children sent to homes of relatives for their education, was practiced widely. In the monasteries established after Christianity came to Ireland schools thrived and many students came from all parts of Europe to study in them.

4. *Education in England:* There were many centers of learning in England during this period: **Canterbury** - here was the center of Roman Christianity. Theodore of Tarsus and Hadrian made this a famous center of learning. **Malmesbury** - here was a monastery founded by Irish missionaries to which was attached a famous school. **Jarrow** - a Benedictine monastery

was located here and from this setting came Bede. **York** - this school produced Alcuin. The leaders of English education at this time were: **Aldhelm** (c. 640-709) - He was educated at Malmesbury and Canterbury and had a wide acquaintance with classical and religious literature. He wrote both in Latin and in Anglo-Saxon. He composed several songs. **Venerable Bede** (673-735) - He wrote commentaries on the Bible, school books, and the famous *Ecclesiastical History*.

THE REVIVAL OF LEARNING UNDER CHARLEMAGNE

1. *Factors Basic to the Revival Were:* The remains of classical learning and culture in Gaul; the work of Latin church Fathers; the Irish and Northumbrian scholars and their missionary work; the efforts of the Carolingian kings for better education, and the peace of the time which gave culture a chance to develop.

2. *The Work of Charlemagne:* Charlemagne was a well-educated man who sought to educate his children, raise the standards of education among the clergy, and improve worship. Charlemagne encouraged scholars to come to his court. Thus, there was established at this court a rich center of learning in which he participated and learned. Much valuable literature and scholarly material were issued from this center. Schools of the times: a) Palace school - Alcuin came from York to be its head (the school having existed from the time of Charles Martel). Children of the court and other boys of promise enrolled. Other scholars worked with Alcuin, teaching, collecting books, and writing. b) Monastic schools - Alcuin became abbot of the monastery of Saint Martin at Tours and head of the school there. This school enrolled both boys who planned to enter the church and boys who desired an education but had no clerical ambitions. The liberal arts, music, writing, and religion were taught. c) Cathedral schools - These taught the liberal arts and stimulated the copying of manuscripts. Music was also stressed The discipline was severe. Improvements in general education: Charlemagne worked through the church which he considered as under his authority. In this manner he sponsored a revision of the *Vulgate,* had sermons prepared for the priests in his kingdom, enforced the Benedictine Rule in monasteries of the kingdom, worked for the establishment of schools in villages and on estates, and issued a number of decrees dealing with education, especially those of 787 and 789.

3. *The Results of the Revival:* It helped restore classical culture to Gaul; libraries were built at many monasteries; many pupils became leaders in the revival of scholarship throughout Europe, and learning never again sank as low as it had been before Charlemagne's times.

THE DEVELOPMENT OF ARABIC LEARNING. The Arabs included people of

Arabia, Syria, Egypt, the Berbers, the Saracens, and the Moors, all bound together by a religion and a culture. The religion was Mohammedanism, the language was Arabic, and the culture was a mixture of strains. There were two capitols, one at Baghdad and the other at Cordova. The Arabs assimilated Greek thought and science, took much from China and India, and made extensive advances along many lines. They passed this all along to Western Europe. Some Christian theology developed in debates between the Christians and the Moslems (see John of Damascus). The Arabs developed Arabic grammar, historical scholarship, oratory, and poetry and did much translating of works in other languages into Arabic. The House of Wisdom was established at Baghdad in 830 by the Caliph al-Ma'mum.

EDUCATION AFTER THE DEATH OF CHARLEMAGNE

1. *Rabanus Maurus* (776-856): He was the most famous pupil of Alcuin. He headed the monastery school at Fulda and later became abbot of the monastery. He did much to build the library at Fulda and to train numerous influential pupils. He also wrote widely.

2. *John the Scot* (810-875): He was sponsored by Charles the Bald. He was a translator and a writer, a freethinker who held that authority comes from reason but that reason and divine authority are not in conflict.

3. *Alfred the Great* (848-901): He became king of Wessex in 866 and set about to revive learning in his kingdom. He laid the foundation for the English language by encouraging literary production in the English tongue.

4. *The Role of the Church in Education:* **The Council of 826** - The bishops began to assume control of education. Thus, church sponsored scholarship increased and education came more definitely under the control of the church hierarchy. **The Council of 853** - This provided for a school in each parish for the teaching of the elements of religion and one at every cathedral for the teaching of the liberal arts. **The Council of Paris (824)** and the **Council of Valens (855)** - Instead of condemning the liberal arts, the church was turning to the teaching of both the liberal arts and the sciences.

5. *Gerbert* (c. 950-1003): He served as Pope Sylvester II from 999 to 1003. He was a scholar of the classical tradition, an inventor, and a teacher of the classics. He built libraries and sponsored the development of learning throughout the church. His pupils included Fulbert, refounder of the cathedral school at Chartres, and Richner, founder of a school of medicine.

Education from 1050 to 1300 A.D.

INTRODUCTION

1. *The Period:* During the 12th and 13th centuries forces with roots in

the early Middle Ages came to full development and resulted in a Medieval
Renaissance. The achievements of the period included: Founding of the
universities; the birth of constitutional monarchy and of parliamentary
government; the climax of Gothic architecture; religious institutions
gained independence from secular authorities; the growth of vernacular
languages and literature, and scholasticism. The characteristics of the
period are: The medieval spirit attained its most complete and rich
embodiment in art, literature, and scholarship; the inspiration for the
period came from Christian and Imperial Rome; the achievements of the
period were within the bounds of authority and the constituted institutions; and this development touched only a small portion of the
population. The political events of the period included: **The Norman
Conquest of England** - This led to the growth of a strong monarchy which
encouraged progress and development along many lines. **The Conquest of
Toledo** - By this Christian scholars were introduced to Arabic learning
and the long-neglected Greek learning then in Arabic translations. **The
Norman Conquest of Sicily** - This made available to western scholars much
classical learning. **The Crusades** did much to change and enrich European
culture while at the same time they impoverished the culture. Developments within the church during the period included: **The Cistercian
Order** - This contributed to unity among the monasteries, emphasized
labor among the monks, and drew many away from the world. Bernard of
Clairvaux, an anti-rationalist, was the leader. He turned from learning
and European monasticism tended to follow his lead. Scholarship and
teaching passed into the hands of secular clerics and cathedral canons.
The Friars - These included the Franciscans, Dominicans, Augustinians, and
Carmelites. They worked in cities and devoted themselves largely to
preaching. Some entered the universities and produced many great
scholars. **The Spiritual Supremacy of the Church** - In fights with secular
rulers a compromise was reached which gave the church authority in
spiritual matters and turned over to secular authorities temporal matters.

INSTITUTIONS OF LEARNING DURING THE PERIOD

1. *The Decline of Monastic Schools:* Teaching in monasteries had always
been secondary to devotion. Their schools and teaching activities
developed largely because there were no other institutions to do the
work. Also, the Cistercian reforms disparaged learning in monasteries.

2. *Learning in Cathedral and Collegiate Churches:* **Organization** - The
cathedral was the center of the diocese and the seat of the bishop. Many
clergy were attached to each cathedral, were organized into a chapter,
and lived under a rule or canon. Thus they were called canons. A Dean was
at the head of each chapter. Under him was a *percentor* in charge of

music, a treasurer, and a schoolmaster (called a *scholasticus* on the continent and a chancellor in England). The collegiate church was a great church with a college of canons but not the seat of a bishop. **Schools in These Churches** - Many scholars were attached to these churches. They conducted schools, including a school of theology, a school for the teaching of the *quadrivium,* a school for the teaching of the *trivium,* and a song school. The **School at Chartres** - here was considerable interest in the classics.

3. *Learning at the Courts of Great Princes:* Princes, needing scholars to help in civil administration, established schools in their courts. They also gave patronage to literary men and encouraged scholarship along many lines.

4. *Learning in the Cities:* Here developed schools of law, medicine, and the liberal arts. Eventually these became the seats of universities.

METHODS FOR THE GROWTH OF SCHOLARSHIP

1. *The Seven Liberal Arts:* The Greeks made a division between studies appropriate for the rational class and those appropriate for the masses. The former included philosophy and the abstract sciences, the "cultural" subjects as distinguished from the useful. The Romans set the pattern of the Seven Liberal Arts. Varro and Quintilian discussed them and Capella, in his *Marriage of Philology and Mercury,* definitely set the number and the content of each. Other writers (Boethius, Cassiodorus, and Isadore) made the division between the *trivium* (grammar, rhetoric, and dialectic) and the *quadrivium* (arithmetic, geometry, astronomy, and music). During the Middle Ages there was considerable development in most of these areas and the schools of the times made them the basis of their curriculums.

2. *Experience and Observation:* As earlier man learned by observation of his world and from his experiences, so the man of the Middle Ages. His learning was not confined wholly to the authoritative statements of the past. Emperor Frederick II (1194-1250) was deeply interested in and encouraged learning from experience. *The Falcon Book* and Jordanus Ruffus' *Horse-Healing* are works based on experience and careful observation. Henry II of England encouraged experimentation and the study of natural phenomena.

3. *Translations:* This was a period of avid translating of the classics both from the Arabic and from the Greek. The Crusades, commerce, and Christian conquest of Toledo, Sicily, and Syria opened the door to sources of the classics. These were translated into Latin. By 1200 most of Greek science and philosophy were in Latin translations and Christian theologians were beginning to effect a fusion of Greek and Christian thought of which the *Summa Theologica* of Thomas Aquinas was the

culmination.

4. *Latin Language and Literature:* Medieval Latin was a living language at this time, growing and yet held to high standards by reference to classical models. A vast amount of literature in Latin appeared, both sacred and profane. Many grammars, plays, poems, epics, satires, legends, biographies, and treatises on religion and government were produced.

5. *Logic:* With the translation of the *Posterior Analytics* of Aristotle, the Middle Ages had a powerful tool for study. This gave scholars the deductive method which they applied to law and theology with much success. It could be employed within the framework of church authority.

THE GROWTH OF SCHOLARSHIP

1. *Scholasticism:* Scholasticism was the movement in Medieval scholarship in which deductive logic was used within the bounds of the authoritative church doctrine to search for truth. Its significance lies in the facts that: a) It developed and refined deductive logic; b) It sharpened meanings; c) It trained many keen thinkers who gradually moved out of Scholasticism to richer scholarship; and d) It added much to knowledge in the fields of theology and law. **The Problem of Universals** - Plato held that the universal is real and that things are mere copies. Neo-Platonism, the Christian modification of Plato, held that concepts caused by universals partake of their reality. Realism was the medieval interpretation of this position, the basis of scholastic philosophy. The Realists held that the reality of an object lies in its essence or substance which is the same for all similar objects. Objects are different because of accidents. This position was vital to the doctrine of the Trinity, the problem of the relation of knowledge to existence, theory of government, and education. Anselm (1033-1109) was the leader of the Realists. Nominalism, lead by Roscellinus (1050-1121), was the position that universals are merely names and individual objects are the true realities. The importance of these doctrines for education lies in the facts that: a) Theology was made the basis for all thinking and men turned away from the study of phenomena as useless, and b) Logic was made the supreme method of study. **Abelard** (1079-1142) - He was a popular teacher at Paris who held that by reasoning one would strengthen his belief in the authoritative doctrines of the church. In his *Sic et Non (Yes and No)* he cited texts for and against 158 theological issues to prove that the arguments for the church's position were stronger than those against. This started many to thinking. He was interested in dialectical study and not science. His significance: a) He stimulated dialectical study to the detriment of literary and scientific study, and

b) He drew world-wide attention to the schools at Paris and stimulated the growth of the University of Paris. **Peter the Lombard** (1100-1164) - He wrote *Four Books of Sentences*. This was an attempt, highly successful, to bring together the pronouncements of various churchmen into a single system of theology. It served as a textbook in theology for many generations and set a pattern for similar books. **The Dominican Order** - This was an order of Preaching Friars founded by Dominic (1170-1221) who was concerned about the Albigensian heresy and believed it could be combatted best by a disciplined and learned priesthood. The discipline of the Order made it powerful in church affairs. Its leaders turned to Aristotle to combat the teachings of the Arabic thinkers, Avicenna (980-1037) and Averroes (1126-1198). Among its leaders were: a) Albert the Great (1193-1280), called Albertus Magnus, who mastered Aristotle and attacked one by one the points of Moslem doctrine; b) Thomas Aquinas (1221-1274), a native of Italy, who was educated at the monastery of Monte Cassino but joined the Dominicans and studied with Albertus Magnus. He mastered Aristotle and wrote the *Summa Theologica* which was made the official philosophical system of the Catholic Church by order of Pope Leo XIII in 1879. He produced a great mass of scholarship which formed the core of studies for the clergy. He also set the pattern of church philosophical studies. **The Franciscian Order** - This Order was founded by Francis of Assisi in 1212 to serve the sick and poor and cultivate mystical religious experiences. Later the Order turned to scholarship, political activity within the church, and missionary work in the cities. It was known in France as the Cordeliers, in Germany as the Barefoot Friars, and in England as the Grey Friars. Among the leaders of the order were: a) Alexander of Hales who sought in a *Summa* to reconcile Aristotle's philosophy and Christian theology. b) Robert Grossetest (1175-1253) who translated many Greek classics. His humanistic leanings influenced English scholarship. c) Roger Bacon (1214-1294) who sought independence from authority and reliance upon observation and experimentation. d) Duns Scotus (d. 1308) who was the extreme realist among the Franciscians. e) William of Occam (d. 1349) who was the extreme nominalist of the Order.

2. *Legal Scholarship:* Roman law had continued into the Middle Ages in codes of the barbarians, at Ravenna, Byzantium, and in Italy. The rise of strong governments, the power of the Papacy and the Italian states stimulated concern with law and legal studies. Scholars turned to the *Digest* of Justinian. Among the legal scholars of the period were: **Irnerius** (d. 1130) who made Bologna a center of legal studies and mastered civil law. **Gratian,** a monk at Bologna, who in 1140 made a compilation of canon law called a *Concord of Discordant Canons* (the

Decretum). He used scholastic methods in his work.

3. *Medical Scholarship:* Greek medical learning had continued in southern Italy and in Sicily during the Middle Ages. Salerno was a center of healing and medical scholarship. Many Greek and Arabic works on medicine were translated into Latin here and thus Western Europe gained possession of the medical lore of the ancients and the Arabs.

The Rise of the Universities
BACKGROUND MATERIAL

1. *Conditions in the Middle Ages Which Made the Universities Possible:* Europe was, with minor exceptions, united under the Roman church. Learning was held in high respect throughout Europe as the key to religious truth. A large body of scholarship had developed and there was a growing number of scholars in Europe. This scholarship was Latin and Christian and took on its particular hue because a) The expanding church and civil bureaucracies were demanding the legalistic mind and professional preparation obtained by the shortest possible route; b) The science of the Middle Ages came not from the Greek directly but through the medium of Arabic translations and commentaries. These lacked the humanistic tone of the originals. And c) The church and the Dominican Friars were more concerned with "divine" truth than with the study of phenomena. Their's was the scholastic point of view.

2. *Distinctive Characteristics of the Medieval University:* It had no buildings or equipment and thus it could maintain its independence and fight for its liberties. Its aim was professional training, usually in law, medicine, or theology. It was not local but had an European character, attracting students and teachers from all Europe, and giving its first allegiance to the Pope.

3. *The Important Features of the Medieval University:* It was a corporation, a society of teachers and scholars. Students from various parts of Europe and teachers united into guilds - masters' guilds and students' guilds - for mutual aid and protection. These had legal status and rights. They were also called "nations." At the northern universities the authority was in the hands of the masters while in the southern universities it was in the hands of the students. It enjoyed certain liberties, privileges, and immunities (grants made by civil rulers or the papacy) in legal matters, freedom from taxation and certain services, and the rights to suspend lectures or to move to another place. It also had authority to deal with certain legal cases and enforce its decisions. It held a monopoly over the license which gave one the right to teach. It presented candidates to church authorities who granted the license. The university vouched for the student's soundness in faith and scholarship

and the church conferred the right to teach.

SOME TYPICAL MEDIEVAL UNIVERSITIES

1. *Introduction:* The great universities, with few exceptions, were not founded nor established, but grew out of the free association of scholars. Their purpose was professional training. Even though the Faculty of Arts, concerned with teaching the Seven Liberal Arts, existed at each institution and formed the basis for other studies, the culminating purpose of the university was found in the professional faculties.

2. *Salerno:* Southern Italy was strongly influenced by the Greeks as early as the 6th century B.C. and remained Greek in many respects through the Middle Ages. The Eastern Empire held authority over Salerno and Byzantine influence was strong. Here also Graeco-Roman medicine survived the collapse of the Roman Empire. Here medicine was practiced and translations of Arabic, Greek, and Jewish medical works were made. Thus a voluntary association of physicians, students, and teachers of the arts developed. This never became a university organization, but received official recognition in 1230 when Frederick II gave its masters the right to examine those wishing to practice or teach medicine in the Kingdom of Sicily. Students were required to spend 5 years studying medicine after completing 3 years in the study of the liberal arts. The doctors were organized under a *praepositue* (later a prior). The curriculum of medical education for the medieval university was built at Salerno, textbooks were written, and teachers were prepared for other universities.

3. *Bologna:* The rise of the city-state in the 11th century was accompanied by a struggle between church authorities, municipal authorities, and feudal lords. Church and municipal authorities appealed to Roman law to support their claims against the feudal lords. This led to: The rise of the University of Bologna out of a) monastic schools in the city; b) the cathedral in the city; and c) the city's system of municipal schools. The revival of Roman law and legal scholarship. Scholars went behind compendiums and codes to study the actual opinions of ancient jurists. Here Irnerius wrote and taught. The motivating forces of this revival were: a) A rebirth of Italian nationalism. b) The revival of Italian commerce with its demand for lawyers. c) The growing influence of the city-states of Lombardy. The establishment of canon law as an exact body of knowledge. Here, in 1140, Gratian brought authoritative pronouncements of the past into a systematic form in his *Harmony of Discordant Decrees* (the *Decretum*) and "founded" the science of canon law. This became the authoritative textbook in the field. Here Irnerius, Gratian, and other legal authorities taught students from all western Europe. The teachers of law formed guilds and other faculties were organized. The

students formed themselves into guilds for mutual protection. These student guilds became the University of Bologna, but the academic functions of the university were under control of the doctors' guilds. The university was recognized by Pope Clement III in 1189.

4. *Paris:* The University of Paris grew out of three schools located at Paris: the cathedral school of Notre Dame, the school of the collegiate church of Sainte Genevieve, and a school conducted by the canons of Saint Victor. The *studium generale* had an ecclesiastical character. Students and masters were clerics, the church determined the rights and privileges, and the organization was an hierarchy. The *licentia docendi* was granted by the chancellors of Notre Dame and Sainte Genevieve. The masters gained control over teaching and study. The charter was granted in 1208. This protected the students and masters and gave them many privileges including that of suspending lectures in protest. After the riot of 1228 the university was dissolved for 6 years. Gregory IX settled the dispute and the university was reopened.

5. *Oxford:* Many schools were located at Oxford before 1150. The town attracted scholars and a teaching and student body grew. The character of the *studium* was English. When, in 1167, Henry II ordered all clerics deriving incomes from English churches to return to England and the King of France expelled all alien scholars from his kingdom, many scholars moved to Oxford. Thus the university developed. The practices at Oxford included: the masters controlled the university; the faculty of arts predominated; students organized "nations," each with a protector; the chancellor was first appointed by the Bishop of Lincoln, but later he was elected by the masters; and "Colleges" grew out of endowed hostels.

6. *Naples:* This university was established by Emperor Frederick II in 1224 to provide trained administrators for the kingdom and also as retaliation against the cities of the north. The university was under political authority.

7. *Rome:* This university was founded by Pope Innocent IV in 1245 to train specialists in civil and canon law. It was called the University of the Roman Court. Theology, Greek, Arabic, Chaldee, Hebrew, philosophy, and medicine were also taught. It was controlled by a college of doctors.

CONDUCT OF THE MEDIEVAL UNIVERSITY

1. *Awards and Degrees:* At first the terms for degrees were used informally and only gradually did they assume definite status. These included: **Inception** - the reception of a teacher into the guild of masters. **Licentia Docendi** - the license to teach. The church nominally held the right to confer this license, but came to accept the recommendations of the faculties. This came in time to include the license to

practice law, medicine, or theology. **Master** and **Doctor** - at first all licensed persons were called master, doctor, or professor. Later these titles came to mean rank and were called degrees. **Bachelor** - this was a title given to students beginning their work. Later it became a degree.

2. *Teaching and Learning Methods:* These included: **The Lecture** - The instructor read the text, gave an exposition, commented upon matters of special interest, and raised problems for discussion. This was all definitely determined and commentaries were written in "glosses" from which there could be no deviation. **Repetition** - This consisted of discussions of lectures by the students. **The Disputation** - This was a debate and was of two kinds: a) One student would present arguments for and against a thesis, seeking to prove one side, and b) Students or masters would engage in debates with each other either as learning exercises or as public argumentation of an important thesis. **Examinations** - These were employed to determine the fitness of a candidate for a degree and were attended with much form and ceremony.

3. *Physical Assets:* The universities had no buildings, libraries, or laboratories. The lectures were given in the streets, public places, or in the homes of teachers.

4. *Studying at a University:* The students mastered books and commentaries. They were not encouraged to do independent research. The time required to complete the work differed widely throughout Europe.

5. *The Rise of Colleges:* These grew out of the living quarters of groups of students. They first took form at Paris. Later endowments were given for the establishment of living quarters for poor students and these eventually grew into colleges. In some places colleges became teaching units within a university while in others they remained merely residence halls.

6. *Women at the Universities:* Although there were a few women of learning and some woman teachers in university towns, the universities were men's institutions and women were excluded from learning at this level.

7. *Life on the Campus:* Students of all ages and all levels of society were in attendance. These engaged in many activities, some good and some bad. There was considerable horseplay, drinking, brawling, and many illegal ventures.

Education in Feudalistic Society

WHO WERE THE NOBLES? The nobles were the governing class of the Middle Ages. They were members of the knightly order.* Knights were mounted troops, the cavalry of the times. Knights held their estates as gifts from overlords to whom they owed military service.

THE HOME OF THE NOBLE. The castle and manor were centers of feudal activity, small, self-contained communities. Castles were great manor houses in which schools were conducted for both boys and girls. The teaching in these schools aimed at training in the code and skills of the noble class, some religion, slight literary knowledge, management of estates, and proficiency in arms. The methods used were participation and some direct instruction.

CHARACTERISTICS OF THE NOBLE. The noble or knight was an army officer who combined in his nature war, religion, and gallantry. Thus he was highly class-conscious, snobbish, selfish, scheming, brutal, crude, and with morals that could not be commended today. There were many knights who lived near to the ideal pictured in the literature of chivalry, but as a class the knights were children of their age.

THE LITERATURE OF CHIVALRY. Chivalry was the ideal of the knightly way of life. This was pictured in both prose and poetry and included works on manners, laws of the knightly class, histories of chivalry, stories of the deeds of knights, and much romantic literature.

THE EDUCATION OF THE NOBLE

1. *A few boys and girls* went to schools but most of the sons and daughters of nobles were educated in the courts or castles of great nobles. Participation and observation were the most popular methods. The boy began his education in his home. At 7 he was sent to the castle or court where he passed through definite stages of training: **Page** (from 7 to 14 years) - he was taught by women and learned the graces, games, deportment, and some intellectual skills. **Squire** (from 14 to 21 years) - he was apprenticed to a knight and learned military skills. **Knight** - at 21 he became a knight after an impressive ceremony.

2. *The Curriculum of Knightly Training:* This consisted of: **Management of Estates and Households.** Both boys and girls learned how to manage the estates upon which they lived. These estates were self-contained communities including many workers and many important activities. **Courtesy and Polite Accomplishments.** Children were trained in the social graces of their class, in music, dancing, chess, falconry and the chase, dice, backgammon, the tournament, and fencing on horseback. **Literary Education.** This was subordinated to practical training. It included feudal law, languages, heraldry, and religion. **Instruction in War.** This included skill in the use of weapons and in the science and art of war. It was very practical and based on participation and contact with an experienced knight.

3. *The Education of Women:* Women were trained very much as the men save that war was eliminated. Their education led to either: **Nun** - she

might enter a nunnery and take a position of leadership, or **Manager of a Household** - this included social leadership, business efficiency, and religion. Also, the woman had some training in the intellectual areas.

Education of the Guild

INTRODUCTION. With the growth of cities and of commerce the place and value of production became more important. Handicraft developed to a high degree of perfection and plans were made to teach the skills to others.

THE GUILDS

1. *What Were the Guilds?* The guilds were associations of workers organized for mutual aid and protection, for social purposes, for common worship, for the protection of the public, and for the regulation of commerce and manufacturing. Some guilds were religious or charitable, some were for artisans, and some were for merchants. There was some legal regulation of the guilds. They were usually self-perpetuating.

2. *How One Became a Member:* In early times he entered as an apprentice, served 7 years without pay and learned the work, became a journeyman who could work for wages, and then became a master who could own his own shop, take apprentices, and hire journeymen. Later sons of masters took over the master's shop and a sharp separation of master and workman was made.

3. *Contributions to Education:* The guilds supported schools, helped poor students, paid the salaries of teachers, and had considerable influence upon municipal support of education.

4. *Apprentice Education:* The master took the apprentice under a certificate of indenture specifying the duties of both the master and the apprentice. The master taught the apprentice the trade or craft and cared for him. Either municipal authorities or the guilds enforced these requirements to protect both the master and the apprentice.

Education of the English Lawyer

ENGLISH LAW. This was a body of learning and a field of professional activity reserved for laymen. Clerics were excluded.

INNS OF THE COURT. Lawyers belonged to societies called inns. These occupied houses near the King's Court. Students, who had completed grammar school and possibly the university, lived in the inns with the lawyers who taught them. These were all Englishmen and their attitude was nationalistic. The expenses were heavy so that law was a profession for the wealthy. Students read law, disputed, and tried mock cases under the supervision of their teachers.

Public Education in the Later Middle Ages

DEVELOPMENT ON THE EUROPEAN CONTINENT

1. *Motivating Factors:* The increasing need for and interest in writing

and reading. This grew out of: a) the growth of civic life, b) the increased volume of guild business, c) the expansion of commerce and business, d) the coming of the universities for training in the higher professions, and e) the spreading interest in religious literature. Skill in writing made one independent of the clergy, who were the official scribes of the times, was basic to success, and opened the door to higher culture. The Latin Grammar schools were not adequate to meet the needs; thus a new type of school was needed.

2. *The Growth of Secular Education:* Schools before the 12th century were attached to cathedrals, monasteries, and parish churches. The *scholasticus* controlled teaching. Factors which contributed to the transfer of this control to lay authorities were: The Italian towns controlled municipal academies and boasted many private schools under lay teachers. Contact with Italy spread the idea of public control of education in northern Europe. The increasing knowledge of Aristotle popularized his advocacy of public education. Temporal rulers had been more or less active in education during the entire Middle Ages. This activity increased during the 12th century and following.

3. *Types of Schools:* **Burgh Latin Grammar Schools** - These were Latin Grammar schools identical with those established by the church but were under municipal control. They supplied education for children of the burgher class, the commercial class, in the conduct of business, government, and guild matters. Latin was also taught. **Writing and Reading Schools** - These were elementary schools for both boys and girls with instruction in the vernacular. The city selected the teachers and supported the schools. The founding of such schools at Brussels in 1320 is typical. **Schools for Girls** - The towns were interested in the education of girls and many established schools for girls along with those for boys. There was some co-education. **Private Schools** - These were established by wandering teachers who collected fees for their teaching. These schools were given various names: Winkel, Klipp, Hedge.

4. *Church Attitude Toward Public Schools:* The church authorities fought the establishment of municipal schools because: They threatened the church's monopoly over education. They decreased the revenue of the church and the *scholasticus*. The battle was bitter. Usually a compromise was reached. The towns established and controlled Latin schools taught by priests. The revenue of the *scholasticus* was protected. The battle was not over doctrinal differences.

5. *Progress of These Schools:* There was bitter competition between schools for pupils and revenue, but municipal schools increased in number. Alms were given for the support of poor students and begging was

permitted. Reading, writing, reckoning, and singing became most popular among the subjects taught.

DEVELOPMENT IN ENGLAND.

1. *Introduction:* The schools which developed in England during the 12th and 13th centuries are important for the history of education in the United States. Here the Latin Grammar school took form. Also a pattern of education was established which was little changed for many generations.

2. *Early English Education:* The church maintained many types of schools: Schools for new converts; schools in monasteries and cathedrals; schools taught by parish priests; schools in collegiate churches; and song schools. All these were under the control of some church authority.

3. *Schools in 12th Century London:* Although most schools were controlled by the church, there were schools under the patronage of prominent individuals and some private schools.

4. *Educational Foundations:* These foundations were religious, but placed control of the schools outside the church. Some of these were: **Chantries** - endowments for charitable purposes. Many were established to support schools. Some chantries were set up by private persons and others came into being through the gifts of associations of individuals. Teachers were under the control of the chantry and not the church. **Colleges -** boarding schools for the classical education of leaders. Sainte Marye college of Winchester, now called Winchester, was founded by William of Wykeham in 1342 as a corporation to maintain a grammar school. Eton was founded in 1440. Others followed. These have become the "public" schools of England. **Guilds -** some guilds established schools under their support and control. In some cases schools were established by private persons and placed under the control of guilds.

5. *Status of the Schoolmaster:* The schoolmaster became an individual of importance and respectability in the community and teaching was on the way to becoming a profession.

6. *Later Developments:* The growth of English control through the breakdown of Norman monopoly and the Great Death; the rise of the English language; English law protected the education of the poor and the lower classes, and the church monopoly of education was broken by the Gloucester Grammar School Case of 1410. This ruling held that the establishment and conduct of a school was "merely an uncertain ministry" and not an estate which should be protected as a monopoly.

Contrast between Europe and England. As the monopolistic control of education by the church was broken, England turned to private and voluntary support and control of schools and resisted all attempts at church or state monopoly. Europe turned to state systems and municipal support and control. Thus two patterns of lay education developed which had tremendous influence in early American education.

BIBLIOGRAPHY

I. Primary Sources:

Aquinas, Thomas, *Basic Writings*. New York, Random House, 1905.

Chase, W.J., *The Ars Minor of Donatus*. Madison, University of Wisconsin, 1926

Chase, W.J., *The Distichs of Cato*. Madison, University of Wisconsin, 1922.

Cubberley, Ellwood P., *Readings in the History of Education,* pp. 64-185. New York, Houghton Mifflin Company, 1920.

Gasquet, F.A., *The Rule of Saint Benedict*. London, Chatto & Windus, 1925.

Jerome, *Letters*. Cambridge, Mass., Harvard University Press, 1933.

Norton, A.O., *Readings in the History of Education: Medieval Universities*. Cambridge, Mass., Harvard University Press, 1909.

Roberts, A., and Donaldson, James, *The Ante-Nicene Fathers*. New York, Charles Scribner's Sons, 1917-1925. (Vol. II, writings of Celement of Alexandria; Vols. III and IV, writings of Tertullian).

2. Secondary Material:

Barnes, Harry Elmer, *An Intellectual and Cultural History of the Western World,* pp. 326-440 and 494-499. New York, Random House, 1937.

Butts, R. Freeman, *A Cultural History of Education,* pp. 133-196. New York, McGraw-Hill Book Company, Inc., 1947.

Cubberley, Ellwood P., *A Brief History of Education,* pp. 63-123. New York, Houghton Mifflin Company, 1922.

Cubberley, Ellwood P., *The History of Education,* pp. 109-235. New York, Houghton Mifflin Company. 1920.

Duggan, Stephen, *A Student's Textbook in the History of Education,* pp. 77-107. New York, D. Appleton-Century Company, 1927.

Eby, Frederick and Arrowood, C.F., *The History and Philosophy of Education, Ancient and Medieval,* pp. 630-835. New York, Prentice-Hall, Inc., 1940.

Graves, Frank P., *A History of Education,* Vol. II. pp. 1-105. New York, The Macmillan Company, 1925.

Graves, Frank P., *A Student's History of Education,* pp. 71-108. New York, The Macmillan Company, 1936.

Melvin, A. Gordon, *Education, A History,* pp. 121-149. New York, The John Day Company, 1946.

Monroe, Paul, *A Brief Course in the History of Education,* pp. 101-158. New York, The Macmillan Company, 1909.

Monroe, Paul, *A Textbook in the History of Education,* pp. 221-347. New York, The Macmillan Company, 1907.

Moore, Ernest C., *The Story of Instruction: The Church, the Renaissance and the Reformation,* pp. 92-381. New York, The Macmillan Company, 1938.

Mulhern, James, *A History of Education,* pp. 189-228. Ronald Press Co., New York, 1946.

Reisner, Edward H., *Historical Foundations of Modern Education,* pp. 223-363. New York, The Macmillan Company, 1928.

Wilds, Elmer H., *The Foundations of Modern Education,* pp. 167-225. New York, Rinehart & Company, Inc., 1942.

CHAPTER VIII

Education During The Renaissance

Introduction

ORIENTATION. Renaissance (rebirth) is applied to a series of movements in the 14th, 15th, and 16th centuries in Western Europe. It is that great general movement in which the human spirit attained "self-conscious freedom." Modern education begins with the Renaissance.

CAUSES OF THE RENAISSANCE

1. *A Change in Attitude Toward the Body:* The earlier religious idea of the body as evil, as the prison-house of the soul, as something that must be denied if the soul is to grow, was displaced by an emphasis upon cultivation of the body in Chivalry, the Crusades, and war.

2. *The Increase of Wealth:* The wealthy supported and encouraged intellectual and artistic talent. Rich and powerful rulers adorned their courts with men of creative ability and of scholarly interest.

3. *Travel and Discovery:* The Crusades, pilgrimages, and other travels brought men in touch with other people and ideas, disclosed new parts of the world, and stimulated the imagination of many. This led to numerous inventions and fired the spirit of adventure.

4. *Growth of the Vernaculars:* Classical Latin, the language of early scholarship, was corrupted by the masses. It became "vulgar" Latin in the Middle Ages. By the 12th century the many dialects of rustic Latin spoken in different parts of southern Europe were fast becoming the Romance languages and a literature in each of these languages began to appear.

5. *Development of Vernacular Poetry and Song:* Chivalry inspired poetry and songs in the vernacular, first in Provence, in southern France, and then in and throughout Europe. Wandering singers (troubadours, minnesingers) appeared. Their literature stressed the romantic emotion, tenderness, and gallantry. This also gave rise to the troubadour knight.

6. *Sex Was Purified and Became Romantic:* The crude attitude toward women and sex of the Middle Ages slowly changed to a purity of passion and gentleness. The "gentleman" and his "lady" were born. The contribution of Ovid's *Art of Love* to this development was great. This movement is contrasted with the ascetic ideal and attitude toward sex of the early church. A literature of the romantic passion arose: Dante, Petrarch.

7. *A New Art Developed:* The church had suppressed natural art in favor of a stilted and ascetic type. Gradually man broke from this shell and

began to create beauty. This was aided by: a more scientific understanding of perspective which gave painting preeminence; a more accurate knowledge of anatomy; a more complete knowledge of oils and water colors; and a new appreciation of the art of the ancients. The result was the creation of beauty in a vast number of fields. Artists sought to harmonize their newer conceptions and spirit with Christianity and the result was marvelous.

8. *The Invention of Printing:* With the invention of printing, books could be multiplied easily and learning circulated at a speed and in an amount never before possible. The Bible, works of classical writers, and the writings of many Renaissance authors were printed in great numbers and circulated widely. This development was opposed by copyists and collectors of hand-done manuscripts.

9. *The Liberation of Man's Spirit:* The human spirit broke the bounds of authority and suppression and asserted itself. Individuality was given free play with no limits set. Thus rivalry was intense and the yearning for fame was all-consuming.

10. *The Growth of Creative Imagination:* In every area of man's life imagination was given free play to create what it would.

The Italian Renaissance

INTRODUCTION. Although the Renaissance was a spirit stirring throughout Europe, the Italian phase has characteristics which are significant.

THE ITALIAN REVIVAL OF LEARNING

1. *Factors Making For the Revival in Italy Were:* The diversity of social and political institutions challenged the regimentation and formality of the Middle Ages. The powerful aristocracy patronized literature and learning to gain prominence. The increase of wealth through commerce made a high standard of living possible. Much of the past still remained in Italy: monuments, schools, literature, and the Latin language. The Renaissance began in Florence.

2. *Petrarch* (1304-1374): The qualities which made him the inspirer of the Italian Renaissance were: a) He saw clearly the failure of medieval institutions. b) He had the soul of a poet. c) He had a deep reverence for the ancients. d) He had untiring energy for research and scholarship. e) He was not afraid of opposition. He collected ancient manuscripts and became a master of classical Latin.

3. *Differences between the Renaissance and the Revival of Learning:* **The Renaissance** - the rebirth of the creative spirit of man. It spread through Europe and was the same in all countries. **Revival of Learning** - the deep interest in the ancient Latin and Greek languages and literature. It is also called "Humanism." It was different in different countries. It

was imitative, a recapitulation of the past. It turned from allegorizing and reading orthodox meanings into the works of the ancients, to direct and simple interpretation of the author's meaning.

3. *The Search for Manuscripts:* Humanistic scholars devoted themselves and their fortunes to collecting classical manuscripts. Petrarch had 200 volumes. Pope Nicolas V collected the nucleus of what became the Vatican library. Much wealth was devoted to the search for manuscripts and copying.

4. *The Re-Discovery of Greek:* Greek had almost disappeared in Italy. There were a few translations of the Greek classics in Latin and in Arabic. Emanuel Chrysoloras (1355-1415) came to Florence from Constantinople and taught Greek from 1396-1400. He was followed by other teachers of Greek. Many Italian scholars went to Constantinople to study Greek. After the fall of Constantinople (1453) many Greek scholars came to Italy and spread knowledge of the Greek language and literature. Greek manuscripts were collected with vigor. However, Greek was never as popular as Latin and interest in it gradually waned.

·5. *Humanism and the Universities:* While courts of the nobles, houses of wealthy merchants, and palaces of the princes of the church rather than the universities were the seats of humanism, some universities - Padua, Pavis, etc. - welcomed humanistic scholars and some universities were founded by Humanists - Florence, Ferrar, etc.

6. *The Rise of Libraries:* Among the libraries established by Humanists were: Petrarch's library of 200 volumes, three libraries founded by Cosimo de Medici, the one at Florence being the most famous, and the Vatican library founded by Pope Nicolas V. Niccoli was the first to open a library to students.

EDUCATION IN THE ITALIAN RENAISSANCE

1. *Introduction:* During the Middle Ages there was a predominance of slavery to tradition in education. Keen interest in the problems of education grew with the Renaissance due to: Pietrus Paolus Vergerius' *On the Manners of a Gentleman* and *On Liberal Studies* written in 1393. He advised the teaching of Latin literature in a liberal curriculum. Guarino da Verona's translation of Plutarch's *On the Education of Children* and the discovery of Quintilian's *Institutes of Oratory,* Cicero's *de Oratore,* Plato's *Republic,* and Aristotle's *Politics.* Quintilian was the most influential.

2. *Renaissance Schools:* **Vittorino da Feltre** (1378-1446) was born near the University of Padua and in a section of country rich in Humanistic development. He spent 25 years at the University in a scholarly atmosphere, becoming a Latin scholar and a mathematician second to none. He had

established a humanistic school at Venice when Gianfrancesco Gonzaga, Marquis of Mantua, invited him to his palace to establish a palace school. He accepted the invitation and established La Giocosa. His pupils included the children of the Marquis, sons of wealthy and powerful persons, sons of great scholars, and several sons of the poor, all ranging from 6 to 27 years in age. He aimed at educating "the complete citizen." The curriculum was humanistic and religious, including Latin, Greek, mathematics, physics, astronomy, music, history, ethics, and physical education. The school set the pattern for humanistic schools throughout Italy. **Guarino of Verona** (1370-1460) established a palace school at Ferrara under the sponsorship of the Marquis, Niccolo d'Este. The aim of the school was the training of young men for the priesthood, professorships, and literary careers. This became the training school for English and German humanists.

3. *Humanistic Educators:* **Petrus Paulus Vergerius** (1349-1430) wrote the first educational treatise in which the study of Latin literature for a liberal culture was advocated. **Leonardo Bruni D'Arezzo** (1369-1444) wrote the first humanistic treatise on the education of girls. **Vittorino da Feltre** (1378-1446) established La Giocosa. **Guarino da Verona** (1434-1513) was the best Greek scholar of the Italian humanists. **Battista Guarino** (1434-1513) taught at Ferrara. **Leone Battista Alberti** (1404-1472) was a many-sided genius. **Aeneus Sylvius Piccolomini** (1405-1458) became Pope Pius II. **Mepheus Vegius** (1405-1458) was a thorough scholar whose educational ideas leaned in the direction of the Church Fathers. **Castiglione** (1478-1529) wrote the *Courtier* which portrays the education of the learned gentleman and lady.

4. *Humanistic Educational Principles:* **The Control of Education** - lay teachers were taking the places of churchmen in the schools so that the church lost its monopoly of education. **The Values of Humanistic Study** - the humanists believed that in the classics were the answers to all their hopes and desires. **The Aim of Humanistic Education** - the development of self-realization, a personality well-rounded, one that excelled in personal glory, service to God, Christian character, literary style, and knowledge. **The Education of Women** - women should have the same intellectual and emotional development as men, but pointed toward the home and its management, the rearing of children, social life, religion, and charity. **Knowledge vs. Style** - though knowledge was emphasized, the goal of education was pure linguistic style.

5. *The Humanistic Curriculum:* The humanists recognized the need for well-trained, healthy bodies and urged physical training as part of the curriculum. In addition, they placed emphasis upon: **Music** - while some

humanists valued music highly, others feared its possible moral effect upon youths· **The Vernacular** - some humanists heartily opposed the use of the vernacular in schools while others saw value in it with the result that no active effort was made to incorporate it into the curriculum. **Greek** - after the appearance of Chrysolorus (1396) Greek spread rapidly in the schools and took its place along side of Latin with emphasis upon the ethical and social content of the classics. **Grammar** - the humanists were in general agreement that education should start with grammar. **Composition** - humanistic education aimed to develop ability to compose in Latin with style and elegance including writing in prose, poetry, and orations. **History** - this was thought necessary as a means of linking the Renaissance Italian with his own past as well as a thing of ethical value. **Arithmetic and Geometry** - the humanists thought of these subjects as means for training in accuracy but failed to appreciate their practical value. **Natural Sciences** - the humanists were little interested in these subjects save as they threw light upon references in the classics even though there were individual humanists who saw value in these areas of human knowledge. **Astronomy** - the humanists felt a need for this as a means of understanding classical writings.

   6. *The Humanist's Attitude Toward Religion and Moral Training:* While the early church had prohibited the reading of pagan literature, the humanists turned to this literature with enthusiasm. Many attempts to justify this new attitude were made in order to prove that the fears of the past regarding the danger of reading this literature were unfounded. But, while the educational leaders of the Renaissance were deeply religious men and sought to instil in their pupils moral and religious virtues, the age was most corrupt.

   7. *The Humanistic Educational Organization:* **Primary** - the subjects learned were reading, spelling, correct speech, Latin vocabulary, Greek vocabulary, arithmetic, religion, morals, and play. **Elementary** - the subjects on this level included the primary subjects, but on a slightly advanced level. In addition, children began memorizing Latin verse and Greek passages. **Secondary** - this included the study of Latin and Greek poets and historians, composition, declamation, and rhetoric. **Higher** - at this level literature was studied for enjoyment, understanding, and appreciation. Grammar study was enlarged and rhetoric was emphasized. Thus grammar, literature, and rhetoric became the cultural subjects. Logic lost its preeminence and became merely an aid to exact thinking.

   8. *Psychology, Child Development, Motivation:* The humanists were not much interested in psychology but followed fairly closely the ideas in Aristotle's *de Anima.* Their knowledge of childhood was very crude and

traditional. a) They held that the qualities which should be trained because they are necessary to scholarship are memory, desire for praise, fear of shame, obedience, industry, thoroughness, alertness, and good social attitude. b) Teaching should be adapted to individual differences. They sought to motivate the pupil by stirring his ambition, the desire for social approval, and the desire to emulate the great men of the past. They also used rivalry and punishment widely, though punishment was reserved for extreme cases.

9. *The Humanistic Instructional Methods:* Since the humanists sought to teach skill in speaking and writing Latin and in appreciation of style, and since books were scarce, the teachers used the following methods: Oral reading and reciting. The teacher often read to the student. Each item was to be learned with understanding. Thus, the humanists employed the inductive method of teaching. Some humanists held that a pupil should study only one subject at a time while others believed that he should diversify his education.

PERIODS OF THE RENAISSANCE

1. *"The Age of Passionate Desire":* This was the early stage of the Renaissance when men like Petrarch and Boccaccio first sensed the glory of the past and desired its return.

2. *The Period of Acquisition:* During this stage scholars and others gathered everything ancient into their possession and worked for the preservation of ancient buildings, tombs, and other public monuments.

3. *The Period of Scholarship:* At this stage men devoted themselves to the critical study and editing of manuscripts and the reading of these to discover their meanings.

4. *Ciceronianism:* This was the final period of the Italian Renaissance when men came to worship pure Ciceronian style. The sole aim of education became that of speaking and writing Latin with the purity and elegance of Cicero's works. This resulted in pure formalism.

WEAKNESSES OF THE ITALIAN RENAISSANCE

1. The work of the schools was not properly fitted to the age and ability of the child, although some leaders aimed at this.

2. There was too great an emphasis upon language. The humanists tended to make language an end rather than a tool for more important ends.

3. The teachers did not understand teaching methods even though they attempted to use those suggested by the ancients.

4. The natural sciences were subordinated to language and literature. Thus education was one-sided.

5. The attempt of humanistic educators to teach morals failed in the face of the general social degeneration.

6. Although educators emphasized social values, they could not stem the tide of individualism.

7. The Italian humanists were aesthetic and formal in their religion, disregarding the ethical and spiritual.

8. The masses were not educated. Humanistic education was reserved for the aristocratic classes and for a few gifted members of the other classes.

The Northern Renaissance

INTRODUCTION. The Renaissance began in Italy but moved north to effect a revolution in the political, economic, religious, moral, philosophical, literary, and institutional areas of human life. The Teutonic races threw off the domination of the Roman world and built a world of their own.

FACTORS MAKING FOR THE REVOLUTION

1. *Discoveries and Inventions:* There were many geographical discoveries, including Columbus' discovery of the new world and Magellan's circumnavigation of the globe. The invention of paper making in the 13th century and of movable type (Guttenberg, 1438). Copernicus's theory of heliocentricity (1543), Vesalius' (1514-1564) considerable work in anatomy, and Cardan's work in algebra.

2. *Changes in Law and Government:* Civil law was strengthened and canon law limited to jurisdiction over matters of a purely religious nature. Thus man was freed from the oppression of church law and placed under the jurisdiction of secular law. Theories of government and education arose: a) Catholic - The church is supreme over the state and education is a function of the church. b) Lutheran - The secular ruler has authority over the church so that he is able to designate the religion of all his subjects and control education. c) Calvinist - The church and state are to carry out the will of God which the church interprets and the state enforces. The education of the child is a function of both church and state. d) Anabaptists - The church and state are separate and neither has control over the other. Education is a state function.

3. *Changes in the Social Pattern:* The medieval social pattern of a spiritual and a temporal hierarchy was challenged by the demand for individual freedom and expression. Institutions based on this older social pattern were collapsing. These were: **Knighthood** - the invention of gunpowder gave the common people a measure of equality with the knights. **Monasteries** - their wealth attracted civil authorities and their overthrow made necessary other means of education. **Church Wealth and Power** - this was largely appropriated by secular authorities. **Begging and Charity** - having become an economic burden under the church, this was placed under civil control. The plan established by the Council of Ypres

(1525) put poor relief under civil authorities and provided for the schooling or apprenticeship of children of the poor.

4. *Rise of the Free Towns:* In the Netherlands free towns sprang up with a growing and industrious population. Manufacture increased and considerable wealth was created. Contact with Italian cities resulted in a growth of the arts and culture and education in the fundamentals (reading, writing, and calculating) was made necessary.

5. *Ominous Stirrings among the Peasants:* Oppressed by the priests, knights, and overlords, the peasants sought to gain freedom and a degree of security. The Peasants' Revolt (1524-1525) was put down by the nobility and conditions of the poor became worse.

6. *Political Factors:* During the Middle Ages the church exercised temporal authority over vast areas, the Holy Roman Empire was powerful, and greater and greater power was being concentrated in the hands of temporal princes. These factors tended toward unification of diverse groups. However, among the Teutonic people there were many free cities and rival civil authorities antagonistic to the church. These led the revolt against the tyrannical and "foreign" church. This was more or less true in all northern lands.

7. *Economic Factors:* The church had become immensely wealthy by milking the people. This aroused the masses to overthrow the church.

THE RELIGIOUS PICTURE. There was a growing protest against the tyranny and corruption of the church. Some groups were formed in rebellion, but these were persecuted by the Church as heretical. Other groups within the Church sought reform. In addition, the general state of the people was that of high excitability, fear, and deepening hatred of the priests.

The Bible was being printed and circulated in Latin and in many of the vernaculars and was being read widely. Tyndale's (1492-1536) New Testament in English appeared in 1526.

Many of the basic doctrines of the church were being disputed by leaders and small groups of deeply religious people. Among these were the doctrine of salvation, the basis of religious authority, the relation between God and the individual, and indulgences.

HUMANISM IN THE NORTH

1. *Contact with Italy:* Members of the Brethren of the Common Life studied in Italy and brought Humanism to the northern countries. It took root at Paris and in England and spread from there to other lands. The scholastics, especially the Dominican and Franciscian Orders, fought the rise of Humanism.

2. *Humanism and the Reformation:* These were two separate movements, agreeing in some respects but antagonistic in others. They were in

agreement: Both opposed scholasticism, formalism, Aristotelian logic, and the corruption of monastic life. Both sought the freedom of the individual. Both were interested in the classics. Both found in classic life and religion interpretations different from those of the Roman church. Both contributed to the growth of secular power at the expense of the Church. Both promoted Biblical scholarship. On the other hand, they were antagonistic and different: Humanism was Italian in origin while the Reformation was northern. Humanism was aristocratic while the Reformation was of the masses. Humanism was intellectual and worldly while the Reformation was emotional, religious, and spiritual. Humanism was interested in the education of the few while the Reformation championed popular education.

3. *Humanism and Scholasticism:* The humanists attacked the traditional culture and education: They ridiculed medieval Latin. Examples are Erasmus' *Praise of Folly* (1509) and *Letters of Obscure Men* (1515-1519). They attacked Aristotelian logic and philosophy. Scholars found that the original Aristotle differed from the Aristotle of the Schoolmen. Peter Ramus (1536) attacked the entire Aristotelian position. They criticized Scholastic teaching methods and curriculum.

4. *Rabelais* (1483-1553): He ridiculed the education of his day in *Gargantua* and suggested a more efficient education in *Pantagruel.*

SCHOOLS OF NORTHERN EUROPE AT THE BEGINNING OF THE NORTHERN RENAISSANCE

1. *Monastic Schools:* These were conducted by monks and trained boys for monastic life. The wealth of the monasteries attracted many students.

2. *Cathedral Schools:* These were schools at the great cathedrals, at smaller churches but under the control of a *scholasticus,* and chantry schools. All gave their instruction in the Latin language.

3. *Burgh Schools:* These were Latin Grammar Schools and vernacular schools established by the towns. Some were free; others charged fees. The church opposed these schools vigorously. The schools were either "common" elementary schools for practical training in reading and writing in the vernacular, arithmetic, French, and bookkeeping for the middle class, or "learned" Latin schools for teaching the higher culture and professional matters to the upper classes.

4. *Schools of the Brethren of the Common Life:* The Brethren of the Common Life was an organization devoted to simple, spiritual living and to service. Its headquarters was in Deventer, Holland. It established a few schools, took over many other schools and introduced in them discipline, orderliness, and the humanistic studies. It helped many poor students by providing work for them while they studied. Many scholars of the times were educated in their schools: Erasmus, Sturm, Luther. They

also established *scriptoria* for copying books and, when printing came into general use, established presses from which came many religious books.

5. *The Teaching of Evangelical Sects:* Many evangelical sects throughout northern Europe conducted schools in the vernacular aiming to teach the masses to read the Scriptures.

DECLINE OF MEDIEVAL SCHOOLS. Attacks made upon medieval schools by Humanists and other Renaissance leaders were effective and the decline of the schools became pronounced in the early part of the 16th century. Reasons for this decline were: The attacks made by the Humanists; the common people came to distrust and hate the products of these schools; as livings furnished by the church declined, people saw little practical value in education offered by the church schools; and the religious bigotry and bitterness of the times.

TYPES OF EDUCATIONAL REFORMERS

1. *Moralistic Humanists:* These leaders considered the classics as rich sources of knowledge which would help them live the good life.

2. *Religious Humanists:* These considered knowledge of the classical languages as a means for the understanding of the Scriptures and the writings of the Church Fathers. This understanding, they held, would reveal true Christianity and expose the errors and corruption of the Church.

3. *Naturalistic Humanists:* These were interested in the classics for the knowledge of the natural world which they revealed.

4. *Stylistic Humanists:* These were influenced by the formalistic phase of Italian Humanism and sought to train pupils to reproduce the pure style of Cicero.

ERASMUS (1467-1563). Educated in the Humanistic tradition and at the University of Paris, a teacher of Latin and Greek at Paris and at Oxford and Cambridge, he was painfully conscious of the corruption of the Church and sought to reform it from within. He was the best scholar of his day and did much to restore exact scholarship to Europe. His educational principles included: mastery of Latin and Greek as the means of producing a man of moral character capable of living a wise and happy life. He wrote many important and popular textbooks, chief of which is his *Colloquies.*

BIBLIOGRAPHY

1. Primary Sources:

Ascham, Roger, *The Schoolmaster* (ed. by D.C. Whimster). London, Methuen, 1934.

Castiglione, Baldassare, *The Book of the Courtier* (tr. by L.E. Opdycke). New York, Horace Liveright, 1929.

Elyot, Thomas, *The Book Named the Governour*. London, Kegan Paul, Trench, 1883.

Watson, Foster, *Vives: On Education*. London, Cambridge, 1913.

2. Secondary Material:

Bax, Clifford, *Leonardo da Vinci*. New York, D. Appleton & Co.; 1932.

Butts, R. Freeman, *A Cultural History of Education*, pp. 197-230. New York, McGraw-Hill Book Company, Inc., 1947.

Cubberley, Ellwood P., *A Brief History of Education*, pp. 129-162. New York, Houghton Mifflin Co.; 1922.

Cubberley, Ellwood P., *The History of Education*, pp. 242-304. New York, Houghton Mifflin Co., 1920.

Cubberley, Ellwood P., *Readings in the History of Education*, pp. 186-235. New York, Houghton Mifflin Co.; 1920.

Duggan, Stephen, *A Student's Textbook in the History of Education*, pp. 113-128. New York, D. Appleton-Century Co.; 1927.

Eby, Frederick and Arrowood, Charles F., *The History and Philosophy of Education, Ancient and Medieval*, pp. 837-939. New York, Prentice-Hall, Inc., 1940.

Eby, Frederick and Arrowood, Charles F., *Development of Modern Education*, pp. 29-78. New York, Prentice-Hall, Inc., 1937.

Graves, Frank P., *A History of Education*, Vol. 2, pp. 106-138. New York, The Macmillan Co., 1925.

Graves, Frank P., *A Student's History of Education*, pp. 112-132. New York, The Macmillan Company, 1936.

Hyma, Albert, *Erasmus and the Humanists*. New York, Crofts, 1930.

Melvin, A. Gordon, *Education, A History*, pp. 151-157, 159-163. New York, The John Day Company, 1946.

Monroe, Paul, *A Brief Course in the History of Education*, pp. 160-187. New York, The Macmillan Company, 1909.

Monroe, Paul, *A Text-Book in the History of Education*, pp. 351-397. New York, The Macmillan Company, 1907.

Moore, Ernest C., *The Story of Instruction: The Church, the Renaissance and the Reformation,* pp. 382-452. New York, The Macmillan Company, 1938.

Mulhern, James, *A History of Education,* pp. 233-245, 252-270. Ronald Press Co., New York, 1946

Reisner, Edward H., *Historical Foundations of Modern Education,* pp. 364-410. New York, The Macmillan Company, 1928.

Robinson, J.H., and Rolfe, H.W., *Petrarch: The First Modern Scholar and Man of Letters.* New York, G.P. Putnam's Sons, 1909.

Sandys, J.E., *A History of Classical Scholarship,* Vol. II. Cambridge, Cambridge University Press, 1908.

Smith, Preserved, *Erasmus.* New York, Harper & Brothers, 1923.

Wilds, Elmer H., *The Foundations of Modern Education,* pp. 249-272. New York, Rinehart & Company, 1942.

Woodward, W.H., *Desiderius Erasmus Concerning the Aim and Method of Education.* Cambridge, Cambridge University Press, 1904.

Woodward, W.H., *Studies in Education during the Age of the Renaissance.* Cambridge, Cambridge University Press, 1906.

Woodward, W.H., *Vittorino da Feltre and Other Humanist Educators.* Cambridge, Cambridge University Press, 1897.

Zweig, Stefan, *Erasmus of Rotterdam.* New York, The Viking Press, 1934.

The Reformation and Education

German Educational Reformers
MARTIN LUTHER (1483-1546)

1. *His Life:* Born at Eisleben in Saxony, son of a poor miner, he obtained an education at Magdeburg, Eisenach, and the University of Erfurt. He became an Augustinian monk. He was called to the University of Wittenberg where he proclaimed his 95 theses in 1517.

2. *His Efforts at Educational Reform:* For Luther educational reform and church reform were phases of the same problem arising from the conditions of his age. Three important writings from his pen are: **The Address to the Christian Nobility** in which he urged the German princes to undertake religious and educational reforms. **The Freedom of a Christian Man** which stimulated the people to demand individual freedom from their overlords and from the Church. **On the Babylonian Captivity of the Church of God,** a bitter condemnation of the papacy. These works set fire to the smouldering antagonisms against the Church and education declined rapidly. This led to Luther's condemnation as a heretic by the Diet of Worms in 1521.

The decline of education made it difficult to obtain trained pastors. Further, parents saw no value in studying the classics since they had the Scriptures in German. To stem this tide, Luther wrote a *Letter to the Mayors and Aldermen of all the Cities of Germany in Behalf of Christian Schools* (1524). This was a definite break with the Church and a turning to civil authorities for support and control of education. In it he urged the establishment of Latin Grammar Schools to lay the foundation for professional training. These schools were to teach Latin, Greek, Hebrew, and religious music.

3. *His Reaction against the Freedom of the Masses:* Luther had sought to free the masses from the tyranny and corruption of the Church. With the overthrow of the Church in Germany and the closing of its schools, learning sank to a new low. The church-school visitation of 1527 revealed the ignorance, indifference, and immorality of the people. The Peasants' War (1524-1525) aroused Luther's anger. He was opposed to armed conflict against civil authority. In addition, the theories of the Anabaptists seemed heresy to him. These experiences caused Luther to change many of his educational views: From his early insistence upon everyone's being able to read the Scriptures and interpret them for himself, Luther came

to believe that such freedom was dangerous. Thus, he wrote the *Short Catechism* and the *Longer Catechism* (1528-1529) for the masses to use in place of the Scriptures. From his early belief in the freedom of each individual, he turned to a conviction that everyone should conform to the religious belief of his prince. From insisting upon the study of German, Latin, Greek, and Hebrew in the schools, he grew to condemn the teaching of the vernacular and to insist that only Latin be taught in the schools. In his *Sermon on the Duty of Sending Children to School* (1530) he condemns parents who send their children to vernacular schools. From belief in the independence of the church, Luther came to believe that the civil authorities should control the church. From a belief that all children should be given an education, Luther came to hold that only those bright enough to be leaders should have training in the Latin schools.

4. *Luther's Educational Principles:* Schools are the responsibility of civil authorities. This laid the basis for state and national control of education. It is a duty of civil authorities to see that schools are established and to force parents to send their children to them. This is necessary for public welfare. Discipline in the home is necessary for the rearing of good citizens, but this must not be unduly severe. School work need not interfere with trade or vocational training. Facilities should be provided for the instruction of girls in religious matters. The curriculum of the elementary schools should include religion (in the vernacular), Latin, History, and music. The universities need to be reformed so as to train the brighter students to become religious leaders. Here he would teach Aristotle's logic, rhetoric, poetry, Latin, Greek, and Hebrew for the understanding of the Scriptures Although Luther would have all children receive vernacular religious instruction in the home, he condemned vernacular schools and popular elementary education. He would suppress private vernacular schools and have all boys attend Latin schools. Nevertheless, he made some important contributions to popular education: a) all children were to be given religious instruction in the vernacular; b) he translated the Bible into High German, and c) he translated Aesop's fables and wrote catechisms in the vernacular.

5. *Luther's Contributions to Education:* He advocated education for all children; he advocated the education of girls at the elementary level in religion; he championed state control and support of schools; he emphasized the educational obligations of parents; he held that physical education is part of general education; he believed that education should be pleasant; he held that religious education was basic to popular

education, and he gave the masses the B‥'e, catechisms, and Aesop's fables in the vernacular.

PHILIP MELANCHTHON (1479-1560)

1. *His Life:* He was the scholar of the Protestant Reformation. Born of a scholarly family, he received his bachelor's degree from Heidelberg at 15, studied at Tubingen, and became a professor at Wittenberg where he joined forces with Luther.

2. *His Contributions to Education:* The school plan for Saxony - This placed education in the hands of civil authorities; held that the purpose of schools was to prepare men for the church and for civil offices; limited teaching to Latin while forbidding the teaching of German, Greek, and Hebrew; and set up schools of three grades. Many towns asked his advice on school matters thus giving him considerable influence upon the type of schools established and the appointment of teachers. He wrote many textbooks on Greek and Latin grammar, rhetoric, dialectic, arithmetic, geometry, music, and astronomy. As a teacher at Wittenberg, he had considerable influence upon the developing Protestant curriculum and teaching methods. His pupils carried his ideas throughout Germany.

JOHANNES BUGENHAGEN (1485-1558). He was the organizer of the Protestant Reformation. He came from northern Germany to become town preacher and a professor at Wittenberg. He drew up school ordinances for several towns. These ordinances provided for: Latin schools, reading and writing schools in the vernacular, schools for girls, and public libraries and lectures. They put control of the schools in the hands of town councils with support coming from fees. They also provided for religious instruction.

JOHANN STURM (1507-1589)

1. *His Life:* Born at Schleiden, his early education was received at the court of Count Manderscheid and at the school of the Brethren of the Common Life in Liege. From here he went to the University of Louvain where he became a devotee of Latin eloquence. Here he taught Latin and established a printing press. In 1529 he went to the University of Paris as student and teacher. Later he became a teacher at the College of France. In 1537 he became rector of the gymnasium at Strassburg where he remained for more than 40 years.

2. *His Educational Aim:* This included piety for everyone with knowledge and eloquence for scholarship and culture. He held that the source of eloquence was Cicero and the Latin tongue.

3. *The Gymnasium at Strassburg:* In 1537 Sturm was invited to survey the three Latin schools of Strassburg and make recommendations for their improvement. He proposed that they be consolidated into one strong school with 10 grades and with boys entering between the ages of 5 or 6 years. The

work of each grade was carefully planned. The curriculum consisted of religion, Latin and Greek language and literature, and logic. This was a narrow course aiming at Latin eloquence - formal Ciceronianism.

4. *His Influence:* This gymnasium became famous throughout the world. European nobility sent its sons to the school and graduates carried Sturm's ideas throughout Europe.

Protestant Educational Reorganization

IN GERMANY

1. *School Reorganization in Free Towns:* Luther's appeal to the mayors and aldermen in 1524 resulted in the reorganization of many town schools; Magdeburg, Eisleben, Nuremberg are examples. Many of the new schools, under Melanchthon's influence, were Latin Grammar Schools. Bugenhagen reorganized the schools in Brunswick and Hamburg following the Saxony school plan of 1528. In these the curriculum included Latin and Greek. German reading and writing schools for boys were established and private schools suppressed. Vernacular schools for girls were established. Also, a free *"lectorium"* was organized. Martin Bucer's work at Strassburg (1524) established the Latin schools which later Sturm consolidated into the gymnasium. He also established elementary schools for the teaching of reading and writing in the vernacular, the catechism, and music. All these schools were under civil control and supported by the revenues from church property which had been taken over by the town, by fees paid by pupils, or by direct appropriations of money by the towns.

2. *School Reorganization in German States:* The German states and principalities used much of the wealth of church foundations and monasteries for education. Schleswig-Holstein had Bugenhagen prepare a school ordinance similar to that of Brunswick. Saxony church-school of 1528 and Pomeranian ordinance of 1535. Duke Moritz of Saxony (1543) established three Latin schools under state control. Duke Christopher of Wurtemberg (1559) established the first complete school system in a German state. This consisted of: local schools in every town and village, a Pedagogium for boys planning to enter the learned professions, Cloister schools for boys planning to enter the ministry or to teach, the University of Tubingen (founded in 1477, but became Protestant). These were all classical schools. Some provision was made for vernacular schools for boys and girls.

3. *Elementary Training:* The catechism was taught to all children as a means of religious indoctrination. Children were taught church music and the reading and writing of German.

4. *Reorganization of the Universities:* The medieval universities in Germany were attacked by the Protestants and suffered greatly, some never recovering. A number of the older universities were reformed: Wittenberg,

Tubingen, Leipzig, Rostock, Heidelberg. Several universities were founded
by the Protestants: University of Marburg (1527), Konigsberg (1544),
Jena (1558), Helmstedt (1576), Gissen (1607), Strassburg (1621). In all
universities the faculties of theology, law, medicine, and philosophy
were changed considerably by Protestant influence.

IN SWITZERLAND

1. *Introduction:* Zwingli (1484-1531) reorganized the schools of Zurich.
Basel organized schools and reestablished its university (1532) under
the leadership of Oecolampadius.

2. *John Calvin* (1509-1564): **His Life:** Born at Nyon in Picardy, the son
of the secretary to the bishop, he studied theology with the intent of
becoming a priest. At Paris he studied under Corderius and at the College
de Montaigu he was under other noted teachers. Though he studied law at
Orleans and Bruges, he returned later to Paris to study classical literature. He broke with the Church and had to leave Paris for Geneva where
he became city pastor. At 26 he wrote the *Institutes of the Christian
Religion*. The reactionaries drove him from Geneva to Strassburg where he
was tremendously influenced by Sturm's gymnasium. Returning to Geneva in
1541, he made the city into a powerful Protestant center. **The Geneva Gymnasium and Academy:** In 1559 Calvin combined Geneva's Latin Schools into
a gymnasium similar to the Strassburg gymnasium but with greater emphasis
upon religion. This was a Latin school supported by tuition fees but
under the supervision of the city. He also established an academy to give
instruction in Greek, Hebrew, ethics, logic, rhetoric, oratory, poetry,
physics, mathematics, and with Corderius as rector. This adademy became
world famous, a source of Protestant preachers and teachers, and influenced
the organization of the University of Leyden, the University of Edinburgh,
Emmanuel College at Cambridge, and Harvard College. **His Theory of Government:** The church interprets the will of God and the state enforces this
will. Family, church, and state are responsible for education. Parents
must teach the catechism and Christian living in the home but under the
eye of the state. The church is also a place of instruction. **His Views
on Mass Education:** Everyone should learn the catechism and religion, but
the schools were Latin and only for boys of superior ability. There was
no Latin education for girls and no compulsory attendance upon schools.
The Ethical Basis for Education: Children are inherently evil and must
be trained rigorously in developing good habits. Education is to be a
complete regimentation of the child to suppress his evil nature and
build good living and thinking.

IN THE NETHERLANDS

1. *Introduction:* The Northern Provinces overthrew their Spanish rulers

and became Protestant and set up the Dutch Republic. Here arose religious toleration and a progressive center of religion, intellectual and artistic development. The wealth of the Church was used to establish and support schools. The Dutch Reformed Church, influenced by Calvinism, cooperated with civil authorities in the establishment of schools.

2. *Schools in the Netherlands:* **Public Schools** - these developed out of the need for popular education, a need growing from commercial life, the necessity for educating all citizens of a democracy, and the Reformation's demand for religious training. The Calvinistic position of unity of church and state implied state support and control of schools, compulsory attendance, and free instruction. **Classical Schools** - many towns established classical schools teaching Latin, Greek, French, mathematics, and philosophy. **Universities** - were established throughout the Netherlands and attracted students from all parts of Europe. Famous among these were Leyden (1575), Amsterdam (1630), and Utrecht (1638). **Influence** - the schools and universities of the Netherlands influenced the development of education in Germany, England, and the American Colonies. The Pilgrims brought many of their ideas to America and incorporated them into their educational structure. (The Pilgrims resided in Leyden).

IN BOHEMIA. The Bohemian Brethren established schools and engaged in printing the Bible, catechisms, and hymnals. Throughout Moravia were parochial schools, higher schools, colleges, and the University of Prague.

IN ENGLAND

1. *Factors Causing the English Reformation:* General desire for a disciplined and preaching clergy and for reform of church abuses. **Evangelicalism** - fervor among the people for purity and simplicity of religion. a) Lollardy - a movement among the masses which was anti-clerical, sought moral reform, was nationalistic and communistic. b) **John Wycliffe** (1320-1384) - leader of the Lollards, taught communism, translated the Bible into English, and sided with Parliament against the Pope. **Rise of the Middle Class** - grew in wealth and power. **Henry VIII** - an ardent Humanist who did much to strengthen humanistic learning in England.

2. *The Reformation in England:* The Act of Supremacy (1534) was the culmination of a long struggle between the English crown and the Church. Its passage put the church under control of the King and his representatives. Cromwell was made vicar-general. Monasteries and preaching orders were abolished, their wealth confiscated, and their schools put under royal patronage. This was followed by a long struggle between Protestant and Roman groups during the reigns of Edward VI, Mary, and Elizabeth. The 39 articles were drawn under Edward, Mary attempted to suppress

Protestantism, and Elizabeth reestablished the Church of England on the basis of the Act of Supremacy and the Act of Uniformity. Schoolmasters were required to conform to the doctrines and practices of the Church of England.

3. *Social Legislation Affecting Education:* **The Statute of Apprentices** (1562-1563) - encouraged instruction in agriculture, animal husbandry, and in the industrial and mechanical arts. It governed the relationships between apprentices and masters. **Poor Laws** - codified in 1601. These dealt with the education and care of the poor.

4. *Educational Theory:* Education was held to be necessary in order to produce a ruling class. The pattern for this education lay in the writings of classical authors. Thus English education was classical and for the ruling class.

5. *Thomas Elyot* (1490-1546): He was a Humanist and an advocate of royal supremacy. He wrote *The Boke Named the Governour,* a Latin-English dictionary, essays, and made many translations. *The Governour* presents a program of education designed to train a young man to be a ruler. This education consists of training in manners, morals, and the use of a tutor to teach humanistic subjects - Latin, Greek, history, and physical training. This became the pattern for English aristocratic training and was developed in many forms by writers who followed Elyot.

Other works dealing with education of the ruling class written at this time and in the same general vein were: *The Institution of a Gentleman* (1557), *Toxophilus* (1545), and *The Schoolmaster* (1572) by Roger Ascham; *Queen Elizabeth's Academy* (1572) by Sir Humphrey Gilbert.

6. *Educational Reforms:* In 16th century England certain reforms of education took place: Endowments from private sources and from dissolved church foundations were given to grammar schools and colleges. English catechisms and primers were put in the schools. All song schools were wiped out. Humanism gained control of secondary schools and universities. Lay control of secondary education increased. The government instituted supervision of schools and teachers. The upper classes were turning to boarding and day schools for education.

7. *The School at Saint Paul's Cathedral:* This school was in existence as early as the 12th century and was an important center of education during the Middle Ages. John Colet, an Oxford humanist, was made dean of the cathedral in 1505 and reorganized the school along humanistic lines. He made William Lily headmaster. In 1511 the school was placed under the control of the Trade Company of Mercers and its endowment supplemented. Colet and Lily, with Erasmus' help, wrote *Lily's Grammar.* The aim of the school was to offer a humanistic and religious education for boys. Religion

was taught in English and no tuition was charged. Manners and morals were emphasized.

8. *English Public Schools:* Many individuals endowed grammar schools to provide free education for poor boys. In time these schools began to take paying pupils and lost their free-school status. Some became England's famous "public schools": Winchester, Eton, Westminister, Saint Paul's, Merchant Taylors', Shrewsbury, Charterhouse, Rugby, and Harrow. They are "public" in that they prepare boys from wide areas of England to become state officials.

IN SCOTLAND. Here Parliament (1543-1560) established a national church, Humanism penetrated the schools and universities, and education came under lay control. Powerful nobles initiated the Reformation here and dominated its development despite popular attempts to democratize the movement.

1. *John Knox* (1505-1572): He was a Calvinist and a popular preacher. He was commissioned to prepare a plan of church organization for Scotland. This plan was his *First Book of Discipline*. This was accepted by Parliament in 1560, but the educational system suggested in the work was too radical for the strong nobles and was rejected. Knox proposed: an autonomous church in control of morals, religion, and education; the donation of the wealth of the monasteries to the Scottish church and schools; the establishing of elementary schools in every congregation, a secondary school in each town, and a university in each city. He proposed that these schools be supported by church endowments and controlled by church officials.

Protestant Influence in Colonial America
THE ECONOMIC AND SOCIAL PATTERN

1. *The Colonists:* Colonization was slow during the 17th century. Immigration increased rapidly during the early years of the 18th century. These immigrants came for: economic opportunity, freedom from religious persecution and economic distress, and slavery.

2. *Their Background:* Most of the settlers were British - from the ruling classes, artisans, small traders, laborers, servants. Groups from other countries were small and scattered throughout the colonies. In the southern colonies large plantations worked by cheap labor, usually slave, prevailed and class distinctions were sharp. Here the Church of England was the established church. In New England agriculture and commerce were important. The land was owned by the town and granted to members of the settlement. The town was democratic. The Congregational Church was the established church.

3. *Their Government:* **Virginia** - Here the House of Burgesses was created

in 1619 and the colony was divided into counties and parishes. There were some important towns. **Massachusetts** - This colony was governed by a Governor, a Council, and a General Court. The colony was divided into towns. Suffrage was limited to property owners. In some colonies other limitations were set. **The New England Town** - all qualified voters had a voice in all affairs of the community. The town was autonomous and was synonymous with the congregation. The members elected all officials in the town meeting. This autonomy led to eventual diversity of religious belief in the colony.

SCHOOLS IN COLONIAL AMERICA

1. *The Southern Colonies:* Virginia is representative. Here efforts to establish schools date at least from 1618. Land and money were appropriated by the English King and the Virginia Company and gifts were made by philanthropic individuals for the education of both English and Indian children. These early efforts came to an end with the Indian massacre (1622) and revocation of the Virginia Company's charter (1625). After 1635 endowed parish schools appeared, teaching elementary subjects and the catechism. Some of these charged tuition while others were free. Also some private tuition schools were established. Clergymen often taught advanced pupils Latin, Greek, and French. Wealthy families often employed tutors.

2. *Apprenticeship:* In all the colonies we find the practice of apprenticeship. Sons of the better families were apprenticed to masters in the highly skilled and remunerative trades after receiving their general education. Poor boys were apprenticed to masters of the less desirable trades.

3. *The Middle Colonies:* Here each church group had its own schools - the parochial system. New Netherlands is representative. This area was settled by members of the Dutch Reformed Church who brought their own schoolmasters with them. The West Indian Company and church authorities supported schools, but the supervision and management were in the hands of the local church. These schools were elementary institutions teaching the vernacular. Some private schools were established. In 1659 a Latin school was established in New Amsterdam.

4. *The New England Colonies:* Here the town established and controlled the schools. The Boston Latin Grammar School was founded in 1635. Ezekiel Cheever served as master of this school. The curriculum of this and all other similar schools was classical. The Massachusetts colony is representative of the development here. It passed laws making the establishment and support of schools obligatory upon the towns. The law of 1642 instructed town authorities to see to the education of children. The law

of 1647 - *The Old Deluder Satan law* - provided for the establishing of elementary and Latin Grammar schools in towns and set a fine for failure to comply.

COLLEGES IN COLONIAL AMERICA

1. *Harvard College:* This grew out of an appropriation made by the General Court of Massachusetts (1636), a legacy from John Harvard, and other smaller gifts. It was opened as a grammar school in 1638 and became a college soon after 1640. In 1650 management was vested in the president, five fellows, and the treasurer. At first the fellows were teachers in the college, but later only laymen were chosen as fellows. The college was supported by grants from the colony, gifts, and certain revenues. The curriculum was classical.

2. *College of William and Mary:* The charter of this institution was granted in 1693 with the Bishop of London as chancellor. In 1729 control of the college was turned over to the president and the professors as a corporation. A board of visitors was set up and eventually, after the American Revolution, it took control. The college was supported by appropriations from England and from the officials of the colony, gifts, legacies, and fees from various tax sources. The college aimed to train ministers and offer a higher education for others. Education of the Indians was part of its responsibility.

3. *Yale College:* This was established as a Collegiate Institute by the General Court of Connecticut in 1701 and grew out of a dispute between conservative and liberal elements in the Congregational Church. The conservatives withdrew their support from Harvard College and founded Yale. The purpose of the college was to train young men in the arts and sciences for service in church and state. The college was supported by gifts and public grants. It was named for Elihu Yale.

Summary of Protestant Education

SIGNIFICANT CONTRIBUTIONS

1. *A New Ideal of Life:* The narrow, repressive, ascetic, other-worldly ideal of the Roman church was replaced by the ideal of the individual living, under the authority of God and the Scriptures, a holy and benevolent life in social relations but in complete control of his baser nature. In education Protestantism took from the past the ideals of knowledge, virtue, and piety and sought an integration into a new Protestant culture.

2. *The Teacher:* Teaching became an honored profession and the teacher was given a high place and dignity among Protestants. Thus Protestantism produced many great teachers.

3. *Administrative Techniques:* Many surveys of school systems and

recommendations for improvement were made. These often resulted in reorganization of the system in question. Supervision of instruction was established both by the Calvinists and the Lutherans. Often teachers were examined carefully before being allowed to teach.

4. *The Education of Girls:* Protestantism gave a fresh and vigorous impetus to the already established practice of educating girls.

5. *The State and Education:* Breaking from the older idea of church authority over education, Protestantism developed three positions regarding the relationship between church and state in education: Civil authority is supreme over the church and education (Luther); the church and the state comprise a single organism with the church determining the aim, methods, and curriculum, and hiring the teachers and the state supporting education (Calvin), and the church and state are completely separate and education is under the control of the state (Anabaptists). This third position tremendously influenced American secular education.

6. *Study of Education:* Protestant leaders turned to study the educational theories of classical times and sought to incorporate their principles into Protestant thinking and practice.

WEAKNESSES

1. Educational progress was hindered by the bitter and violent religious conflicts of the period.

2. Elementary education was largely confined to the large centers of population while elsewhere lack of education and ignorance were general. Many Reformation leaders opposed the vernacular schools.

3. The work of Latin schools was largely formal and did not result in high moral living and deep appreciation of literary beauty.

4. Ciceronianism came to dominate education.

5. Although both Humanism and Protestantism began with great promise of intellectual and spiritual freedom, they turned gradually to formalism and narrow orthodoxy. However, the stranglehold of the Church was broken.

The Catholic Reformation

INTRODUCTION. The Roman church realized the import of revolutionary tendencies in Europe and sought to reform the Church, correct abuses, and unify all religious forces under Rome. The Council of Trent (1545-1563) sought to spread the Catholic faith to non-Christian areas, to destroy heresy, to win back the Protestants, to discipline the clergy and members of the church, and settle differences in theology. This council encouraged teaching congregations and urged school reforms.

THE SOCIETY OF JESUS (JESUITS)

1. *Early History:* The Order was founded by Ignatius of Loyola (1491-1556) in 1534. The Constitution of the Order was completed in 1556. The

section devoted to education, the *Ratio Studiorum*, was developed during 1586-1599. The Order was organized on military lines and devoted itself to teaching, study, preaching, and pastoral care.

2. *Growth of the Order:* The Jesuits became powerful, wealthy, and influential. Thus they made many enemies within the Church. As a result, the Order was suppressed by the Pope in 1773 and remained so until it was allowed to reform in 1814. The *Ratio Studiorum* was revised in 1832.

3. *Jesuit Colleges:* The Jesuits were interested only in secondary and higher education. They established lower colleges similar to the Latin Grammar Schools of the times and higher colleges similar to the universities. These schools were supervised carefully and all textbooks and teaching planned for religious ends. Many great minds were educated in these schools.

4. *Teaching Methods:* The methods used included a thorough study of the material assigned and discussion by both teacher and pupils. The methods of prelection and repetition were used. The aim was complete understanding of the text. Reviews and summaries were considered important.

5. *Motivation:* Emulation and rivalry were stressed. Also, appeal was made to the pupil's love and respect for his teachers and parents, to his sense of duty, and to his love for superior attainment.

6. *Preparation of Teachers:* The candidate for teaching had to be a graduate of the lower college. He devoted 16 to 19 years to study and cadet teaching under careful supervision before he was ready for ordination. Careful records were kept of his work.

7. *Results of Jesuit Education:* This training was highly successful in accomplishing what was desired. The graduates were able to read and speak Latin, were devoted Catholics, and were devoted to the Order. However, they tended to be limited, to lack individuality, to disparage modern scientific developments, and to miss a truly liberal education.

THE EDUCATION OF WOMEN. Convents increased in importance. Also, teaching orders for women were established. The Order of Ursulines, 1635, is typical. The aims for the education of women were: to fit women to function as mistresses of households and members of fashionable society, to develop Christian character, and to train for refinement in taste and manners. Fenelon wrote *On the Education of Girls.*

BIBLIOGRAPHY

I. Primary Sources:

Cubberley, Ellwood P., *Readings in Public Education in the United States,* pp. 1-96. New York, Houghton Mifflin Company, 1934.

Cubberley, Ellwood P., *Readings in the History of Education,* pp. 236-315. New York, Houghton Mifflin Company, 1920.

Luther, Martin, *Works* (6 volumes). Philadelphia, A.J. Holman & Company, 1915-1932.

2. Secondary Material:

Barnard, Henry, "Ezekiel Cheever," in *American Journal of Education,* vol. I, pp. 297-314.

Barnard, Henry, *German Teachers and Educators.* Hartford, Brown and Gross, 1878.

Barnes, Harry Elmer, *An Intellectual and Cultural History of the Western World,* pp. 546-596. New York, Random House, 1937.

Bruce, G.M., *Luther as an Educator.* Minneapolis, Augsburg Publishing House, 1928.

Butts, R. Freeman, *A Cultural History of Education,* pp. 231-305. New York, McGraw-Hill Book Company, Inc., 1947.

Cox, F.A., *The Life of Philip Melancthon.* London, Gale, 1817.

Cubberley, Ellwood P., *A Brief History of Education,* pp. 164-202. New York, Houghton Mifflin Company, 1922.

Cubberley, Ellwood P., *Public Education in the United States,* pp. 1-76. New York, Houghton Mifflin Company, 1934.

Cubberley, Ellwood P., *The History of Education,* pp. 306-377. New York, Houghton Mifflin Company, 1920.

Duggan, Stephen, *A Student's Textbook in the History of Education,* pp. 131-153. New York, D. Appleton-Century Company, 1939.

Dunshee, Henry W., *History of the School of the Collegiate Reformed Dutch Church in the City of New York.* New York, Aldine Press, 1883.

Eby, Frederick and Arrowood, Charles F., *The Development of Modern Education,* pp. 80-199. New York, Prentice-Hall, Inc., 1937.

Eby, Frederick, *Early Protestant Educators.* New York, McGraw-Hill Book Company, Inc., 1931.

Edgar, John, *History of Early Scottish Education.* Edinburgh, James Thin, 1893.

Eells, Hastings, *Martin Bucer.* New Haven, Yale University Press, 1931.

Fitzpatrick, Edward A., *St. Ignatius and the Ratio Studiorum.* New York, McGraw Hill Book Company, Inc., 1933.

Fulop, Miller R., *The Power and Secret of the Jesuits.* New York, Viking Press, 1930.

Graves, F.P., *A History of Education, During the Middle Ages and the Transition to Modern Times,* pp. 179-237. New York, The Macmillan Company, 1925.

Graves, Frank P., *Peter Ramus and the Educational Reformation of the Sixteenth Century.* New York, The Macmillan Company, 1912.

Graves, F.P., *A Student's History of Education,* pp. 135-160. New York, The Macmillan Company, 1936.

Hart, Joseph K., *Creative Moments in Education,* pp. 232-237. New York, Henry Holt and Company, 1931.

Heatwole, C.J., *A History of Education in Virginia.* New York, The Macmillan Company, 1916.

Hughes, Thomas A., *Loyola.* New York, Charles Scribner's Sons, 1904.

Jackson, Samuel M., *Huldreich Zwingli.* New York, G.P. Putnam's Sons, 1903.

Kilpatrick, W.H., *The Dutch Schools of New Netherland and Colonial New York.* Washington, Government Printing Office, 1912.

Laurie, Simon S., *Development of Educational Opinion,* pp. 86-93. New York, The Macmillan Company, 1903.

Lindsay, T.M., *Luther and the German Reformation.* New York, Charles Scribner's Sons, 1900.

Marique, Pierre J., *History of Christian Education,* Vol. II, pp. 122-162. New York, Fordham University Press, 1926.

Martin, G.H., *Evolution of the Massachusetts Public School System.* New York, D. Appleton, 1894.

McCabe, Joseph, *A Candid History of the Jesuits.* London, E. Nash, 1913.

McCrie, Thomas, *The Life of John Knox.* Edinburgh, J. Ogle, 1813.

Melvin, A. Gordon, *Education, A History,* pp. 157-173. New York, The John Day Company, 1946.

Messenger, James F., *An Interpretative History of Education,* pp. 127-140. New York, Thomas Y. Crowell Company, 1931.

Monroe, Paul, *A Brief Course in the History of Education,* pp. 189-214. New York, The Macmillan Company, 1909.

Monroe, Paul, *Thomas Platter and the Educational Renaissance of the Sixteenth Century.* New York, D. Appleton, 1904.

Monroe, Paul, *A Textbook in the History of Education,* pp. 401-439. New York, The Macmillan Company, 1907.

Moore, Ernest C., *The Story of Instruction: The Church, the Renaissance and the Reformation,* pp. 453-563, New York, The Macmillan Company, 1938.

Mulhern, James, *A History of Education,* pp. 245-252, 276-279, 282-287. Ronald Press Co., New York, 1946.

Painter, Franklin, *Great Pedagogical Essays,* pp. 169-202. New York, American Book Company, 1905.

Painter, Franklin, *A History of Education,* pp. 153-194. New York, D. Appleton-Century Company, 1904.

Painter, F.V.N., *Luther on Education.* St. Louis, Mo., Concordia Publishing House, 1928.

Paulsen, F., *The German Universities and University Study.* Tr. by Frank Thilly and WilliamW. Elwang. New York, Charles Scribner's Sons, 1906.

Peirce, Benjamin, *History of Harvard College.* Cambridge, Mass., Brown, Shattuck and Company, 1833.

Quick, Robert H., *Educational Reformers,* pp. 32-62. New York, D. Appleton-Century Company, 1890.

Reisner, Edward H., *Historical Foundations of Modern Education,* pp. 364-501. New York, The Macmillan Company, 1927.

Richard, James W., *Philip Melanchthon, the Protestant Preceptor of Germany.* New York, G.P. Putnam's Sons, 1898.

Puccius, Walter M., *John Bugenhagen Pomeranus.* Philadelphia, The United Lutheran Publishing House, 1916.

Schwickerath, Robert, *Jesuit Education; Its History and Principles.* St. Louis, Mo., B. Herder, 1903.

Small, W.H., *Early New England Schools.* Boston, Ginn and Company, 1914.

Walker, Williston, *John Calvin.* New York, G.P. Putnam's Sons, 1906.

Ward, A.W., *The Counter Reformation.* London, Longmans, Green, & Co., 1889.

Wilds, Elmer H., *The Foundations of Modern Education,* pp. 276-308. New York, Rinehart & Company, Inc., 1942.

CHAPTER X

Realism and Education

The Early Stages of Realism

INTRODUCTION. Humanism and the Renaissance were preparatory stages for Realism, a 17th century movement. The Realists were interested in the discovery of reality and for this they turned to science and exploration. They used classical writings only as sources of knowledge, but they reserved the right to contradict the ancients whenever their own discoveries warranted.

EARLY EDUCATIONAL REALISTS

1. *Juan Louis Vives* (1492-1540): He was a Spaniard, born of noble parentage in Valencia, and received the best possible education of the times at the University of Paris, at Bruges, and at Louvain. He was a Catholic Humanist. He lectured at Oxford and served as supervisor of the education of Princess Mary. He wrote extensively on education (*On a Plan of Study for Youth* and *On Instruction of a Christian Woman*), on poor relief (*On Poor Relief*), on teaching (*Concerning the Teaching of the Arts*), and on psychology (*Concerning the Mind*). He was interested in learning how the mind works and applying this knowledge to teaching. His educational principles included: The child should be studied and school work fitted to his ability; the vernacular should be taught as a basis for other learning; Latin should be taught for scholarship, but there should be no subservience to the past, and women should be educated in the vernacular, Latin, religion, morals, conduct, household management, and the care and education of children. The aim of education for him was: religion, personality development, and business competency. He emphasized the practical in education.

2. *Francois Rabelais* (1494-1553): Born at Chinon, in Touraine, he became a monk but later left the monastic life. He studied medicine. He used satire and humor to criticize the practices of his day and suggest new ways of educating. In *Gargantua* (1533) he criticized medieval education severely and suggested more efficient ideas and practices. In *Pantagruel* he outlined his theories on education and on the curriculum. For him education must be based on the natural activity of the child. He would substitute spontaneity and interest for formalism and authority, nature and daily activity for the classroom, observation and direct contact with the world for textbooks, and reasoning for mere memorizing of authorities.

113

3. *Peter Ramus* (1515-1572): Son of a noble family, he studied at Paris and gained powerful support among churchmen and nobles. He became a brilliant teacher at the University of Paris, turned Protestant, and was murdered during the massacre of Saint Bartholomew. He held that all learning should have practical value and maintained that the classics should be studied for their content. He worked for the reform of higher education in both the liberal arts and professional areas. His principles of educational reform were: All the material for study should come from experience with nature; only pertinent materials should be included within each field of knowledge; teaching should move from general principles to particulars, and the pupil should use whatever he learns. He laid out a plan for the school day consisting of two periods of six hours each. He countered scholastic logic with a new logic based upon the working of the mind as revealed in great literature. This logic was analytical and creative and had considerable influence at the time.

4. *Richard Mulcaster* (1530-1611): Head of Merchant Taylors' School and later of Saint Paul's School, he wrote *Positions* and *The Elementaire*. He held that education should be wide-spread and adapted to the needs of each individual, suggested a plan of elementary education, opposed the use of tutors, insisted upon vernacular education, and worked for the complete education of women. He advocated vernacular education for all, and Latin training for those who could profit by it. He held that teachers should be well prepared and well paid and stressed the need for special care in the teaching of young children.

5. *Francis Bacon* (1561-1626): He was a popularizer of work the scientists were doing. He criticized the Middle Ages and the Renaissance and proposed the use of science. He believed in authority in the field of theology but use of the senses to observe and learn in other fields. For him the goal of the sciences was to make human living better and happier. He outlined his ideas in *The New Atlantis,* a utopian scheme of scientific research.

THE GROWTH OF SCIENCE IN THE 17TH CENTURY

1. *Mathematics:* Advances in this area which made scientific growth possible include: Arabic notation, the decimal system, algebra, logarithms, geometry, and trigonometry. This development began in the 13th century and was expanded greatly during the 16th and 17th centuries. The invention and use of printing made possible the distribution of books in the field.

2. *Astronomy:* This was used by medieval scholars to calculate the calendar and dates of Church festivals. Later it was used in astrology. Copernicus (1473-1543) published his heliocentric theory in 1543. This

theory was condemned by the Church, many Protestant theologians, and most scientists. By 1596 it was generally accepted. Other scientists, using mathematics, worked from this theory to a defintie heliocentric astronomy: Tycho Brahe, Kepler, Galileo, and Newton who wrote *The Celestial Mechanics.*

3. *Other Physical Sciences:* Slow advances were made in mechanics and magnetism. Scientists were turning from philosophizing to careful experimentation: Stevin, William Gilbert, Harvey, Torricelli, Boyle. These were using the inductive method. Many scientific instruments for exact measurement were invented: the thermometer (1597), the telescope, the compound microscope, the micrometer, the thermoscope, the barometer, the air pump, and the pendulum clock.

4. *Geography:* A globe was made in 1492. Mercator (Gerhard Kremer) (1512-1594) made maps, globes, and astronomical instruments. The first atlas was published by his son in 1595.

5. *Medicine:* This began to break away from the authority of Hippocrates and Galen. Vesalius dissected the human body and published drawings of what he found. Harvey discovered the circulation of the blood in 1616. Botany became part of medical science. Doctors began to search for material causes of diseases.

6. *The Pattern of the Sciences:* Sciences during the 17th century developed together and were interrelated. Great mathematicians were students of medicine and astrology was necessary to medicine. Mathematics was basic to art. Mathematics applied to astronomy produced Newton's *Principia* (1687) The sciences spoke with an unquestioned authority lacking in earlier times.

7. *Rise of Scientific Academies and Societies:* Several societies or academies for the furthering of scientific research and the exchange of information appeared during this period. These include: *Academia Secretarum Naturae* (1560) at Naples, *Academia dei Lincei* (1603) at Rome, *The Royal Society of London* (1660), *Academie des Sciences* (1660) at Paris, and the *Berlin Academy* (1700).

RENE DESCARTES (1596-1650). Born in Touraine of a noted family, he was educated by the Jesuits at La Fleche. Dissatisfied with the narrowness of his training, he turned to mathematics where he found certainty. He sought to apply this principle of certainty to other fields. His three criteria of scientific knowledge were: 1. Accept nothing as true which is not free from all possibility of doubt. 2. Analyze every problem into its parts. 3. Work from the simple to the complex. He assumed that the basic axioms of all knowledge are inherent in the nature of the mind and that learning consists in developing their implications by the deductive method. Learning, for him, was rational thinking. This is the doctrine of innate ideas and is thus a rationalistic position.

THE NEW SCIENTIFIC METHODS. With both the Protestant churches and the newly developing sciences contradicting Aristotle and proving him wrong at many points, authoritarianism was crumbling. This left the door open for a new source of certainty. Two methods were presented for arriving at certainty:

1. Descartes' deductive development of innate and certain truths.

2. Bacon's inductive thinking: He studied the human mind and attempted to counter the traditional "organon" of Aristotle with a *Novum Organum* (1620). In this he emphasized observation and thought of human benefit as the aim of all knowledge.

Realistic Educational Theories

THE UTOPIANS

1. *Introduction:* With the crumbling of medieval complacency and authority many imaginative minds turned to dreaming of utopias in which society could be reconstructed through education.

2. *Thomas More* (1478-1535): He wrote his *Utopia* in 1515-1516 suggesting political reform and communism. Here is seen a belief in the improvement of human life in England.

3. *Tommaso Campanella* (1568-1639): He wrote *The City of the Sun* in which he follows Plato's *Republic* in constructing an ideal community. Here is one book, an encyclopedia of all knowledge, read by everyone. Here the walls of the city are covered with pictures, children are taken to the shops of craftsmen to learn in terms of their interests. Here the home is spurned and state breeding and training are advocated.

4. *Johann Valentin Andrea* (1586-1654): He was a brilliant Christian pastor and educator who wrote the *Christian City* (1619). In this he conceived of a city ruled by Christian principles. In the city was Christian communism, everyone was educated equally, and the chief aim of all was service. Education was compulsory and the schools were supported and controlled by the people. He emphasized sense impressions as basic to learning. The aim of education, for him, was piety, virtue, and knowledge.

5. *Francis Bacon* (1561-1626): He wrote the *New Atlantis* (1629) in the center of which he imagined Solomon's House, a great research center with emphasis upon science. This book was not completed; thus, the educational phase of the utopia is not completed.

6. *James Harrington* (1611-1677): He was an English political philosopher who wrote *The Commonwealth of Oceana* (1656) in which he suggested compulsory education in free schools.

WOLFGANG RATICH (RATKE) (1571-1635)

1. *His Life Story:* Born at Wilster in Holstein, he was educated at the gymnasium in Hamburg and at the University of Rostock. He was a devout Lutheran and studied for the ministry, but turned to education. He announced a new method for teaching the classical languages and High German so that all might learn and thereby establish one language, one government, and one religion. His plan was studied by high educational authorities. Prince Ludwig von Anhalt-Kothen established a school for him in Kothen, but this was a failure.

2. *His Method of Teaching:* He sought a method which would be true to the nature of the mind. He argued that if one understood the mind he could develop a method of teaching which would convey knowledge easily and surely. This he believed he had. Thus, he suggested principles of teaching in line with this understanding: Teach everything in terms of the working of the child's mind. Master one thing at a time. Constant repetition will fix the knowledge in the child's mind. Learn first in the mother tongue and then in the original. Learn rules of grammar from the teacher, not from books. Compulsion causes the child to hate studies; therefore, teach without force. Do not teach by rote. Be sure that the child understands what he is learning. Teach similar subjects in the same way. Learn a thing first, then move to analysis and explanation. All learning must come through experience and experimentation.

3. *His Influence:* He was a fanatical Lutheran and hated other faiths. He was selfish, offering his new discoveries for a price only. He was suspicious of others, quarreled with his subordinates, and promised far more than he could deliver. In spite of all this, his influence was wide. The most important phase of his influence is that which he exerted upon Comenius.

JOHN AMOS COMENIUS (1592-1670)

1. *His Life Story:* Born at Nivnitz, in Moravia, of Slav ancestry, he was a member of the Moravian Brethren, followers of John Huss. He received a poor education in the village school. At 20 he entered the College of Herborn in Nassau to study for the ministry. Here he came under the influence of John Henry Alsted and the ideas of Ratich. He spent some time in Amsterdam. He was devoted to helping the Moravians during their persecutions at the time of the Thirty Years' War and was forced to settle in Lissa, Poland. Here he became rector of a gymnasium and wrote the *Great Didactic, Gate of Tongues Unlocked, The Vestibule.* He visited England and Sweden, wrote numerous textbooks for Latin schools in Sweden, and spent his last years in Amsterdam writing and helping the scattered Moravian Brethren.

2. *The Pansophic Dream:* Commenius sought to correlate all knowledge and stimulate advances in every field of learning by: Compiling an encyclopedia of universal knowledge; establishing a college for research in all fields of endeavor, and developing a method of teaching which would enable everyone, as far as he is capable, to learn in all areas of knowledge. He would teach everyone everything. This dream was based on: Comenius' confidence that in every individual are the seeds of knowledge, virtue, and piety, and that these are capable of unlimited cultivation given the correct education, and his belief in the "Christian Republic," a society of equality and democracy.

3. *His Educational Plan:* The aim of education is to teach all men everything to the end that each will become "as like to Christ as possible." This aim necessitated good textbooks, good teachers, and good methods of teaching. Education is essential to make the individual human. The organization necessary consists of four schools of six years each: a) The School of the Mother's Knee; b) The Vernacular School; c) The Latin School or Gymnasium, and d) The University and travel. He advocated instruction of children in groups and held that each child should have his own textbook.

4. *The Schools Proposed:* **The School of the Mother's Knee** - Since education begins at birth, the first school is the home. He wrote *The School of Infancy.* He sought to teach each child everything he could learn at his age, develop his senses, give him social training, and instruct him in religion. **The Vernacular School** - He believed that all children should be educated in the same school, be compelled to attend, and devote six years to the study of the vernacular before beginning the study of Latin. In this school the child should be trained in all the arts of common humanity. **The Latin School or Gymnasium** - All boys who wish to be more than unskilled laborers should attend this school for training of the higher faculties of the mind. The school should teach Latin, Greek, Hebrew, and an encyclopedic knowledge of the arts and sciences. **The University and Travel** - Only the brightest boys should attend the University to train the will and prepare for the professions, to become teachers and leaders. Travel should complete one's education.

5. *His Educational Psychology:* He held that teaching should follow the order of nature. The mind, for him, was composed of "faculties." Nevertheless, he developed principles of psychology resembling the more modern functional position: All knowledge comes through the senses; imagination is an inner sense; the faculty of memory can be trained by practice, but before a child tries to memorize he must have a clear understanding of the meaning of the material he is to memorize; the faculty of reason

deals with material gained through the senses; the child's emotions must be appealed to so that he will like what he is learning and will want to learn. This influences the will; deal with the child in terms of his individuality; adapt instruction to the level of the child's development by grading the work carefully, and the child's powers grow by exercise of specific functions. This last is the theory of formal discipline.

6. *His Pansophic Curriculum:* Everyone should learn the principle ideas in every subject at his level of development. Comenius advocated study of the vernacular; some knowledge of Latin, Greek, and Hebrew, though he was not a Humanist; study of the *trivium* and *quadrivium,* physics, geography, chronology, history, morals, religion, and the manual arts. He favored play and physical activity. All knowledge, he held, is useful.

7. *His Method of Learning and Teaching:* Reacting against the poor methods under which he had studied, Comenius took his ideas from nature. Some of these are of great value: All learning comes through the senses, therefore use as many senses as possible in teaching. Subject-matter must be graded on the basis of the child's ability so that each thing learned leads to the next more difficult thing. Do not force a child to learn, but stimulate inner desire, interest, and curiosity. The learner should communicate what he learns so as to impress it upon his mind. Thus, learning should be a group activity. Integrate the material learned. Begin with what the pupil knows and move to what he does not know but is to learn. Plan the work so that the child sees unity and is not confused by his learning.

8. *The Writings of Comenius:* Books dealing with educational principles: *The Great Didactic, The School of Infancy.* Textbooks: *The Gate of Tongues Unlocked (Janua), Vestibule to the Gate of Tongues Unlocked (Vestibulum), The Inner Room (Atrium), The Palace of Authors (Palatium), The World of Sensible Things Pictured (Orbis Pictus).*

Realism and Educational Reform among the Protestants
REALISM IN PROTESTANT EUROPE

1. *The Synod of Dort* (1618-1619): This was a general council of the Reformed Church meeting at Dordrecht in Holland and working under the influence of Calvinistic interest in education. It urged promotion of schools by civil authorities, the establisment of schools in outlying areas, and religious instruction in the home, school, and church.

2. *The Weimar Plan:* Dutchess Dorothea Maria sponsored the school order of 1619 which required compulsory attendance at school of all boys and girls between six and twelve years of age, enforcement by civil authorities, and the learning of the vernacular before Latin.

3. *Duke Ernst of Gotha:* The son of the Duchess Dorothea, he took school

reform out of the hands of the church and placed it under civil authority. He became Duke of Gotha in 1640, near the close of the Thirty Years' War (1618-1648) and sought to revive education after the war. His reforms included: a minimum income for teachers, higher standards for teaching, and a general school law. Andreeas Reyher, rector of the Gotha gymnasium, prepared a plan of school organization which was adopted in 1642. This provided for better teachers, milder discipline, a longer school term, compulsory attendance for all children from 5 to 12 years of age, and a program of class periods and study. Reyher wrote textbooks and manuals of instruction in the realistic subjects. Stress was placed upon sense impressions in learning. Supervision of the schools was under state control and for state interest.

REALISTIC EDUCATION IN ENGLAND AND IN SCOTLAND

1. *Introduction:* The 17th century saw the struggle in England between the Crown and Parliament and the production of many literary and scientific monuments. The era was marked by: Realistic subjects were introduced into the schools; English grew as a school subject; education was spread among the people, and education outside the established church was tolerated.

2. *The Social Pattern:* The Commonwealth was established and sought school reforms which failed because of the conditions of the times. The Scottish General Assembly petitioned Parliament in 1639, 1641, and 1646 for school reform and spread of elementary education. The war with Cromwell made enforcement of education laws impossible and led to domination of education by the English church. The Act of Uniformity (1665) suppressed teaching by dissenters and led to the founding of dissenting academies. The Revolution of 1688 resulted in toleration of dissenters, a Protestant English church. In Scotland it resulted in the establishment of the Presbyterian church and school legislation by the Scottish Parliament (1696).

3. *Educational Theorists:* **Edmund Coote** - He wrote *The English Schoolmaster,* an early English speller aimed at teaching the English language. **John Brinsley** - He wrote *The Grammar Schoole* (1612) and *A Consolation for Our Grammar Schooles* (1622). He advocated the Ascham method of double translation in teaching English and Latin. He believed in mild discipline, that the child should have a clear understanding of the material he was learning, class organization of schools, and thoroughness in teaching. **Samuel Hartlib** (1600-1670) - He was the son of a Polish merchant and a leading figure in the Commonwealth. He wrote *Description of the Famous Kingdom of Macaria,* a utopia in which children are educated in the arts, sciences, and manufacturing, *Considerations Tending to the*

Happy Accomplishment of England's Reformation in Church and State, holding that the civil authorities must see that schools are built, maintained, and supervised, and *An Essay for the Advancement of Husbandry Learning.* He popularized the ideas of Comenius in England. **John Milton** (1608-1674) - He wrote *Of Education* (1644). He was a classicist and a Puritan, a Humanistic Realist, who advocated the study of the classics and wanted classical academies established for boys to study everything through reading the ancients. Travel completed his scheme of education. He fought for religious toleration and freedom of the press. **John Drury** (1598-1680) - He wrote the *Reformed School* and *A. Supplement to the Reformed School.* He was a sense Realist who advocated teaching with objects, a practical education, and teaching adapted to the mind of the child. **William Petty** (1623-1687) - He wrote *The Advice of W.P. to Mr. Samuel Hartlib for the Advancement of Some Particular Parts of Learning.* In this he advocates a realistic education and the establishment of three educational institutions: a Literary Workhouse or common school in which all would learn to read, write, and earn a living, a College of Trades-men or school for teaching the mechanical arts and manufacturing, and an Academy or combined botanical garden, museum, and zoological area. He advocated universal education and religious freedom. **Charles Hoole** (1610-1667) - He wrote *A New Discovery of the Old Art of Teaching School* and many textbooks. He was a sense Realist and advocated an enriched elementary school curriculum. **Daniel Defoe** (1659-1731) - He wrote an *Essay on Projects* (1697) in which he advocated the establishing of an academy of letters similar to the French Academy, a Royal Academy for Military Sciences, and academies for the liberal education of women. He also wrote *The Complete English Gentleman.*

4. *Types of Realistic Schools:* **Universities** - Oxford declined but showed signs of turning in the direction of the realistic studies, mathematics and the sciences. However, it remained conservative. Cambridge experienced difficulties but was the center for the work of Isaac Barrow and Isaac Newton. Mathematics and chemistry flourished. **Grammar Schools -** Latin was gradually declining in prominence and English translations were being used with the result that greater emphasis was placed upon the mastery of grammar. This domination by the grammarians was opposed by many educators. **Elementary Schools -** In most instances these were taught by poor, incapable persons and little was accomplished. Some educators pleaded for better beginning teaching. **Charity Schools -** Many philanthropists financed schools for the poor. The Society for Promoting Christian Knowledge (S.P.C.K.) was founded in 1699 and the Society for the Propagation of the Gospel in Foreign Parts (S.P.G.) was founded in

1701. These organizations promoted many charity schools. They were Church of England agencies for academic, trade, and religious training of children. **Dissenting Schools** - Dissenters, driven out of pulpits and universities by the Act of Uniformity (1662) and other repressive legislation, established schools for the teaching of their own children. These grew and became very popular. Academies established by these dissenters offered work similar to that of Oxford and Cambridge. Those established between 1663 and 1690 had one tutor and 30 to 40 pupils. English and the classics were emphasized as well as work in the foreign languages and the sciences and logic. These academies influenced early American education. Between 1690 and 1750 the academies offered work in commercial areas and increased their offerings in mathematics and science.

PIETISM AND EDUCATION

1. *Introduction:* Pietism was a 17th century religious movement which began in Germany and spread throughout Europe and to America. Philip Jacob Spener (1635-1705) was the founder of the movement.

2. *Causes of the Pietistic Movement:* The degradation and immorality of the times, the dissension within religious bodies, and the cold ritualism of religion gave birth to Pietism as an expression of a longing for freedom. It was a normal reaction to the religious formalism and rationalism and general distress following the Thirty Years' War. It remained within the Lutheran church and was the religious aspect of Realism.

3. *Spener's Criticism of Schools:* Schools neglect the cultivation of a living religious faith. Schools devote too much time to Latin and not enough to Greek and Hebrew. Schools give too little attention to the Scriptures. Schools substitute Aristotle for Christian morals. Teachers must be more concerned with the morals of their pupils.

4. *August Hermann Francke* (1663-1727): **His Life** - He was a brilliant, highly educated teacher at the University of Leipzig where he experienced an intense emotional conversion and joined the Pietistic movement. He was expelled from Leipzig and became a teacher at the University of Halle and pastor in the village of Glauchau. **His Educational Background** - He was reared in Gotha, lectured on education at Leipzig, and was greatly influenced by Johannes Winckler and his infant school in Hamburg. This led him to the conviction that education is necessary to make men better. **His Educational Aim** - To honor God through religious training and education. He believed that all learning should contribute to Christian living. **His Educational Institutions** - a) An elementary school for poor children; b) An elementary school for burgher children; c) A Padagogium or school for children of the nobility; d) An orphanage for boys and one for girls; e) A gymnasium for boys of the middle well-to-do class; f) A

Teachers' Seminar to train common school teachers and a Select Seminar
to train teachers for Latin schools; g) The Canstein Bible Institute for
publishing books and tracts, and h) An apothecary shop. **The Curriculum -**
Religion was the basic field of study. Sciences were taught as were also
Latin, Greek, and Hebrew. The realistic subjects were prominent. There
was much vocational teaching. **His Influence upon Prussian Education -** He
influenced Johann Julius Hecker (1707-1768) in establishing the *Realschule*
(1747). He wrote school laws, stimulated interest in orphanages, and his
pupils spread his ideas throughout Germany. **His Influence in America -** The
Salzbergers and Moravians who settled in Georgia and in Pennsylvania, as
well as many other groups and individuals, brought his ideas and institutions to America. The work of Count Zinzendorf among the Moravians in
Pennsylvania and of Henry Melchior Muhlenberg among the Lutherans in
that same state grew out of the Pietistic influence.

5. *The Results of Pietism:* A new emphasis and value was put on emotions
in religion and in other aspects of life. The Scriptures were studied for
conduct rather than for doctrinal orthodoxy. Laymen had a greater part
in the church services. It stimulated church music. It stimulated
interest in philanthropy and missionary work. It created a new interest
in Christian education. It championed education for all children, rich
and poor alike.

EDUCATION OF THE PRINCES. The *Ritteracademien* (knightly academies)
were established in Germany to train the sons of German princes in
courtly manners, to prepare them for military service, and to educate
them in statecraft and administration. The realistic studies were included in the curriculum. These academies died after the development of
the modern gymnasiums.

17TH CENTURY GERMAN UNIVERSITIES. Pietism and the realistic movement
combined to give the German universities new life. The University of
Halle was founded in 1694. It employed the German language, disregarded
ancient authorities and emphasized free investigation. A group of
distinguished teachers joined the faculty - Thomasius, Wolff, Francke -
and soon the influence of the university was felt in other German
institutions.

Realism and Educational Reform among the French Catholics
THE TEACHING ORDERS

1. *Introduction:* The teaching orders of the Catholic church gained
almost total control of French education.

2. *The Oratory:* The French Oratory was founded in 1611 by Cardinal de
Berulle to improve the discipline and scholarship of the priests. It
gradually undertook general education through the college level. It was

influenced by Descartes' philosophy and offered instruction in religion, mathematics, physics, the natural sciences, history, geography, Latin, French, Greek, Hebrew. It encouraged mild discipline. Leaders of the Order included: Father Thomassin who sought to reconcile Christianity and the classical writings, and Nicolas Malebranche (1638-1715) the philosopher of the Order.

3. *The Port Royalists:* **Founding** - Jean Duvergier de Hauranne (Saint Cyran) (1581-1643) and Cornelius Jansen (1585-1638), working at Port Royal near Paris, began the religious movement called Jansenism. They sought to reform the Catholic Church but were so zealous that the Order was dispersed in 1661. **The Little Schools** - These were organized by 1646 as Latin schools for the training of leaders. Each school took no more than 50 boys. **Educational Aims** - They held that human nature is corrupt and can be made pure by education; one should study only to prepare for service of God. They taught sciences and literature and used mild discipline but held complete control over their pupils. **The Curriculum** - They had a Christian Humanistic curriculum which included French, Latin, Greek, mathematics, the sciences, history, geography. The teachers sought to make the work interesting to the pupils. **Teaching Methods** - Proceed from what cannot be doubted to that which is to be known (the Cartesian method), give clear impressions through the senses, be sure that pupils understand what they are learning, and cultivate the power of reasoning.

EDUCATION OF THE POOR

1. *Introduction:* Catholic education of the poor in the 17th century was haphazard and meager. Charity and parochial schools were poorly taught and supported, although there were some efforts made to improve conditions: **The Sisters of Notre Dame** was founded in 1598 by Peter Fourier for the education of the poor. **The Congregation of Saint Charles** was founded in 1666 by Father Demia for the education of the poor children of Lyons. He also established a school for teacher training.

2. *Brothers of the Christian Schools:* This Order was founded by Jean-Baptiste de La Salle (1651-1719) in 1684 to provide free instruction for the poor in the elementary subjects. The Order established a teacher training school at Reims in 1685.

EDUCATION OF GIRLS

1. *Order of Ursulines:* This Order, founded in 1535 by Angela Merici (1470-1540), was concerned with the education of girls to be devout Christians. It aimed to prepare girls for religious orders or for their duties as wives and mothers. The Order spread to Quebec (1639) and New Orleans (1727).

2. *Port Royal:* The education of girls by the Port Royalists was very

repressive. Jacqueline Pascal gives a vivid picture of the practices of the Order in her *Rules for the Pupils of Port Royal.*

3. *Francois de Salignac de La Mothe Fenelon* (1651-1715): He wrote *On the Education of Girls* (1687). In this he held that girls should be educated for the career of motherhood and family life. This education included ability to manage estates. He believed that education in the home was better than that in a convent.

4. *Saint Cyr:* This was a boarding school for girls founded in 1686 by Madame de Maintenon (1635-1719). It took girls of noble families and aimed to prepare them for careers as mothers. At first the curriculum was liberal and included much intellectual training. In 1692 the school was reorganized as a convent under the Order of Saint Augustine and became very repressive with intellectual education being minimized in favor of practical training.

The 17th Century in Retrospect
CHANGES IN CULTURE AND THOUGHT

1. *Growth of Religious Toleration:* Catholics and Protestants fought bitterly during this century and then divided Europe up between themselves, each having more or less control of specific areas. In many countries the principle of religious toleration was gaining ground.

2. *Need for Psychological Knowledge:* The limited knowledge of the mind of the child at this time hampered educational development and gave rise to many unsatisfactory practices. Education was waiting for a thorough exploration of this area.

3. *Theory of Knowledge:* The dominant position was that knowledge was innate (Descartes' theory). However, there was a growing realization that knowledge was advanced through observation and experimentation (employment of the senses).

4. *Growth of Liberty and Autocracy:* During this period the theory of political liberty was gaining ground, but it was fought in practice by political organizations and by certain theorists in the field of government. John Milton pleaded for freedom in his *Areopagitica.* This led to a growing respect for man as an individual. Here is the basis for the modern idea that everyone should have the opportunity to develop his capacities.

RISE OF VERNACULARS. Gradually Europe was turning away from the exclusive use of Latin to use of the vernaculars. A vernacular literature was arising and books were being printed in these languages. Dante's *The Divine Comedy,* Luther's translation of the Bible into High German, the appearance of the King James version of the Bible in English, and the writings of Shakespere are examples of this development.

GROWING CONCERN FOR THE EDUCATION OF THE MASSES. In the 16th century cultural education was reserved for the upper classes while the masses received only religious and apprentice training. In the 17th century movements arose which championed the enlightenment of the common people. These were fought bitterly by the aristocratic and ruling groups in many countries. In Germany several attempts were made to establish schools for the masses and force them to attend, but the fight for and against mass education remained intense. The work of philanthropic organizations in the direction of mass education helped to spread the idea and increase the demand for general education.

EDUCATIONAL ADVANCES IN THE 17TH CENTURY

1. The weaknesses of classical Humanism were more clearly seen and Latin gradually lost its dominance in Europe.

2. Use of the vernaculars became more popular and vernacular literatures were developing. These languages and their literatures were competing with Latin for a position in the school curriculum.

3. There was considerable progress in the scientific fields - mathematics and the physical sciences.

4. Rationalism and Empiricism both claimed to be the way to true knowledge and had to be reconciled in an effort to construct a scientific method.

5. Realism demanded that work of the schools be guided by the principle of use, utility.

6. Theories of human progress appeared in the utopias of the century.

7. There was a growing attempt to justify government by founding it upon human nature rather than upon authority.

8. Religious toleration made possible the development of charity schools by religious bodies.

9. In the work of Comenius and that of the Knightly Academies was the conflict between democratic and aristocratic educational policies.

10. Greater emphasis was placed upon the education of girls.

11. Several profound educational theories were developed during the century.

12. Teacher education was undertaken by several groups and teaching Orders.

13. Educational ideas and institutions were carried to America by the colonists and transplanted in this new soil.

BIBLIOGRAPHY

I. Primary Sources:

Bacon, Francis, *Advancement of Learning and Novum Organum.* Boston, Ginn and Company, 1904.

Bacon, Francis, *New Atlantis.* London, A.T. Flux, 1899.

Brinsley, John, *Ludus Literarius; or The Grammar Schoole.* London, Constable and Company, Ltd., 1917.

Comenius, John Amos, *The Labyrinth of the World and the Paradise of the Heart.* Chicago, National Union of Czechoslovak Protestants of America, 1942.

Cubberley, Ellwood P., *Readings in the History of Education,* pp. 316-359. New York, Houghton Mifflin Co., 1920.

Defoe, Daniel, *Essay on Projects.* London, Thomas Cockerill, 1697.

Descartes, Rene, *Discourse on Method,* in Harvard Clasics, vol. 34. New York, P.F. Collier & Son, 1910.

Fenelon, F. de S., *On the Education of Girls.* Translated by Kate Lupton. Boston, Ginn and Company, 1891.

Harrington, James, *The Commonwealth of Oceana.* Edited by S.B. Liljeren. Heidelberg, Winters, 1924.

Hoole, Charles, *A New Discovery of the Old Art of Teaching School.* Syracuse, C.W. Bardeen, 1912.

Milton, John, *Of Education.* London, Thomas Dring, 1673.

Montaigne, M. de, *Education of Children.* New York, D. Appleton & Co., 1899.

Mulcaster, R., *Positions.* London, Longmans, Green and Co. 1888.

Mulcaster, R., *The Elementaire.* Oxford, Oxford University Press, 1925.

Rabelais, F., *Gargantua.* London, Chatto and Windus, n.d.

Watson, F., (Translator), *Vives: On Education.* Cambridge, Cambridge University Press,

2. Secondary Material:

Bardeen, C.W., *The Orbis Pictus of John Amos Comenius.* Syracuse, C.W. Bardeen, 1887.

Barnard, H.C., *The Little Schools of Port Royal.* Cambridge, Cambridge University Press, 1913.

Barnes, Harry Elmer, *An Intellectual and Cultural History of the Western World,* pp. 668-705. New York, Random House, 1937

Becker, Carl, *The Heavenly City of the 18th Century Philosophers.* New Haven, Yale University Press, 1932.

Butts, R. Freeman, *A Cultural History of Education,* pp. 309-346. New York, McGraw-Hill Book Company, Inc., 1947.

Cadet, Felix, *Port Royal Education.* London, S. Sonnenschein & Co., 1898.

Cubberley, Ellwood P., *A Brief History of Education,* pp. 205-226. New York, Houghton Mifflin Co., 1922.

Cubberley, Ellwood P., *The History of Education,* pp. 379-425. New York, Houghton Mifflin Co., 1920.

De la Fontainerie, F., *The Conduct of the Schools of Jean Baptiste de la Salle.* New York, McGraw-Hill Book Company, Inc., 1935.

Dircks, Henry, *A Biographical Memoir of Samuel Hartlib.* London, J.R. Smith, 1865.

Duggan, Stephen, *A Student's Textbook in the History of Education,* pp 156-188. New York, D. Appleton-Century Co., 1936.

Eby, Frederick and Arrowood, Charles F., *The Development of Modern Education,* pp. 200-384. New York, Prentice-Hall, Inc., 1937.

Graves, Frank P., *A History of Education, During the Middle Ages and the Transition to Modern Times,* pp. 240-305. New York, The Macmillan Co., 1925.

Graves, Frank P., *A Student's History of Education,* pp. 163-181. New York, The Macmillan Co., 1936.

Graves, Frank P., *Peter Ramus.* New York, The Macmillan Co., 1912.

Held, Felix Emil, *Johann Valentin Andrea's Christianopolis.* Urbana, University of Illinois, 1914.

Keatings, M.W., *Comenius.* New York, McGraw-Hill Book Co., Inc., 1931.

Keatings, M.W., *The Great Didactic of John Amos Comenius.* London, Adam and Charles Black, 1896.

Masso, Gildo, *The Place of Education in Utopias.* New York, Teachers College, Columbia University, 1927.

McClure, M.T., *Bacon Selections.* New York, Charles Scribner's Sons, 1928.

Melvin, A. Gordon, *Education, A History,* pp. 173-194. New York, The John Day Company, 1946.

Messenger, James F., *An Interpretative History of Education,* pp. 141-155. New York, Thomas Y. Crowell Co., 1931.

Monroe, Will S., *Comenius and the Beginnings of Educational Reform.* New York, Charles Scribner's Sons, 1900.

Monroe, Will S., *Comenius' School of Infancy.* Boston, D.C. Heath and Co., 1896.

Monroe, Paul, *A Brief Course in the History of Education,* pp. 215-253. New York, The Macmillan Co., 1909.

Monroe, Paul, *A Text-Book in the History of Education,* pp. 442-502. New York, The Macmillan Co., 1907.

Mulhern, James, *A History of Education,* pp. 262-276. Ronald Press Co., New York, 1946.

Painter, Franklin, *A History of Education,* pp. 195-230. New York. D. Appleton-Century Co., 1904.

Watson, F., *Louis Vives, El Gran Valenciano.* Oxford, Oxford University Press, 1922.

Watson, F., (Editor), *Vives and the Renascence Education of Women.* New York, Longmans, Green and Company, 1912.

Wilds, Elmer H., *The Foundations of Modern Education,* pp. 313-349. New York, Rinehart & Co., Inc., 1942.

CHAPTER XI

The Era of Transition

John Locke (1632-1704)

HIS LIFE AND WRITINGS. Born at Wrington, the son of a Puritan attorney, Locke received a good education at Westminister School and at Christ Church College, Oxford. After 1667 he attached himself to the Earl of Shaftesbury as friend, secretary, physician, and tutor of his son and later his grandson. He traveled widely, spent an exile, after the fall of Shaftesbury, in Holland, and returned to England with William of Orange. His writings in the fields of philosophy, government, economics, education, and religion show him to be one of England's deepest and most influential thinkers. In the field of government he urged: the doctrine of the divine right of kings is false (see his *Two Treatises on Government,* 1690); there must be complete separation of church and state and freedom of worship and of conscience (see his *Letters Concerning Toleration,* 1685, 1690, 1692, and 1706). In the field of philosophy he wrote the *Essay Concerning Human Understanding,* 1690, which deeply influenced European thinking. In the field of education he wrote *Some Thoughts Concerning Education* (1693), *Conduct of the Understanding, Some Thoughts Concerning Reading and Study for a Gentleman, Instructions for the Conduct of a Young Gentleman, Of Study,* and *Working Schools.*

HIS PSYCHOLOGICAL THEORY

1. *There are no Innate Ideas:* Locke held that there are no innate ideas since he could find no ideas that were universally known. He held that the mind is a "white paper" *(tabula rasa).* Ideas come to the mind from experience (the senses) and from the workings of the mind as it deals with the material of sensations. The mind works up experiences by discrimination, analysis, and association, into concepts (generalizations, abstractions, relations, and general principles).

2. *Some Implications of This Position:* It denies the old theological doctrine of innate total depravity, and it provides a psychological basis for the theory of human development. If there are no innate ideas, the child is vastly different from the adult in intellectual possessions. His mind develops as he grows in experience. The child gradually builds knowledge and the ability to think in abstract terms.

3. *What is Innate?:* Locke assumed the innate existence of the soul or mind, all the appetites, and mental faculties. Activity is caused by inner needs (appetites) and is directed by the effort to avoid pain or

obtain pleasure. These inner needs are experienced as desires: **Ordinary necessities** (hunger, heat, weariness, etc.); **Fantastical uneasiness** ("itch for honor, power, riches," etc.). The most important drives are a sense of shame and a desire for honor. The faculty of reason combines sense material into concepts and judgments. It functions for the sake of the moral good of the individual. Man is a rational being.

4. *Theory of Language:* Words are symbols of ideas, standing for the ideas which the individual who speaks has. They are chosen arbitrarily. One should get ideas first and words afterward. Do not teach words before children have the ideas to give them meaning. As far as possible one should think without words.

HIS THEORY OF EDUCATION

1. *Whence Came His Ideas?:* From Montaigne, some from ancient writers, but mostly from the English practices in educating the upper classes.

2. *Aims of Education:* The education in which he was concerned is that of the gentleman or the aristocratic class. Thus, he emphasizes: **Virtue -** good character built from the proper religious training. This included reverence for God, love of truth, and good will toward others. **Wisdom -** prudence, sound judgment, and foresight in practical matters. **Breeding -** manners in accord with English tradition, proper self-respect and respect for others. **Learning -** knowledge. Locke realized the importance of learning, but he disparaged the scholar in favor of the man of practical judgment.

3. *The Means of Education:* Private education in the home and under a tutor is superior to public education. Physical education is most important (a sound mind in a sound body). This should lead to the hardening of the body. Develop the habit of self-control, moral discipline, through forcing the child to be obedient to his elders. Every element of the curriculum must find justification in its contribution to present and future life. Thus, the child should study many broad, general courses in a variety of fields. One should master the English language, then French, and perhaps Latin. In addition, he should study drawing, writing, shorthand, geography, geometry, chronology, anatomy, history, philosophy, science, ethics, psychology, and some manual arts.

4. *Education of the Masses:* Poor children should be educated in "working schools" away from their parents until their 14th year, then apprenticed. In these schools children should learn religion and simple handicrafts.

THE THEORY OF MENTAL DISCIPLINE

1. *Introduction:* Many have held that Locke was the first to advocate the doctrine of formal mental discipline. Paul Monroe takes this position.

2. *Was Locke a Mental Disciplinarian?:* **Mental Discipline -** One can

strengthen the power of memory by practicing memorizing. **Locke** - Memory is due to the power of the mind to retain impressions and this power cannot be increased by practice. It is innate. **Mental Discipline** - practice of perceiving strengthens the power to perceive. **Locke** - in perceiving the mind is passive. Thus it cannot be strengthened. **Mental Discipline** - the power of attention can be strengthened by training in attending. **Locke** - attention cannot be strengthened, but by training one can so master his mind that he can direct attention from one thing to another. This is the power of switching or directing attention which comes through training. **Mental Discipline** - learning, strengthening of the faculties, comes through compulsion and hard work. **Locke** - there must be no compulsion. All learning is to be made easy. Compulsion may cause the child to dislike learning. **Mental Discipline** - there are special faculties of the mind which can be strengthened by exercise and then can be used in learning any subject. **Locke** - he did not believe in general powers of the mind. One may reason well today and about "one sort of matter" and may not be able to reason at all about others. The child acquires special skills, not general powers.

3. *Training of the Rational Faculty:* Locke was seeking a method for making all other fields as certain as mathematics. He believed that the study of mathematics brings the rational potentialities of the child to maturity, makes the mind critical, reveals the necessity for analyzing every problem, emphasizes the need for excluding all irrelevant matter in reasoning, emphasizes the need for impartiality, and reveals the value of a connected series of propositions. In the study of mathematics one discovers a method of reasoning which he then has as a model for his reasoning in other fields.

4. *Locke was not a mental disciplinarian because:* He wanted learning made easy and recognized the place of the child's spontaneous interests. He would teach only that which is useful and not subjects that "strengthen the mind." He wanted the pupils to study many subjects, no one too thoroughly. He made an appeal for the development of reason and judgment. He was against memorizing by rote. He held that the child has a general capacity but that he develops habits or skills by exercise and independently. He held that mathematics gives one a model for reasoning which he may use in other areas.

LOCKE'S INFLUENCE: In the field of philosophy he influenced David Hume and Bishop Berkeley in England, the Enlightenment in France, and the idealistic movement of Kant, Fichte, and Hegel in Germany. In the field of education he influenced the thinking of Rousseau, Basedow, Pestalozzi, and Herbart.

The Enlightenment

INTRODUCTION. France in the 18th century was the center of a revolution that had world-wide repercussions and produced a deeper knowledge of man and a new philosophy of human life and social institutions.

FACTORS CAUSING THE REVOLUTION

1. *Revolt against Domination of Classical Literature:* Charles Perrault (1628-1703) championed the modern writers over against the classics. This led to considerable creativity in French literature.

2. *The Effects of Rationalism and Empiricism:* Voltaire (1694-1778) and the Encyclopedists gave France a new conception composed of the Rationalism of Descartes and the Sensationalism of Locke. They held that truth comes only by reason and that reason is enlightened by the senses alone. They abandoned revelation as a source of knowledge. They came to worship reason. What reason had accomplished in the world of physical nature they held could be accomplished in all other areas. Thus, they sought a science of human nature.

3. *Sensuality:* French life was sensual, materialistic, and atheistic. Man was held to be a machine built wholly out of sensations. The spiritual was abandoned and the material was made supreme.

4. *The Revolt against Christianity:* The Christianity of France was the Catholic Church and the Jesuit Order. These were corrupt and oppressive and conspired with the King to hold power over the people. They were opposed to all enlightenment and progress. Thus, leaders of the Enlightenment reacted violently against Christianity. Voltaire fought the Church bitterly, turned to deism, and held that intelligent people did not need religion. Religion was for the masses, to keep them in order morally. The result was a theory of complete separation of church and state, state control of education, expulsion of the Jesuit Order, atheism, and a turning on the part of many from the formalism of established religion to a religion of inner light and ethical meaning.

5. *Social Conditions:* The rich and powerful were corrupt, brilliant, and heartless. The poor lived in abject poverty. The peasants worked hard but had to support the court, nobility, and the Church. A bourgeoisie class was arising and from this came the first rumblings of political discontent. Montesquieu (1689-1755) wrote *The Spirit of Laws.*

THE FUNCTION OF ENLIGHTENMENT. Leaders began to realize that release from these conditions lay in the spread of enlightenment. Through knowledge man could save himself and create a new and wonderful society. Although a great many despised the masses and held that enlightenment was for the upper classes only, there were those who sought to disperse knowledge among the masses.

The Physiocratic Movement

INTRODUCTION. The Physiocrats, or Economists, recognized the need for economic reorganization and sought to work out an economic theory for betterment of the working classes. Leaders of the movement were Francois Quesnay (1694-1774), Jean Claude de Gournay (1712-1759), and P.S. Dupont de Nemours (1739-1817). This school of economists attempted to apply the principle of natural law to economics. Its members founded the science of economics and introduced the doctrine of economic individualism and freedom.

DOCTRINES OF THE SCHOOL

1. Agriculture is the sole source of wealth. It alone has real value.

2. Everyone has the natural right to work and enjoy the rewards of his labor. This is an inalienable right. Happiness lies in an abundance of things fitted to enjoyment and in complete freedom to enjoy them.

3. Production must be free to follow its own inherent laws without governmental restrictions. This is the *laissez-faire* doctrine.

4. The job of government is to protect life and property and administer justice. It must never interfere with production or trade.

5. Individual ownership of property and security are basic to any economic freedom.

RESULTS OF THE MOVEMENT. Better conditions for the poor were advocated, agriculture gained in dignity, and training for industrial and farm life was stimulated. Benevolent despots sought to better conditions of the poor, freed trade, and attempted to educate the people to become productive workers.

BIBLIOGRAPHY

I. Primary Sources:

Adamson, J.W., (editor), *The Educational Writings of John Locke*. Cambridge, Cambridge University Press, 1912.

Cubberley, Elloowd P., *Readings in the History of Education*, pp. 392-407. New York, Houghton Mifflin Co., 1920.

Holbach, Paul Henri, *The System of Nature*. (translated by H.D. Robinson). Boston, J.P. Mendum, 1853.

Montesquieu, Charles Louis, *The Spirit of Laws*. (translated by Thomas Nugent), New York, Colonial Press, 1899.

Quick, R.H., (editor), *Some Thoughts Concerning Education*. Cambridge, Cambridge University Press, 1913.

Voltaire, Francois, *The Best-Known Works of Voltaire*. New York, Blue Ribbon Books, 1931.

2. Secondary Material:

Bourne, H.R. Fox, *The Life of John Locke*. London, Henry S. King and Co., 1876.

Browning, Oscar, *A History of Educational Theory*, pp. 102-118. New York, Harper & Brothers, 1905.

Butts, R. Freeman, *A Cultural History of Education*, pp. 309-346. New York, McGraw-Hill Book Company, Inc., 1947.

Cubberley, Ellwood P., *A Brief History of Education*, pp. 230-232 and 259-261. New York, Houghton Mifflin Co., 1922.

Cubberley, Ellwood P., *The History of Education*, pp. 433-437 and 471-486. New York, Houghton Mifflin Co., 1920.

Duggan, Stephen, *A Student's Textbook in the History of Education*, pp. 182-198. New York, D. Appleton-Century Co., 1936.

Eby, Frederick and Arrowood, Charles F., *The Development of Modern Education*, pp. 386-440. New York, Prentice-Hall, Inc., 1937.

Graves, Frank P., *A History of Education, During the Middle Ages and the Transition to Modern Times*, pp. 305-313. New York, The Macmillan Co., 1925.

Graves, Frank P., *Great Educators of Three Centuries*, pp. 52-66. New York, The Macmillan Company, 1912.

Hart, Joseph K., *Creative Moments in Education*, pp. 246-252. New York, Henry Holt and Co., 1931.

Higgs, Henry, *The Physiocrats*. London, Macmillan and Co., Ltd., 1897.

Laurie, Simon S., *Development of Educational Opinion*, pp. 181-234. New York, The Macmillan Co., 1903.

Messenger, James F., *An Interpretative History of Education*, pp. 156-163. New York, Thomas Y. Crowell Co., 1931.

Monroe, Paul, *A Brief Course in the History of Education*, pp. 254-270. New York, The Macmillan Co., 1909.

Monroe, Paul, *A Text-Book in the History of Education*, pp. 505-529. New York, The Macmillan Co., 1907.

Mulhern, James, *A History of Education*, pp. 257-259. Ronald Press Co., New York, 1946.

Painter, Franklin, *A History of Education*, pp. 230-238. New York, D. Appleton-Century Co., 1904.

Thayer, Vivian T., *The Misinterpretation of Locke as a Formalist in Educational Philosophy.* Madison, University of Wisconsin Press, 1921.

Wilds, Elmer H., *The Foundations of Modern Education*, pp. 353-374. New York, Rinehart & Co., Inc., 1942.

CHAPTER XII

Jean Jacques Rousseau (1712-1778)

Rousseau the Man

HIS LIFE STORY. Born in Geneva of a French father and a Swiss mother who died when he was one week old, Rousseau was reared by his father, an eccentric and sentimental watchmaker. His father taught him to read but did not train him in the conventional habits and attitudes of normal life. Thus, he stole, lied, played dirty tricks, was indolent, ill-bred, and unprincipled. His father left Geneva when Rousseau was 10, and the boy went to Bossey to school. Returning to Geneva several years later, he failed as a clerk, was apprenticed to an engraver but ran away at 16 and became a vagabond. He became a Catholic, met Madame de Warrens, attempted to find himself in the priesthood, in music, and in teaching, but failed in each case. His wanderings showed him the miseries of the peasants and his studies introduced him to the current thought regarding social and philosophical problems. In 1741 he went to Paris, entered the society of leaders of the Enlightenment, and lived with Therese Lavasseur who bore him five children. His genius awakened with a flash in October, 1749. He wrote the prize essay, *Discourse on the Arts and Sciences.* This was followed by: *What is the Cause of Inequality Among Men?, The New Heloise, The Social Contract, Emile, Confessions.* His life was a psychological puzzle - highly emotional, erratic, a creative genius, a man of reprobate and perverted nature, an idealist, passionately devoted to the down-trodden and to liberty.

Rousseau the Political and Social Theorist

HIS REVOLT AGAINST CIVILIZATION. The Academy of Dijon offered, in the *Mercure de France,* a prize for an answer to the question: "Has the restoration of the Arts and Sciences had a purifying effect upon morals?" Rousseau answered that in all ages the arts and sciences had caused the downfall of morals.

HIS THEORY OF SOCIAL DEVELOPMENT

1. *Natural Man:* Original man in the state of nature is an animal. His aim is to avoid pain and death and to satisfy his physical wants for food, a mate, and rest. He is motivated by the impulse for self-preservation (*amour-de-soi* or self-love). All men are equal and free at this stage and no one is dependent upon another.

2. *Savage Man:* Reason makes man more than an animal and he develops speech, family life, and simple arts, but he is independent, has few

wants, and his virtues are greater than his vices.

3. *Civilized Man:* Man's imagination brings new desires and he creates civilization. Primitive self-love gives way to a calculated and ambitious love of self (*amour-propre*). This creates all the evils of society and leads to man's degradation. Man's reason leads to inequality and destroys the primitive state of innocence. Thus, Rousseau prayed for deliverance from " the fatal arts and sciences of our forefathers" and a return to "ignorance, innocence, and poverty which alone can make us happy."

4. *The Way to Happiness:* To rescue man from this condition, Rousseau called for reforms in state, church, marriage, family life, and the schools. **In the State:** Liberty is a natural right. By a social contract man established the state. This state must protect man and preserve his original freedom. The state must be governed by a direct democracy and all laws should be a direct expression of the general will. This doctrine shows development between his writing of the *Discourse on the Arts and Sciences* and *The Social Contract.* **In the Church:** In his *Profession of Faith of a Savoyard Vicar* he pleads for a religion based on nature and reason. **In Marriage and Family Life:** In *The New Heloise* he condemns marriages arranged by parents without the consent of the children. He holds that marriage should be based upon natural feelings and affections.

HIS DOCTRINE OF EVIL. Rousseau opposed the doctrine of original sin and held that "everything is good as it comes from the hands of the author of nature." Vice begins when man enters into human relations. These relations create self-centered interests which conflict with those of other individuals. The home, school, and social environment give children artificial desires that result in conflicts and evils. To realize desires men use others and social inequality results, leading to degeneracy and evil in society and in the individual.

Rousseau the Educational Theorist
ROUSSEAU'S REVOLUTIONARY POINT OF VIEW

1. *Introduction:* Education must be determined by the spontaneous interests and activities of the child and be guided by the development of the child.

2. *The Old Position is False:* The old idea that the child's education is to be governed by adult interests and activities is false. This old idea leads to untruths. **The Child is a Little Adult.** This is false, for the child is an individual wholly different from the adult. Thus, education is not the acquiring of what adults wish, but is furnishing the child with the proper environment for growth in terms of his true inner nature. **The Interests of Society are Above Those of the Individual.** This is false, for it means the crushing of the individuality of a child. The

individual is a precious entity that is to be bent to no outer will. The needs and interests of the individual are above those of organized society. **The Child's Nature is Unimportant.** This is false, for all true education is based upon understanding of the nature of children and their environment.

3. *The Recapitulation Theory:* In the individual's development from childhood to adulthood he lives again each epoch in the history of civilization. These stages are definite and clear, sharply marked from each other: **Animal stage** (from birth to 5). **Savage stage** (from 5 to 12) when self-consciousness emerges. **Rational stage** (from 12 to puberty) when the rational faculty emerges and the higher sentiments develop. **Social stage** (from puberty to adulthood) when sex emerges and social relations properly begin. Here also religious life properly develops Each stage is a complete unit of development and does not lead on to the next. The education of the child is not preparation for adult life. At each stage the child is to be taught what is useful for him at that stage only.

ROUSSEAU'S EDUCATIONAL AIMS. His fundamental aim was preservation of man's natural goodness and creation of a society which would insure its most complete development. Rousseau conceived . form of education for an ideal state organized in accord with the nature of man with education a public function and available to every child. Its aim is to foster natural virtues and a sense of social unity. This ideal is developed in his *Discourse on Political Economy, The Social Contract,* and *Considerations on the Government of Poland.* He also conceived a form of education for a society such as his own. Here education must protect the child from the evils of society until he is able to protect himself. This is developed in *Emile.* Here education is for the higher classes and aims at a generous, liberal cultivation of the child's natural endowments and avoids specialization. It seeks to fit the child for a changing environment. Since we do not know the future, we must educate in terms of the child's present needs. If this is well done, he will be able to meet the future adequately.

ROUSSEAU'S EDUCATIONAL INSTITUTIONS

1. *Public Education:* Rousseau favored public education that leads to social unity and a sense of equality. This leads to nationalism.

2. *Family Education:* The family educates in cooperation with the state. This is the Calvinistic position. Education should begin with the family and later be taken over by the state.

3. *The Isolation of Emile:* This is education of the wealthy boy who is to be educated as a savage to enter society as it is. He must be protected until he is able to resist successfully the society of his day.

THE STAGES OF MAN'S GROWTH

1. *Infancy* (from birth to 5): This stage is concerned with growth of
the body, motor activities, and the beginnings of sense perception and
feeling. Here one should follow the methods of nature. The child's
individuality must be respected. He must be freed from restraint, but
his body must be hardened by nature's methods. The adult must permit the
child to become self-dependent. During this period the child's education
consists of the free and unhampered expression of his natural activities
in relation to his physical environment. The child should be permitted to
act naturally and to experience directly the results of his actions.

2. *Childhood* (from 5 to 12): Rousseau criticized the methods used by
schools of his day at this level. He held that the concentration upon
books was wrong and he would eliminate books and expose the child to
things. Education must be negative - "do nothing and allow nothing to
be done." Let the child develop as his inner nature demands and protect
him from outer interference. The child cannot reason. Thus, experience
is his only teacher. He learns through necessity directed by his natural
development. The curriculum at this level should consist of natural
activities. The child will pick up reading incidentally; he will learn
his mother tongue naturally; he will develop his organs, senses, and
powers.

3. *The Age of Reason* (from 12 to 15): At this age reason emerges. The
child's strength has outrun his needs and reason emerges as a "check to
strength." Here education by human agencies begins. They direct the unfolding process. We must not try to educate the child through reason; we
must not use authority in place of the child's mental efforts, but help
him to make his reason the authority; and we must not make the mistake
of thinking that reason is the driving power of life. The motivating
factors at this level are the desire to learn (curiosity) and the
usefulness of knowledge (utility). The curriculum at this level is drawn
from *Robinson Crusoe* and consists of exercising the intelligence in the
world of nature - geography, astronomy, physical sciences, agriculture,
manual arts, and crafts. Rousseau was not concerned so much with learning
material as with the acquiring of a correct method of thought, a desire
for knowledge, and clear and accurate ideas. Nothing is to be learned
from the authority of others but rather through experience, by direct
observation and discovery. The child should make all his own materials
for study.

4. *Social Stage* (from 15 to 20): Here sex emerges and with it the
social urge. This is the period when perception of human relations,
appreciation of beauty, the sense of moral and social life, religion, and

the higher virtues awaken in the child. Sex demands a companion, and human relationships become dominant. Here the youth studies psychology, sociology, ethics in concrete life situations. Natural religion emerges.

ROUSSEAU'S THEORY OF THE EDUCATION OF GIRLS. In this he contradicts all he has advocated for Emile. The girl is educated to please the man and everything that she is to learn is relative to men.

BIBLIOGRAPHY

I. Primary Sources:

Boyd, William, *The Minor Educational Writings of Jean Jacques Rousseau.* London, Blackie and Son, Ltd., 1910.

Eliot, Charles W., (editor), *Profession of Faith of a Savoyard Vicar,* in Harvard Classics, Vol. 34. New York, P.F. Collier & Son.

Foxley, Barbara, (translator), *Emile: or Education.* New York, E.P. Dutton & Co., 1911.

Payne, William, (translator), *Rousseau's Emile or Treatise on Education.* New York, D. Appleton, 1895.

Rhys, Ernest, (editor), *Confessions of Jean Jacques Rousseau; Discourse on Political Economy; Discourse on the Arts and Sciences; Discourse on the Origin of Inequality; The New Heloise; The Social Contract.* In Everyman's Library. New York, E.P. Dutton & Co.

2. Secondary Material:

Adams, John, *Evolution of Educational Theory,* pp. 250-282. London, Macmillan & Co., Ltd., 1912.

Archer, R.L., *Rousseau on Education.* New York, Longmans, Green & Co., 1912.

Boyd, William, *The Educational Theory of Jean Jacques Rousseau.* London, Longmans, Green & Co., 1911.

Browning, Oscar, *History of Educational Theory,* pp. 135-150. New York, Harper & Brothers, 1905.

Compayre, Gabriel, *Jean Jacques Rousseau and Education from Nature.* Translated by R.P. Jago. New York, Crowell, 1907.

Cubberley, Ellwood P., *The History of Education,* pp. 530-538. Boston, Houghton Mifflin Co., 1920.

Duggan, Stephen P., *Student's Textbook in the History of Education,* pp. 203-219. New York, D. Appleton-Century Co., 1936.

Eby, Frederick and Arrowood, Charles F., *The Development of Modern Education,* pp. 443-510. New York, Prentice-Hall, Inc., 1937.

Graves, Frank P., *A History of Education, In Modern Times,* pp. 5-25. New York, The Macmillan Co., 1927.

Graves, Frank P., *A Student's History of Education,* pp. 215-225. New York, The Macmillan Co., 1936.

Graves, Frank P., *Great Educators of Three Centuries,* pp. 77-121. New York, The Macmillan Co., 1909.

Hart, Joseph K., *Creative Moments in Education,* pp. 252-261. New York, Henry Holt and Co., 1931.

Hoffding, Harold, *Jean Jacques Rousseau and His Philosophy.* London, H. Milford, Oxford University Press, 1930.

Hudson, William H., *Rousseau and Naturalism in Life and Thought.* New York, Charles Scribner's Sons, 1903.

Knight, Edgar W., *Twenty Centuries of Education,* pp. 347-356. Boston, Ginn and Co., 1940.

Melvin, A. Gordon, *Education, A History,* pp. 195-203. New York, The John Day Co., 1946.

Messenger, James F., *An Interpretative History of Education,* pp. 164-181. New York, Thomas Y. Crowell Co., 1931.

Misawa, Tadasu, *Modern Educators and their Ideals,* pp. 59-144. New York, D. Appleton-Century Co., 1909.

Monroe, James P., *The Educational Ideal,* pp. 153-178. Boston, D.C. Heath and Co., 1906.

Monroe, Paul, *A Brief Course in the History of Education,* pp. 273-296. New York, The Macmillan Co., 1909.

Monroe, Paul, *A Textbook in the History of Education,* pp. 533-585. New York, The Macmillan Co., 1905.

Morley, John, *Voltaire and Rousseau.* London, Macmillan & Co., 1909 and 1910.

Morley, John, *Rousseau and His Era.* London, Macmillan&Co., 1923.

Mulhern, James, *A History of Education,* pp. 305-317, 346-362. Ronald Press Co., New York, 1946.

Painter, Franklin, *Great Pedagogical Essays,* pp. 321-250. New York, American Book Co., 1905.

Parker, Samuel, *History of Modern Elementary Education,* pp. 161-206. Boston, Ginn and Co., 1912.

Quick, Robert H., *Educational Reformers,* pp. 239-289. New York, D. Appleton-Century Co., 1904.

Reisner, Edward H., *The Evolution of the Common School,* pp. 151-178. New York, The Macmillan Co., 1930.

Wilds, Elmer H., *The Foundations of Modern Education,* pp. 378-400. New York, Rinehart & Co., 1942.

CHAPTER XIII

Educational Reformers in 18th Century: Germany

Johann Julius Hecker (1707-1768). Hecker was influenced by Francke while a student at the University of Halle and a teacher in the *Padagogium*. He became pastor of Trinity Church in Berlin (1739), improved the schools of his parish, and (1747) opened a school of realistic studies (a *Realschule*) for training in the trades. He also established a school for training teachers. In 1763 he drew up general school regulations for Frederick the Great establishing an elementary school system for Prussia.

Johann Bernhard Basedow (1724-1790)

HIS LIFE. Basedow was born in Hamburg of a father who was a poor wig-maker and of a mother who suffered from melancholia. He was eccentric, vulgar, a drunkard, and heterodox. He ran away from home and later studied for the Lutheran ministry but was too unorthodox. He became tutor of the son of Herr von Quaalen of Holstein, an experience which turned him to educational reform. This led to several teaching positions in all of which he was a failure. He was influenced by Rousseau, La Chalotais, Comenius, Locke, and Francke.

HIS WRITINGS. He wrote an *Appeal to the Friends of Mankind and to Men of Power Concerning Schools and Studies and Their Influence on Public Welfare* (1768), an appeal for funds to write a book for the guidance of parents. This was successful and considerable money was made available for him. With this he wrote his *Book of Methods for Fathers and Mothers of Families and for Nations (Methodenbuch)*. He also wrote an *Elementary Book (Elementarbuch)* the same year (1770). Later these two books were combined (1774) in four volumes treating of the education of the child from birth to 18 years. The work contained 100 engravings.

THE PHILANTHROPINUM. Prince Leopold of Anhalt-Dessau furnished buildings and money for a school and (1774) Basedow opened an institution for boys of the upper classes. It became famous for a while, but failed because of Basedow's personality and his ineptitude as an administrator. The aim of the school was to prepare children of the upper classes for useful and happy living as citizens of Europe with broad patriotism and religious attitudes.

HIS EDUCATIONAL THEORY. The state should control education and schools should be open to all religious groups. He pieced together a theory of method from the works of other writers: 1. Teach through objects, pictures, and models. Make a direct appeal to the senses. 2. Teach words along with objects or pictures, never apart from them. He taught languages by the conversational method and through games. 3. Education through discipline and a good environment is more significant than mere learning. 4. All education must be useful in preparation for life. 5. Discipline should be mild. Make learning pleasant and give rewards rather than lashes. Further, he held that the curriculum should be broad, including Latin, French, German, arithmetic, geography, geometry, history, natural history, anatomy, physics, and carpentering. He believed that children should learn by visiting places of value and seeing what is being done. Religion should be undenominational. Textbooks should be on the level of the child's ability to understand and should be thorough and simple enough for the untrained to use. This idea stimulated the writing of a literature for children. He held that physical training is important and should aim at strengthening and hardening the child.

RESULTS OF BASEDOW'S WORK

1. It coordinated the growing but scattered interest in education among the philanthropically inclined.

2. It stated a precise pattern of educational reform and developed a definite program. This was copied in many parts of the world with considerable success.

3. It provided impetus toward complete control of education by the state.

4. It made the *Realschule* a modern humanistic school with emphasis upon real studies and physical education and aiming at a high realistic culture.

Baron von Rochow (1734-1805). He was a wealthy German nobleman with a missionary interest in the welfare of the poor in rural areas. In 1772 he wrote a *School Book for Children of Country People and for the Use of Village Schools.* This was planned to improve the skill of teachers. He also wrote the *Children's Friend, Schools for the Poor, Abolition of Public Beggary,* and *Formation of National Character by Popular Schools.* He believed that the state should provide education for all children.

BIBLIOGRAPHY

I. Primary Sources:

Basedow, J.B., *Elementarwerk*. Stuttgart, Verlagsbureau, 1849.

Cubberley, Ellwood P., *Readings in the History of Education,* pp. 436-439. New York, Houghton Mifflin Co., 1920.

2. Secondary Material:

Barnard, Henry, *Great Teachers and Educators,* pp. 457-490, 497-508. Hartford, Brown and Gross, 1878.

Cubberley, Ellwood P., *A Brief History of Education,* pp. 294-296. New York, Houghton Mifflin Co., 1922.

Cubberley, Ellwood P., *The History of Education,* pp. 533-538. New York, Houghton Mifflin Co., 1920.

Duggan, Stephen, *A Student's Textbook in the History of Education,* pp. 216-219. New York, D. Appleton-Century Co., 1936.

Eby, Frederick and Arrowood, Charles F., *The Development of Modern Education,* pp. 512-529. New York, Prentice-Hall, Inc., 1937.

Graves, Frank P., *A History of Education, In Modern Times,* pp. 25-22. New York, The Macmillan Co., 1927.

Graves, Frank P., *A Student's History of Education,* pp. 225-229. New York, The Macmillan Co., 1936.

Monroe, Paul, *A Brief Course in the History of Education,* pp. 297-300. New York, The Macmillan Co., 1909.

Monroe, Paul, *A Text-Book in the History of Education,* pp. 577-583. New York, The Macmillan Co., 1907.

Mulhern, James, *A History of Education,* pp. 403-406. Ronald Press Co., New York, 1946.

CHAPTER XIV

American Education (1700 TO 1830)

Events and Institutions

THE REVOLUTION. The American Revolution was part of a revolution throughout the western world against conservatism. In America it meant the realization that American conditions demanded indigenous institutions. The institutions imported from Europe were not suited to the American scene. It also meant that the entire culture and social life of America was changing.

EARLY 18TH CENTURY SCHOOLS

1. *The Dame Schools:* Private dame schools, primary schools preparing children for the writing and grammar schools, flourished. Some towns had public dame schools.

2. *Public Schools:* New England town schools and parish schools were supported both by tuition fees and some public funds. They were under nominal public control.

3. *Private Schools:* Among private schools of the early 18th century were: private teachers employed by families to teach their children; schools supported by local societies; many private secondary schools in cities, and mathematical and English schools to train boys for business and trades. Some of these were held after working hours for apprentices. Girls were given instruction in some of these schools in English grammar, modern languages, bookkeeping, and needlework.

CHARITY SCHOOLS. Many elementary charity schools were established by the Society for the Propagation of the Gospel in Foreign Parts (S.P.G.). Their first school was in New York City in 1704. Poor children were admitted to these schools without charge. In Pennsylvania the schools sought to teach English to German colonists, but their efforts were resisted even though many schools were established.

THE ACADEMY. Latin Grammar Schools and colleges were not meeting the educational needs of America. Benjamin Franklin (1749) proposed a more useful institution in his *Proposals Relating to the Education of Youth in Pennsylvania.* The school, called an academy, opened in 1715, was chartered in 1753, and was chartered as a college in 1755. Its features were: it stressed the English language and literature, oratory, offered scientific subjects, and was non-sectarian. The first medical school in the United States opened here in 1765. The institution was made the University of Pennsylvania in 1791.

Academies sprang up throughout the country to supplant the Latin schools. They were private institutions, but with some public support. There were academies for boys and for girls and some were coeducational. They taught a variety of subjects and ranged from poor to very good college preparatory institutions. Early academies included: Dummer's (1761), Phillips Andover (1778), Phillips Exeter (1783). Many academies eventually became colleges. The high schools eventually drove most academies out of business.

TEXTBOOKS. The *New England Primer* (1685-1690) was an adaptation of the *Protestant Tutor*. Isaac Greenwood (1729) published the first arithmetic to appear in this country. Webster's *Blue Back Speller* appeared in 1783. Jediah Morse wrote an *American Universal Geography*. Many books were brought to America from England and used until American books appeared. Gradually the American theme and color appeared in textbooks.

American Educational Thought

INTRODUCTION. The philosophy of the American revolutionists was educational. Its basic ideas were: man is capable of improvement; the government must make the people secure in their natural rights so that this improvement can take place; activities of the government must conform to natural law. Education is the chief means for insuring public welfare. Two views of the educational system necessary to accomplish these ends appeared: 1. A highly centralized, government-controlled system indoctrinating all citizens in the particular ideas and ideals of the country. 2. A localized system with government merely making possible and protecting freedom of thought and speech. This emphasized the free cultivation of the mind.

BENJAMIN FRANKLIN (1706-1790). He had little formal schooling, but educated himself to become a leader in many areas of American and world life. He believed in self-education and that education should aim at utility, but not a narrow utility. He was the leader in the founding of the American Philosophical Society, a society for the exchange of information, and the University of Pennsylvania.

THOMAS JEFFERSON (1743-1826). Born on the American frontier, he was well educated and held many important offices, including the Presidency of the United States. As a member of the Virginia House of Burgesses he worked for a state educational system. He sought complete separation of church and state. His plan for a state educational system included free elementary schools in each locality, secondary tuition schools, and a state university. The plan was not adopted by the state. He was the founder of the University of Virginia.

PLANS FOR EDUCATION

1. The American Philosophical Society's prize essay contest produced many schemes for school systems reaching all the people and culminating in a national university. Samuel Knox and Samuel Harrison Smith made such proposals. 2. George Washington attempted to start a national university. 3. The American trend was away from centralization of education toward local control of elementary schools and private control of colleges and universities.

Federal Laws and Education

THE CONSTITUTION. It contains no reference to education, but the first and tenth amendments assure control of education by states and the secularization of public education.

SCHOOLS IN AREAS WEST OF THE APPALACHIANS. As the new land was opened for settlement, laws were passed setting aside land or revenue for the support of schools. The Northwest Ordinance (1787) provided for setting aside lot 16 in each township for support of a school and two townships for a university.

State Laws and Education

STATE CONSTITUTIONS AND EDUCATION. Many state constitutions made direct and liberal provisions for education: Pennsylvania (1776 and 1790), North Carolina (1776), Georgia (1777 and 1798), Massachusetts (1780), New Hampshire (1784), and Vermont (1793). Though other states made no reference to education in their constitutions, many, as New York and Connecticut, were very active educationally.

MASSACHUSETTS. The constitution of 1780 made liberal provisions for Harvard College. The revised school law of 1789 legalized the district system, required the establishing of an elementary school in each town of 50 or more families and a Grammar School in each town of 150 or more families, required teachers to be college graduates or certified by the Congregational ministers, limited teaching to American citizens, set fines for towns neglecting schools, and chartered academies and gave them land. In 1798 academies meeting set standards were given endowments of land and a recognized place in the public school system.

NEW YORK. There was no mention of education in the New York state constitution until 1894, but interest in education was high from early times. A state educational system was begun by Governor Clinton in 1784: 1. Unappropriated lands were surveyed and 690 acres in each township were set aside for the support of schools. 2. The Board of Regents of the University of the State of New York was established to promote and oversee secondary and higher education. 3. King's College was changed to Columbia University. The Regents chartered academies. In 1790 a state school fund was established and state aid for education inaugurated. In 1795 state aid was increased and machinery was set up for distributing the funds. Elementary education was also encouraged.

Growth of the American College

INTRODUCTION. The early colleges were patterned after English models since they had to meet the requirements of English officials and received their support largely from England. Most administrators and teachers were from English institutions.

HARVARD. This college was founded by the General Court of Massachusetts in 1636 and was established in 1638. Its founders and teachers were English in training and spirit and the institution was dedicated to the training of ministers. Its pattern was Cambridge and Oxford. Students lived in dormitories under masters, attended daily religious services, their conduct was strictly regulated, a master taught his group all subjects, formal discipline of mind and morals was emphasized, and students were listed according to the rank and social standing of their families.

SPREAD OF THE COLLEGE IDEA. Colleges were founded throughout the country by private interests and church groups: William and Mary (1693), Yale (1754), Princeton (1746), Dartmouth (1769), King's College (1754), Brown (1764), Rutgers (1766). Enrollments were small and the work taught was narrow and attracted students of the secondary age level. Gradually these colleges became more liberal, gave up sectarian requirements, and broadened their curricula to include more modern subjects.

Rise of the American University

THE UNIVERSITY. Early institutions of higher education were colleges under church control. The university was secular and aimed at a broad education leading to the professions. States sought to establish state universities offering secular, free education. These included: North Carolina (1776), Virginia (1779), Pennsylvania (1791), Kentucky (1798), Northwest Territory (1802), Louisiana (1805), Michigan (1817). Some plans were proposed to unite all educational activities of a state under a University of the State.

UNIVERSITY OF THE STATE OF NEW YORK. In 1784 the New York legislature passed an act establishing a state university system consisting of all levels of schools. Some hoped that King's College would be the head of this centralized system. This failed, but the rest of the system was established in the present University of the State of New York.

UNIVERSITY OF NEW ORLEANS. In 1805 the Louisiana legislature established the University of New Orleans and sought to set up a system of education in the state consisting of academies and libraries. The university was established, but the rest of the plan was soon abandoned.

UNIVERSITY OF MICHIGAN. The Act of 1817 established the University of Michigan with power to found educational institutions throughout the state, control teachers and other employees, and pay all salaries from the treasury of the university. Some schools and a college in Detroit were established.

SOURCE OF THE UNIVERSITY IDEA. The French plan of state education was highly influential in America in the 18th century. Many leaders of American education were enthusiastic about this plan: Benjamin Franklin, John Adams, Thomas Jefferson, John Jay, and Ezra L'Hommedieu. They worked for state systems in this country and Jay and L'Hommedieu originated the University of the State of New York. Many French teachers and educational leaders came to America. Dupont de Nemours wrote *National Education in the United States*. Although the French plan was not successful in America, definite contributions were made to education in this country: 1. Institutions of higher learning were called "universities." 2. State support and control of education was recognized as necessary for democratic government. 3. Higher education turned from the exclusive training of ministers to professional training. 4. Secular education began to take the place held before by church-controlled religious training. 5. Education became freer. 6. The educational system was thought of as comprising schools, libraries, museums, etc., and all these articulated into a whole. 7. The curriculum was broadened. 8. A system of schools consisting of elementary, secondary, and higher developed.

BIBLIOGRAPHY

I. Primary Sources:

Dupont de Nemours, *National Education in the United States of America.* Newark, Deleware, University of Deleware Press, 1923.

Ford, Paul L., (editor), *The Works of Thomas Jefferson.* New York, Charles Putnam, 1895.

Cubberley, Ellwood P., *Readings in Public Education in the United States,* pp. 97-128. New York, Houghton Mifflin Co., 1934.

2. Secondary Material:

Arrowood, Charles F., *Thomas Jefferson and Education in a Republic.* New York, McGraw-Hill Book Co., Inc., 1930.

Barnard, H.C., *The French Tradition in Education.* Cambridge, Cambridge University Press, 1922.

Cubberley, Ellwood P., *Public Education in the United States,* pp. 82-116. New York, Houghton Mifflin Co., 1934.

Eby, Frederick and Arrowood, Charles F., *The Development of Modern Education,* pp. 530-573. New York, Prentice-Hall, Inc., 1937.

Graves, Frank P., *A Student's History of Education,* pp. 252-290. New York, The Macmillan Co., 1936.

Monroe, Paul, *Founding of the American Public School System,* pp. 165-221. New York, The Macmillan Co., 1940.

Mulhern, James, *A History of Education,* pp. 273, 279-281, 287-299. Ronald Press Co., New York, 1946.

Tewksbury, D.G., *The Founding of American Colleges and Universities Before the Civil War.* New York, Teachers College, Columbia University, 1932.

Thwing, C.F., *A History of Higher Education in America,* Chs. IX-XV. New York, D. Appleton-Century Co., 1906.

Woody, Thomas, *The Educational Views of Benjamin Franklin.* New York, McGraw-Hill Book Co., Inc., 1931.

CHAPTER XV

Nationalization of Education

Introduction. During the last half of the 18th and the early part of the 19th centuries the individual was attaining a new dignity and sense of worth. Rousseau's plea for the emancipation of the individual from social bondage was taken up by Immanuel Kant (1724-1804) in his famous statement, "Be a person and reverence all others as persons." The right of each individual to develop his capacities was being recognized. Two plans of government to insure an education that would develop the capacities of each individual were proposed: **A Benevolent Despotism** - Influenced by the French Encyclopedists and the Physiocrats, the belief developed that benevolent despots could interpret natural law in the social order. This idea dominated lands east of the Rhine. It implied education for obedient subjects. **Democracy** - Influenced by British and French political thinkers, this conception dominated France and America and implied an education to produce intelligent citizens of a free government.

Nationalization in France. Early French education was controlled by the Jesuits. When the Order was suppressed (1764) many plans for a system of national, highly centralized schools were proposed. These plans, in general, suggested:

CONTROL. Education under control of the state, not the church.

EDUCATION FOR ALL, not divisions as to the amount. The common people should have education, but not beyond their needs. Primary education should be universal and free.

THE AIMS OF EDUCATION are enlightenment, development of a national spirit, and creation of the ability to protect one's rights and serve the state.

INSTRUCTION should be secular, not religious indoctrination.

GRADES OF SCHOOLS should include primary, secondary, institutes or colleges, professional, and a National Society of Sciences and Arts.

FREE EDUCATION. Writers differed as to how high free education should go.

COMPULSORY EDUCATION. Some would regiment all children in Spartan fashion.

FREEDOM OF TEACHING, uniformity of instruction, adult education, and scholarship were emphasized.

Popular interest in a national system of primary and secondary schools was high by 1790. Napoleon (1806) established the University of France, a national system of secondary education as an instrument of national propaganda.

Nationalization in Germany

THE ENLIGHTENMENT IN GERMANY. In Germany the Enlightenment, Physiocracy, and Naturalism were confined to the ruling classes and did not reach the masses. The German nobility copied French life and customs, and some were benevolent rulers.

THE RISE OF PRUSSIA

1. *Frederick William I:* He was influenced by Francke to work for better schools and more efficient teaching. He made education compulsory in 1717.

2. *Frederick William II:* He was a freethinker and an enlightened despot, wanted to improve the lot of his subjects, and supported the work of Hecker who wrote a general code for the regulation of rural schools (1763). This code provided for: compulsory attendance, supervision, child accounting, free education for the poor, religious and secular instruction, and the licensing and regulating of teachers.

THE NEW HUMANISM. The old Humanism of the Renaissance had become formal when Johann Winckelmann (1717-1768) aroused new interest in the beauty of Greek art. This began a revival of interest in the spirit of the classics and led to a German literature and an ideal of culture emulating the Greek spirit. This new Humanism was introduced into German schools and the profession of teaching began to assume dignity and to demand respect as one of the learned professions. The school law of 1787 put Prussian schools under a supreme school board; established three types of schools - rural, town, and higher gymnasiums; inaugurated "leaving-examinations" for pupils completing the gymnasium and entering the university. The law of 1794 reaffirmed state regulation and centralization of education.

Nationalization in Austria. Maria Theresa (1717-1780) sought to follow the pattern of educational reform set by Frederick the Great in Prussia and enlisted the aid of Felbinger. Joseph, Maria's son, sought to unite the Austrian universities with the elementary and secondary schools of the country into one system under governmental control. The curriculum was revised and teachers made civil servants. This was a highly paternal-istic system with considerable censorship.

Nationalization in Sweden and Baden

SWEDEN. Gustavus III sought to introduce the reforms of the Physiocrats into Sweden. He inspired Mercier de la Riviere to write *Of Public Education* (1775).

BADEN. Charles Frederick put into operation the ideas of the Physiocrats

in an effort to raise the economic level of the peasants of his princi-
pality.

Nationalization in Spain and in Spanish America. Charles III, influenced
by the French Enlightenment, introduced many reforms into 18th century
Spain.

EXPERIMENTS IN AGRICULTURAL COLONIES. Ideal communities were established
with the clergy excluded and the farmers permitted to live free and
under the laws of nature. These had little success and were eventually
abandoned.

EDUCATIONAL REFORMS IN SPAIN. Education was taken away from the clergy
and put under control of the state with examinations for teachers and
other reforms in the system.

EDUCATIONAL REFORMS IN SPANISH AMERICA

1. *In Louisiana:* A "director" and three teachers were sent to Louisiana
to open a school in New Orleans. The "director" became a sort of city
superintendent.

2. *In California:* Colonies were established in which educational work
was done by the Franciscians. Schools were introduced by Father Lazuen
(1784). Similar schools were opened elsewhere, notably in Saint Augustine, Florida (1785).

Nationalization in Switzerland. Franz Urs Balthasar (1758) published
*The Patriotic Dreams of a Confederate of a Way to Rejuvenate the Old
Confederation* in which he recommended a national institute of education.
This inspired the Helvetic Society (1762), a member of which was
Pestalozzi, an organization working for liberty, unity, and education. In
1798 the Helvetic Constitution was adopted and the Swiss Directorate
established. Albrecht Stapfer was made minister of arts and sciences and
began to centralize education under federal control. Pestalozzi worked
with him, published a paper on educational reform, established an
orphanage and school at Stanz, and later founded his famous school at
Burgdorf. Stapfer organized the Society of the Friends of Education which
supported Pestalozzi's work.

Nationalization in England

INTRODUCTION. In the England of 1750 religion was at low tide, but the
Methodist church and Unitarianism were about to take form out of the
growing evangelical fervor and the liberalism and scientific thinking of
the times. Economic conditions were improving and population increasing,
literature was attaining high quality and a large reading public was
appearing. However, education was poor and largely formal.

THE SOCIAL AND ECONOMIC PATTERN. Inventions ruined the small cottage

workers and made possible the Industrial Revolution. This led to the
employment of women and children in factories, bad working conditions,
little time for education of the worker, and virtual industrial slavery. A
series of acts, beginning in 1802, were passed by Parliament to protect
the workers and make their condition better. These acts established the
principles that officers of the state have the right to control the lives
and training of children and that children have the right to care, food,
education, and protection from cruelty. Parliament ceased to be a tool
of the privileged few and became representative of the people. The
religious revival led by John and Charles Wesley and a group of Oxford
students made a strong appeal to the poor. Out of this come the Methodist
church. This church led in efforts for popular education, abolition 6f
slavery, temperance, and the emancipation of women.

THE CULTURAL PATTERN. Among the leaders of English scholarship during
this period were David Hume (1711-1776), Sir William Blackstone (1723-
1780), Jeremy Bentham (1748-1832), Edward Gibbon (1737-1794), Adam Smith
(1723-1790). There was also the work of Priestly, Richard Price, and a
host of writers and poets. These men produced material which the schools
had to consider and include in their curricula.

EDUCATIONAL THEORY. Great concern for education was reflected in the
writings of the times. Priestly wrote an *Essay on a Course of Liberal
Education for Civil and Active Life* (1765). The theory of utilitarianism
(all education must be useful) dominated education in England and spread
to America. Richard Lovell Edgeworth and his daughter, Maria Edgeworth,
wrote many books of interest to children, presenting information necessary
for their education. Among these was *Harry and Lucy*. The Edgeworths also
wrote *Early Lessons, Practical Education* (1798), *Parent's Assistant,* and
Popular Tales.

EDUCATIONAL REFORMS

1. *In Dissenting Academies:* These institutions began to open their
doors to young men preparing for many fields of activity and to offer a
wide curriculum. The work of Dr. Phillip Doodridge at Northampton and of
Joseph Priestley at Warrington was important. Later these academies
began a decline.

2. *In Universities:* Leaders were dominating reforms in the universities
where corruption and general neglect had been general. Many new subjects
were introduced into university curricula.

PHILANTHROPY IN EDUCATION

1. *The Sunday School Movement:* Robert Raikes (1780) opened a school at
Gloucester, England, on Sundays for poor children. This was a charity
school teaching reading, writing, arithmetic, spelling, hymns, the

catechism, and the Scriptures. The idea spread and the Society for the Establishment and Support of Sunday Schools Throughout the Kingdom was organized in 1785. The Methodists and Baptists supported many such schools. Later these schools gave up secular work and were incorporated into the program of religious education of many churches.

2. *Societies for Education:* The need for elementary education was greater than could be met by the existing schools. The monitorial system solved this problem. Andrew Bell (1753-1832) brought the monitorial system from India and added the idea of military organization. Joseph Lancaster (1778-1838) conceived a similar plan later. These men invented materials for use in schools working under this plan. The Society for the Promotion of Christian Knowledge (S.P.C.K.) and the National Society for Promoting the Education of the Poor in the Principles of the Established Church Throughout England and Wales (1811) established many schools using the monitorial system. Also the British and Foreign School Society entered this field. Government grants for education were usually distributed through these organizations. The monitorial system made possible better elementary schools and better education than was generally available, but it had many defects: It was mechanical in teaching methods; it lacked direct contact on the part of the pupils with well-trained teachers, and the monitors were not paid for their work.

3. *The Infant School Movement:* Robert Owen (1771-1858), a cotton manufacturer at New Lanark, Scotland, opened a school for the free education of children from 5 to 10 years of age. James Buchanan took the idea to London and inspired Samuel Wilderspin to spread the idea in London. In 1824 the Infant School Society was founded with Wilderspin as agent. Many infant schools were established. In 1826 the Glasgow Infant School Society was founded under the leadership of David Stow.

4. *Dame Schools:* These were elementary schools taught by women in their homes. A fee was charged each child. The curriculum consisted of the Lord's Prayer, the Apostles' Creed, the alphabet, the catechism, and simple reading.

STATE SUPPORT OF SCHOOLS. In 1802 Parliament passed a law requiring education for all apprentices in reading, writing, and arithmetic. Teachers were to be paid and school rooms provided by the masters of apprentices. Much agitation for government aid to elementary education culminated in 1833 in financial aid being made available by Parliament.

BIBLIOGRAPHY

1. Primary Sources:

Cubberley, Ellwood P., *Readings in the History of Education,* pp. 370-391, 454-541. New York, Houghton Mifflin Co., 1920.

Wilderspin, Samuel, *Infant Education; or Practical Remarks on the Importance of Educating Infant Poor.* London, Simpkin and Marshall, 1929.

2. Secondary Material:

Adamson, J.W., *English Education (1789-1902).* Cambridge, Cambridge University Press, 1930.

Allen, W.O.B. and McClure, E., *Two Hundred Years; History of the S.P.C.K., 1698-1898.* London, Christian Knowledge Society, 1898.

Binns, Henry B., *A Century of Education, 1808-1908. History of the British and Foreign School Society.* London, J.M. Dent and Co., 1908.

Cubberley, Ellwood P., *A Brief History of Education,* pp. 239-247, 254-267, 275-284, 308-350. New York, Houghton Mifflin Co., 1922.

Cubberley, Ellwood P., *The History of Education,* pp. 437-458, 472-494, 552-650. New York, Houghton Mifflin Co., 1920.

Eby, Frederick and Arrowood, Charles F., *The Development of Modern Education,* pp. 575-617. New York, Prentice-Hall, Inc., 1937.

Graves, Frank P., *A History of Education, In Modern Times,* pp. 35-75. New York, The Macmillan Co., 1927.

Graves, Frank P., *A Student's History of Education,* pp. 232-249. New York, The Macmillan Co., 1936.

Graves, Frank P., *Great Educators of Three Centuries,* Chapter XII. New York, The Macmillan Co., 1912.

Harris, J. Henry, *Robert Raikes; the Man and His Work.* New York, E.P. Dutton and Co., 1899.

Jones, Lloyd, *The Life, Times, and Labours of Robert Owen.* London, Swan, Sonnenschein and Co., 1905.

Melvin, A. Gordon, *Education, A History,* pp. 278-287. New York, The John Day Co., 1946.

Montmorency, J.E.G. de, *The Progress of Education in England,* Chapter IV. London, Knight and Co., 1904.

Mulhern, James, *A History of Education,* pp. 281-282, 305-332, 395-411. Ronald Press Co., New York, 1946.

Salmon, D., and Hindshaw, W., *Infant Schools, Their History and Theory.* London, Longmans, Green and Co., 1904.

Salmon, D., *Joseph Lancaster.* London, Longmans, Green and Co., 1904.

Wilds, Elmer H., *The Foundations of Modern Education,* pp. 404-450. New York, Rinehart & Co., Inc., 1942.

CHAPTER XVI

Johann Heinrich Pestalozzi (1746-1827)

His Life Story

EARLY PERIOD. Born at Zurich, the son of a capable physician and a gifted mother, Pestalozzi's father died when he was 5 and he was reared by his mother and an old servant and in strained financial circumstances. This emphasized the feminine characteristics of Pestalozzi. He attended the customary elementary and Latin schools, but was unhappy and did not distinguish himself. Visits with his grandfather, Andrew Pestalozzi, at Honegg impressed upon him the degradation of the poor and awakened in him a desire to help.

COLLEGE YEARS. He attended the *Collegium Humanitatis* and the *Collegium Carolinum* at Zurich. Here his teachers inspired him with a passionate love for justice and liberty and a deep asceticism. His attainment in scholastic fields here was not high.

THE UNCERTAIN YEARS. Pestalozzi determined to devote his life to helping the poor. He tried the ministry, but failed. Then he turned to law and politics, but was branded a radical and was feared by those he wanted to help. Then he turned to agriculture, hoping to operate a model farm and teach the people how to raise their standard of living through more scientific farming. He borrowed money, bought a 100-acre farm near Birr, and established Neuhof (1769). He married and in 1770 his son was born. By 1775 the venture was a failure. Neuhof then became an orphanage, but this also failed.

YEARS OF DECISION. Pestalozzi had been interested in education since his college days. The *Emile* had influenced him tremendously. At Neuhof he sought to combine intellectual and vocational training. *Leonard and Gertrude* appeared in 1782. It was a success as a novel but not as a portrayal of his educational ideas. After 10 years of poverty, he met Fichte (1792) and Immanuel Kant. At the suggestion of Fichte he wrote *My Investigations Into the Course of Nature in the Development of the Human Race*. This work convinced him that teaching was his field and he determined to be a schoolmaster. Put in charge of an orphanage at Stanz (1798) he began to work out his conviction that by awakening in each individual self-respect and a sense of power he could regenerate society. He moved to Burgdorf where he conducted a boarding school for boys from 1800 to 1804, and then to Yverdun where he worked from 1805 to 1825.

YEARS OF TRIUMPH. At Yverdun he operated a boarding school for boys

159

from all countries of Europe. The atmosphere was that of a home. Discipline was mild and no coercion to learn was evident. The school became world famous and thinkers, educators, and rulers from all parts of the world visited it and some enrolled as students to learn from the master.

YEARS OF DECLINE. After 1810 Yverdun began to decline. Pestalozzi's wife died and he seemed to weaken mentally. His assistant, Schmidt, drove his best teachers away, lawsuits and disputes increased, and eventually the institution was closed. Pestalozzi retired to Neuhof, then owned by his grandson, and died in 1827.

His Educational Principles

INTRODUCTION. Pestalozzi worked against inexpressibly bad conditions among the poor. Poverty, ignorance, disease, fear, and vice were rampant. Teachers were untrained and many cared nothing for their work. Pestalozzi desired to aid these people. He believed that the way lay along the lines of better education. Thus, he laid down three basic principles of relief:

1. Reform must begin with the individual rather than with the social pattern. To change society will be useless unless each individual is given a sense of personal dignity and of ethical importance.

2. Reform of the individual comes only by giving him the power to help himself. Philanthropy is weakening. We must teach the individual to help himself.

3. The means to this end is development of the innate powers of the individual. Education merely furnishes the situation for the unfolding of the child's nature.

HIS THEORY OF ORGANIC DEVELOPMENT. The individual is a natural organism that may unfold its inner nature according to definite laws if given the proper environment. Though an organic whole, the individual has three aspects:

1. *The Intellectual* (head): This develops in terms of the experiences furnished through sense impressions.

2. *The Physical* (hand): Motor activities growing out of wants.

3. *Moral and Religious* (heart): Relationships with other individuals and with God.

Each develops in its own way, but as part of the whole. The educator must discover the laws of this development and use them in teaching. This leads to his general principles and methods: 1. All three aspects must develop together and in harmony with each other. The individual is a unity and an over-development or under-development of one aspect throws the organism out of balance. 2. Education that is general must come before that which gives one vocational competency. General education uplifts and ennobles the individual. To neglect this for the development of skills is degrading. 3. Education must aim at the increase of the child's power to make his own judgments rather than knowledge of the judgments of others. Intellectual training rather than the mere increase of knowledge is the aim. 4. The child's powers grow from within as his inner nature develops. We must not force the child before he is ready. We must study the laws of this development. 5. Work must be graded in terms of this development. The teacher must move by slow steps from the easy to the more difficult and insist upon mastery at each step. 6. All method must follow the plan of nature. The educator is like a gardener who supplies nothing, but follows the plan of the nature of the plant and provides the environment which will stimulate full development of that nature.

DEVELOPMENT OF THE "HEAD". Knowledge comes through sense impressions. Thus, the child must experience objects. The mind is active, dealing with sense impressions and building concepts. This is the basis of Pestalozzi's "object lessons." All instruction begins with form, number, and language. These are the "elementary means of instruction." From these he builds his curriculum. Intellectual instruction must: 1. Proceed from the known to the unknown, and 2. Proceed from the concrete to the abstract. Pestalozzi sought a logical order of subject-matter and failed to recognize that the child learns psychologically rather than logically. This is seen in his methods of teaching language and drawing.

However, Pestalozzi made many important changes in the teaching of many subjects:

1. *Arithmetic:* He began with concrete objects and moved to an understanding of symbols, insisting upon drill and mastery at each step. Thus, he brought arithmetic down to the first grade and developed mental arithmetic.

2. *Geography:* He began with the natural world around the child, made clay models of the surrounding land and rivers, then turned to maps to broaden the child's knowledge.

3. *Drawing:* He held that drawing was an introduction to writing. It trained the child in accurate observation and clear thinking. Further, in drawing he began with simple lines and moved to more complex figures.

4. *Language:* He would teach objects and meanings before words and would begin with the vernacular.

5. *Music:* He would begin with perception of tone and move on to time and melody.

DEVELOPMENT OF THE "HAND". He believed that the child learns by doing and emphasized the training of skills and development of the ability to produce. He would begin with movements of the limbs and move on to more complicated activities.

DEVELOPMENT OF THE "HEART". He would begin with the instinctive feelings of the child toward his mother. These result in dependence and love, trust and gratitude, patience and obedience. From these develop the higher aspects of man's moral, social, and religious life. Right development results in a feeling of dependence upon others and upon God, sympathy and altruism, and a sense of the ideal and of conscience. Thus, religion is based upon development of the emotions. Consequently, it cannot be taught. The development of the fundamental emotions comes before intellectual growth. We talk about religion after we have experienced it, not before. This development is fundamental and furnishes the power and motive for harmonious development of the "head" and "hand."

His Success Amid Failure
WHY HE FAILED

1. *His Personality:* He had many peculiarities, was talkative, highly emotional, slovenly, a muddled thinker.

2. *Language Difficulty:* Both French and German were spoken at Yverdun.

3. *Great Popularity:* Pestalozzi's fame turned his head and instruction at Yverdun suffered from publicity. The school at Yverdun became a show place.

4. *The original home atmosphere of the school was lost* as it became famous.

5. *Discord increased* among Pestalozzi's assistants.

HIS ENDURING LEGACY. 1. He had a great faith in education as the only means for making better people and a better society. 2. He realized that sound education must rest upon a sound knowledge of the psychology of child development. He began the psychologizing of education. 3. He thought of education as an organic development of the child's nature. 4. He turned attention to the beginnings of all growth and to the necessity of starting education here. 5. He emphasized the necessity of moving from the concrete to the abstract in thinking. 6. He emphasized the need for gradual unfolding of the powers of the child through graded experiences. 7. He saw that religion develops from man's emotions and not from creeds or dogmas. 8. He introduced many new methods and devices for teaching such as letters on cards, use of the slate and pencil, and class instruction. 9. He held that discipline must be based upon the mutual sympathy between teacher and pupil. 10. He stimulated interest in teacher training and in the study of the science of education.

HONORS BESTOWED UPON HIM. 1792 - He was made a Citizen of the French

Republic.

1814 - He was knighted by Tsar Alexander of Russia.

He was reverenced and praised by the great minds of his day.

His Influence in Europe

IN PRUSSIA. Fichte urged a defeated Prussia to adopt the methods of Pestalozzi (1807-1808). The Prussian government sent select young men to be trained at Yverdun. Further, Pestalozzi's methods were employed in many schools of Prussia and teachers were trained in the use of these methods.

IN SWITZERLAND. Cantons adopted Pestalozzian methods in schools and established teacher training schools. Baron von Fellenberg (1771-1844) founded an agricultural and industrial institute at Hofwyl on Pestalozzian ideas.

IN FRANCE. Pestalozzi's ideas were spread in France by M.A. Jullien, Chavennes, and Maine de Biran.

IN ENGLAND. J.P. Greaves introduced Pestalozzianism to England. Dr. Charles Mayo and Elizabeth Mayo spread a mechanized and formalized Pestalozzianism throughout England through the Home and Colonial Training College and their work influenced American education.

His Influence in America

WILLIAM MACLURE (1763-1840) and JOSEPH NEEF (1770-1854). Maclure, a Scotchman who came to the United States and became wealthy, visited Yverdun and Hofwyl and brought Neef to Philadelphia in 1806 to conduct a Pestalozzian school. He discussed Pestalozzi's ideas in the *National Intelligencer* (1806) and in a *Sketch of a Plan and Method of Education* (1808). The school was opened near Philadelphia in 1809. At first a success, the school moved to a place near Chester, Pennsylvania, and soon failed. Meeting Robert Owen at New Lanark, Scotland, Maclure persuaded this philanthropist to cooperate with him in a communal and educational experiment at New Harmony, Indiana. Neef conducted the school. This venture was a failure.

WRITINGS ON PESTALOZZIANISM. *Method of Instructing Children Rationally in the Arts of Reading and Writing* (1813), by Neef. Articles appearing in *The Academician* in 1819. *A Year in Europe* (1823), by John Griscom. *American Annals of Education* (1794-1845), edited by William C. Woodbridge. Published reports of Victor Cousin, Calvin E. Stowe, A.D. Bache, Henry Barnard, Horace Mann.

TEACHING OF SPECIAL SUBJECTS

1. *Geography:* William C. Woodbridge published *Rudiments of Geography* and *Universal Geography.* Arnold H. Guyot (1807-1884) lectured on the

teaching of geography under the auspices of the Massachusetts State Board of Education and wrote texts on the subject.

2. *Music:* Woodbridge influenced Lowell Mason (1792-1872) who developed public school music education to a high level of skill in America.

3. *Drawing and Arithmetic:* William Russell founded the *American Journal of Education* in which appeared many articles on Pestalozzianism. He also brought Hermann Krusi, Jr., son of Pestalozzi's assistant, to this country to teach in his normal school at Lancaster, Pennsylvania.

THE OSWEGO MOVEMENT. Edward A. Sheldon (1823-1897), superintendent of schools at Oswego, New York, learned of Pestalozzi's work through an exhibit of the materials and object lessons employed by the Mayos in the Home and Colonial Training College in London. He employed Miss M.E.M. Jones of the College to introduce the work at Oswego. She was followed by Hermann Krusi, Jr., who continued the work for 25 years. Thus, Oswego became the center of Pestalozzian influence in the United States.

BIBLIOGRAPHY

I. Primary Sources:

Cubberley, Ellwood P., *Readings in the History of Education*, pp. 439-454. New York, Houghton Mifflin Co., 1920.

Pestalozzi, J.H., *How Gertrude Teaches Her Children*. Translated by Lucy E. Holland and Francis C. Turner. Syracuse, C.W. Bardeen, 1894.

Pestalozzi, J.H., *Letters on Early Education,* Addressed to J.P. Greaves. Syracuse, C.W. Bardeen, 1898.

Pestalozzi, J.H., *Leonard and Gertrude*. Translated by Eva Channing. Boston, D.C. Heath and Co., 1897.

2. Secondary Material:

Anderson, Lewis F., *Pestalozzi*. New York, McGraw-Hill Book Co., Inc., 1931.

Bennett, Charles A., *History of Manual and Industrial Education up to 1870,* Chapters IV-VII. Peoria, Ill., Manual Arts Press, 1926.

Biber, E., *Henry Pestalozzi*. London, John Souter, 1831.

Compayre, G., *Pestalozzi and Elementary Education*. Translated by R.P. Jago. New York, Crowell, 1907.

Cubberley, Ellwood P., *A Brief History of Education,* pp. 297-306. New York, Houghton Mifflin Co., 1922.

Cubberley, Ellwood P., *The History of Education,* pp. 539-547. New York, Houghton Mifflin Co., 1920.

Dearborn, Ned H., *The Oswego Movement in American Education*. New York, Teachers College, Columbia University, 1925.

DeGuimps, Roger, *Pestalozzi: His Life and Work.* Translated by J. Russell. New York, D. Appleton-Century Co., 1895.

Duggan, Stephen, *A Student's Textbook in the History of Education,* pp. 225-243. New York, D. Appleton-Century Co., 1936.

Eby, Frederick and Arrowood, C.F., *The Development of Modern Education,* pp. 619-677. New York, Prentice-Hall, Inc., 1937

Graves, Frank P., *Great Educators of Three Centuries,* Chapter IX. New York, The Macmillan Co., 1912.

Graves, Frank P., *A Student's History of Education,* pp. 295-314. New York, The Macmillan Co., 1936.

Graves, Frank P., *A History of Education, In Modern Times,* pp. 120-163. New York, The Macmillan Co., 1927.

Green, J.A., *Pestalozzi's Educational Writings*. London, Edward Arnold, 1916.

Green, J.A., *Life and Works of Pestalozzi*. London, University Tutorial Press, Ltd., 1913.

Green, J.A., *The Educational Ideas of Pestalozzi*. London, University Tutorial Press, Ltd., 1911.

Hollis, Andrew P., *The Contribution of the Oswego Normal School*. Boston, D.C. Heath and Co., 1898.

Holman, H., *Pestalozzi: An Account of His Life and Work*. London, Longmans, Green and Co., 1908.

Knight, Edgar W., *Reports on European Education by John Griscom, Victor Cousin, Calvin E. Stowe.* New York, McGraw-Hill Book Co., 1930.

Krusi, Hermann, Jr., *Pestalozzi; His Life, Work, and Influence*. New York, American Book Co., 1875.

Melvin, A. Gordon, *Education, A History*, pp. 204-224. New York, The John Day Co., 1946.

Monroe, Paul, *A Brief Course in the History of Education*, pp. 307-319. New York, The Macmillan Co., 1909.

Monroe, Paul, *A Text-Book in the History of Education*, pp. 597-622. New York, The Macmillan Co., 1907.

Monroe, Will S., *History of the Pestalozzian Movement in the United States*. Syracuse, C.W. Bardeen, 1907.

Mulhern, James, *A History of Education*, pp. 362-368. Ronald Press Co., New York., 1946.

Parker, Samuel C., *History of Modern Elementary Education*, Chapters XIII-XVI. Boston, Ginn and Co., 1912.

Stettbacher, Hans, ed., *Pestalozzi, a Pictorial Record for the Centenary of His Death*. Zurich, Zentralbibliothek, 1928.

Wilds, Elmer H., *The Foundations of Modern Education*, pp. 457-462. New York, Rinehart & Co., Inc., 1942.

CHAPTER XVII

Education in 19th Century: Europe

The German School System

EVENTS IN GERMAN HISTORY. 1. Prussia was overcome by Napoleon. 2. Fichte (1806) urged the people to adopt the Pestalozzian school system as a basis for national regeneration. 3. Prussia rose to power among the German states and the German Empire emerged in 1870.

THE VOLKSSCHULEN (the common people). Prussia followed Fichte's advice and established the best schools in Europe. Elementary schools were free and public; attendance was made compulsory; teachers were selected carefully; the work of the schools was aimed at building national ideals. The curriculum was enriched to include both tool subjects and cultural materials. There were separate schools for boys and for girls. The *Volksschulen* provided education for the lower classes, but gifted children in these classes could receive higher instruction.

THE SECONDARY SCHOOLS. Secondary education was confined largely to the classical *gymnasium* and the realistic schools were of little importance. By 1850 this state was being challenged by: 1. The demand for inclusion in secondary education of the growing scientific knowledge and its application to industrial production. 2. The Industrial Revolution which led to the vast industrial empire of the Germans and made industrial education necessary. 3. The democratic spirit which led to the Revolution of 1848 and the constitutional government. Thus, the monopoly of the classical *gymnasium* was broken and the *Realgymnasien* rose to prominence. In 1890 William II challenged the gymnasium for its classical aim and urged education to "bring up young Germans and not young Greeks or Romans."

ORGANIZATION AND CURRICULUM. Children taking secondary education began by studying in a special primary school (from 6 to 9 years of age). Then they might enter the gymnasium, taking a classical course and preparing for the learned professions; or, they might enter the *Realgymnasien,* taking a combined modern scientific course and classical course; or, they might enter the *Oberrealschule,* taking a course consisting of modern languages and scientific studies and training for higher technical and commercial vocations. The curricula in all these schools were planned to meet the training needs of those entering vocations.

The English School System

EVENTS IN ENGLISH HISTORY. 1. The reign of Queen Victoria, 1837-

1901. 2. The British Empire was created and became wealthy. 3. England became highly industrialized and dependent upon its empire for raw materials and trade.

ENGLISH EDUCATION BEFORE 1832

1. *Elementary Education:* This was very poor. Some work was being done by school societies and local groups, but the majority of children received no education.

2. *Secondary Education:* There were private schools for middle class children, but many of these were very poor. The school foundations were negligent and the curricula were divorced from the life of the people.

3. *Higher Education:* This met the needs of only a small sector of English youths. The University of London was founded in 1828 with emphasis upon the sciences.

THE DEVELOPMENT OF ELEMENTARY EDUCATION

1. *Progress to 1870:* Money was appropriated by the ministry for educational purposes and Dr. James Kay was made assistant secretary of a Privy Council committee to supervise its allocation. He was instrumental in establishing school inspection, a system of teacher training called the "pupil-teacher system," and certification of teachers. By the Grammar School Act of 1840 charity foundations for education were recognized as elementary schools fitted to the needs of the times. An Educational department was created in 1856 to have responsibility for education and take over the work of the Privy Council Office. The Newcastle Commission (created in 1858 and reported in 1861) recommended grants on the basis of results shown in standard examinations in reading, writing, spelling, and arithmetic. This plan had many evil results and was abandoned in 1904.

2. *Elementary Education Act of 1870:* This grew out of the failure of the voluntary school system and of pressure by the National Education League for a system of free, universal, compulsory, non-sectarian elementary schools. The act required voluntary societies to provide adequate schools in each district. Where this was not done, school boards were established to found and supervise schools supported by taxation and tuition fees. These were called "board schools."

3. *Progress from 1870 to 1902:* The "board schools" gradually took over elementary education and the standards were raised and many attempts made to institute compulsory education. Government grants were increased so that by 1891 elementary education became virtually free. The Board of Education was established in 1899 as a result of the Bryce Commission's recommendation (1894) for consolidation of educational authority.

4. *The Education Act of 1902:* The councils in counties, county boroughs,

and urban districts were made the local school authorities working through school committees approved by the Board of Education. Thus, England had developed a national system of public schools.

DEVELOPMENT OF SECONDARY EDUCATION

1. *Thomas Arnold:* He reformed teaching at Rugby and influenced teaching at the nine English public schools - Eton, Shrewsbury, Harrow, Rugby, Merchant Taylors', St. Paul's, Charterhouse, Westminister, Winchester.

2. *The Clarendon Commission* (1861-1864): This commission studied the nine public schools and made recommendations which resulted in the Public School Act of 1864 reforming administration of these schools.

3. *The Taunton Commission* (1864-1867): This commission uncovered abuses of educational endowments, showed inadequacies in the classical curriculum, and recommended changes in supervision and administration.

4. *Tax Support of Secondary Education:* The Technical Instruction Act of 1889 and the Local Taxation Act of 1890 permitted taxation for manual and technical instruction. This was interpreted freely and many other subjects were encouraged under these acts. Elementary schools extended their courses. The Act of 1902 placed secondary education under the control of the city council.

DEVELOPMENT OF THE UNIVERSITIES. A system of provincial universities was established to further scientific learning and spread liberal education among the people. Oxford and Cambridge became more liberal and their curricula broadened to include the scientific areas.

The French School System

EVENTS IN FRENCH HISTORY

1. *Napoleon Made First Consul* (1799): He gave France an efficient government based upon an administrative system and code of laws that proved sound.

2. *Louis Napoleon Made Emperor in 1852:* This resulted from a series of governmental changes including the constitutional monarchy, the reign of Charles X and Louis Philippe, and the establishment of the republic. France became prosperous under this reactionary government which was eventually overthrown and the Third Republic established. The Republican government was in complete control by 1879.

EDUCATION UNDER NAPOLEON (1799-1815). Napoleon's aim was a system of education that would train loyal and obedient subjects and produce scientific and military leaders. The Law of 1802 left responsibility for primary schools in the hands of the *communes,* provided for the establishment of *lycee* (state secondary schools) and *colleges* (municipal or private secondary schools). Thus, this law laid the foundation for the French educational system. The laws of 1806 and 1808 founded a system of education under the Imperial University headed by a Grand Master directly responsible to the Emperor. The nation was divided into academies, each headed by a Rector who had charge of all education in the academy. Napoleon also founded technical schools and the Superior Normal School.

EDUCATION UNDER THE RESTORATION MONARCHY (1815-1830). Napoleon's administrative plan was retained; the name of Grand Master was changed to Minister of Education; the Superior Normal School was suspended; and 12 schools for the training of elementary teachers were established.

EDUCATION UNDER THE JULY MONARCHY (1830-1848). Francois Pierre Guillaume Guizot (1787-1874) was made minister of education and Victor Cousin (1792-1867) was made a member of the Council of Public Instruction. Cousin studied the Prussian education system and, in 1830, wrote his *Report on the State of Public Education in Prussia.* This caused wide interest. The Law of 1833 provided for a system of publicly controlled primary schools throughout France. It also provided for normal schools for the training of elementary teachers. These schools were to be supported by tuition fees, taxes, and national grants.

EDUCATION UNDER THE SECOND REPUBLIC AND SECOND EMPIRE (1848-1870). The law of 1850 abolished the state monopoly of secondary and higher education as well as the higher primary schools. In 1852 Napoleon II took control of education and the present administrative machinery in French education was established.

EDUCATION UNDER THE THIRD REPUBLIC (1870-1937). Fees in public lower primary schools were abolished and compulsory attendance instituted. The earlier system of state education was perfected with the minister of education responsible to the Chamber of Deputies and advised by a superior council placed at the head of the system; academies became teaching universities with the Rector at the head; and departments set up headed by a prefect and an advisory council.

BIBLIOGRAPHY

I. Primary Sources:

Cubberley, Ellwood P., *Readings in the History of Education*, pp. 455-541. New York, Houghton Mifflin Co., 1920.

2. Secondary Material:

Adamson, J.W., *English Education, 1789-1902*. Cambridge, Cambridge University Press, 1930.

Alexander, Thomas, *The Prussian Elementary Schools*. New York, The Macmillan Co., 1919.

Alexander, Thomas, and Parker, Beryl, *The New Education in the German Republic*. New York, John Day Co., 1929.

Archer, R.L., *Secondary Education in the 19th Century*. Cambridge, Cambridge University Press, 1921.

Becker, Carl H., *Secondary Education and Teacher Training in Germany*. New York, Teachers College, Columbia University, 1931.

Birchenough, Charles, *History of Elementary Education in England and Wales*. London, W.B. Clive, 1925.

Bolton, F.E., *The Secondary School System of Germany*. New York, D. Appleton-Century Co., 1905.

Butts, R. Freeman, *A Cultural History of Education*, pp. 385-439. New York, McGraw-Hill Book Co., Inc., 1947.

Cubberley, Ellwood P., *A Brief History of Education*, pp. 309-350. New York, Houghton Mifflin Co., 1922.

Cubberley, Ellwood P., *The History of Education*, pp. 552-650. New York, Houghton Mifflin Co., 1920.

De Montmorency, J.E.G., *State Intervention in English Education*. Cambridge, Cambridge University Press, 1902.

Duggan, Stephen, *A Student's Textbook in the History of Education*, pp. 408-448. New York, D. Appleton-Century Co., 1936.

Eby, Frederick, and Arrowood, C.F., *The Development of Modern Education*, pp. 679-704. New York, Prentice-Hall, Inc., 1937.

Farrington, F.E., *French Secondary Schools*. New York, Longmans, Green and Co., 1910.

Farrington, F.E., *The Public Primary School System of France*. New York, Teachers College, Columbia University, 1906.

Graves, Frank P., *A History of Education, In Modern Times*, pp. 256-316. New York, The Macmillan Co., 1927.

Graves, Frank P., *A Student's History of Education*, pp. 433-491. New York, The Macmillan Co., 1936.

Kandel, I.L., *Comparative Education.* Boston, Houghton Mifflin Co., 1931.

Melvin, A. Gordon, *Education, A History,* pp. 257-276. New York, John Day Co., 1946.

Meyer, Adolph, *The Development of Education in the Twentieth Century.* New York, Prentice-Hall, Inc., 1939.

Mulhern, James, *A History of Education,* pp. 429-467. Ronald Press Co., New York, 1946.

Paulsen, Friedrich, *German Universities and University Study.* New York, Charles Scribner's Sons, 1906.

Reisner, E.H., *Nationalism and Education Since 1789.* New York, The Macmillan Co., 1923.

Smith, Frank, *History of English Elementary Education Since 1760.* London, University of London Press, 1931.

CHAPTER XVIII

Education in 19th Century: America

Growth of the Free School System
BACKGROUND MATERIAL

1. Though free school systems were developing throughout the western world during the 19th century, that of the United States differed from others in several respects: The schools were more sensitive to popular demand; social class distinctions were largely abolished; the teaching of religion in the schools was banned; a large number of pupils had access to the higher levels of education; the American plan of control kept the schools close to the people, and there was no national system of education, but 48 different state systems.

2. *Conditions Influencing the Educational Development Included:* Leadership in education was exerted by those areas which were settled earliest; the great diversity of cultural backgrounds in the population; the work of outstanding leaders such as Horace Mann and Henry Barnard; the great wealth of the United States built upon rapid exploitation of natural resources, and the vastness of the country and the diverse living conditions.

3. *Status of Schools at the Beginning of the 19th Century:* Educational opportunities for the masses were varied and often poor and inefficient. The more wealthy employed tutors and private teachers. Though some public money was being distributed among schools, their chief support came from tuition fees. The school buildings were poor and not at all well equipped. Teachers, with few exceptions, were poorly trained and considered teaching as a means to other ends.

4. *The Social Pattern of the Times:* Territorial boundaries of the nation were being extended and the population was increasing rapidly; the country was changing from an agricultural to an industrial economy, and the franchise was being extended under pressure from those wishing to establish wide political democracy.

CONSTRUCTING THE SCHOOL SYSTEM

1. *Beginnings in New York:* The Common School Fund was established in 1805 and the Literary Fund begun in 1813. The New York Free School Society was organized in 1805 and its work prospered under the leadership of DeWitt Clinton (1769-1828). The School Law of 1812 provided for a state superintendent of schools, town school commissioners, district trustees, and distribution of the common school fund. Gideon Hawley was

made the first state superintendent.

2. *Beginnings in Other States:* **Massachusetts** - Under the school law of 1789 town school committees were permitted. In 1826 the towns were required to appoint school committees, but opposition to this was so great that the law was changed the next year. In 1827 support of schools by taxation was made compulsory. **Pennsylvania** - In 1802 a pauper school act was passed permitting overseers and guardians of the poor to collect taxes for the education of their charges. A free school system was established by the law of 1834. **Ohio** - The state received a square mile from each township for education. Laws were passed establishing universities and the district system. The law of 1825 laid the foundation for a school system. In 1827 a school fund was established. **North Carolina** - The school fund was established in 1825 and a system of elementary schools set up in 1839.

3. *Educational Publications:* A vast amount of material on education appeared in America between 1815 and 1860. This included: *Year in Europe* (1819) by John Griscom, *Report on the State of Public Education in Prussia* by Victor Cousin, and reports made by William C. Woodbridge, Calvin E. Stowe, Horace Mann, and Henry Barnard. Also, several educational journals began publication: *The Academician* (1818), *The American Journal of Education* (1826-1831) which was continued after 1831 as the *American Annals of Education* (1832-1839).

4. *Educational Associations:* Many associations propagandizing for education were organized during this period: The Western Academic Institute and the Board of Education, both founded at Cincinnati in 1829, The American Institute of Instruction founded in Boston in 1830. These, and others of similar concern, issued publications, drew up resolutions for legislatures, and organized sentiment for better education.

5. *Education in Massachusetts:* Massachusetts led in the development of a school system. In 1834 the foundation of her system was laid. Leaders in the thought on education of the times included John Quincy Adams, Ralph Waldo Emerson, George Ticknor, and William Prescott. James G. Carter (1795-1849) suggested educational reforms in his *Letters to the Hon. William Prescott on the Free Schools of New England* (1821), founded a private normal school, helped organize the American Institute of Instruction, served in the state legislature, and drafted the law of 1837 which established the Massachusetts State Board of Education. Horace Mann (1796-1859) left the presidency of the state Senate to become Secretary of the Massachusetts State Board of Education, published annual reports dealing with educational problems (his *Seventh Annual Report* is a classic), established the *Massachusetts Common School*

Journal, worked for better teachers, higher salaries, an enriched curriculum, improved school buildings, school libraries, better administrative procedures, and non-sectarian schools.

6. *Education in Connecticut:* Henry Barnard (1811-1900) was the scholar of early American education. He served as secretary of the Connecticut State Board of Education from 1838 to 1842 and also as a member of the state legislature. He established the *Connecticut Common School Journal.* From 1843 to 1849 he helped organize the educational system of Rhode Island. Then he returned to Connecticut to head the school system of that state. He published the *American Journal of Education* (begun in 1855), a storehouse of information about American and European developments in education, served as chancellor of the University of Wisconsin (1858-1860), and became the first United States Commissioner of Education in 1867 and filled that office until 1870.

GROWTH OF THE ELEMENTARY SCHOOL. The Pestalozzian influence in the United States resulted in an increase in the number of elementary schools and in an enriched program at this level. Gradually a graded plan for these schools developed because of the spread of class instruction, the grading of subject matter, the spread of the monitorial system, and the employment of trained teachers. in addition, many leading educators were advocates of having a teacher for each class and a system of grading. John Philbrick (1847) built, in Quincy, Massachusette, the first school with separate rooms for each class. By 1890 the educational system of this country consisted of eight years of elementary schooling and four years of high school work. The work of each unit covered one year.

GROWTH OF THE HIGH SCHOOL. The Latin Grammar School was the early American secondary school. This was supplanted by academies offering courses in English literature, history, mathematics, and the sciences. The Boston English Classical School, established in 1821 for boys planning merchantile and technical careers, offered no Latin nor Greek and emphasized English. In 1827 Massachusetts passed a law requiring a similar school in each town of 500 families. Attempts to establish schools of this type for girls failed. The high school movement spread throughout the country but was opposed in many quarters. The Kalamazoo Case (1872) challenged the right to use tax money for high schools. The Supreme Court of Michigan ruled in favor of taxation for high school support. Thus, higher education was made a proper part of a state's free school system.

The Federal Government and Education

IN THE EARLY YEARS OF THE COUNTRY. There was much interest in a federal system of education but efforts to establish such a system failed. Plans to endow state colleges from funds obtained by the sale of federal lands were defeated.

THE MORRILL ACT (1892). This law provided for a grant of land to each state on the basis of the number of Congressmen from that state, the proceeds from such land to be used for establishing a state college in which agriculture, the mechanical arts, and military science were to be taught. However, a state might, if it desired, establish departments for teaching these subjects in existing institutions. Schools established under this act are known as "land-grant colleges." In 1890 Congress established a plan for giving direct annual grants to these colleges.

THE UNITED STATES COMMISSIONER OF EDUCATION. This office was established in 1867 by Congress as part of a national department of education. In 1868 this department was put in the Interior Department. Later it became the United States Office of Education.

The Growth of American Colleges

INFLUENCE OF THE GERMAN UNIVERSITIES. German universities at the beginning of the 19th century were centers of free research and teaching. The great minds of Germany were connected with her universities and these institutions put great emphasis upon work in their schools of medicine, law, philosophy, theology. The purpose of the German universities was to produce learned scholars rather than to give a general education or turn out technicians in practical fields.

THE EARLY PERIOD OF GERMAN INFLUENCE (1810-1875). Reports on German education, including that of Victor Cousin, began to appear and stimulate interest in this hitherto unknown area. Many students went to Germany for their advanced training and came back with glowing reports of work done there. Some of these came to hold leading educational posts in this country. Further, a number of German scholars came to this country and were given important educational posts. Dr. Henry P. Tappan (1805-1881), president of the University of Michigan from 1852-1863, sought to build in the west a university on the German model. Charles W. Eliot (1834-1926), president of Harvard University from 1869 to 1909, built a small New England College into one of the great American institutions of learning. These developments and the increased German influence resulted in drawing the line between the college and the university clearly. Harvard and the University of Michigan made gradual reforms in the direction of the German university plan. The inauguration of Eliot at Harvard marks the dominance of German ideals in American university education, the beginning of the modern period. Noah Porter, president of Yale University, attacked this entire concept in his *The American College and the American Public*. He championed the traditional American college over against the German University.

LATER PERIOD OF GERMAN INFLUENCE (1875 to the present). The elective system and coeducation were established at many colleges. A number of universities became colleges with additional work weakly imitating the German universities. The development of graduate work under the leadership of Johns Hopkins University (opened in 1876) and Clark University, with G. Stanley Hall as president, was evident in many other places. Gradually professional schools grew up around colleges. The result is the American university with a college of arts attacked from below by the secondary schools, from about by the professional schools, and from above by the graduate schools.

Development of the "Educational Ladder"

INTRODUCTION. The present system of education in the United States was not planned. It grew as different units, founded for specific purposes, were gradually articulated into a whole.

GROWTH OF THE ELEMENTARY SCHOOL. The primary school was consolidated with the reading and writing school. Since 14 was generally accepted as the upper limit of free schooling and children began their schooling at approximately 6 years of age, the grades in the elementary school were usually 8. This school was not planned to prepare a pupil for high school, but rather to give a common school education to the great mass of children. It was not thought that the child would go beyond this.

GROWTH OF THE HIGH SCHOOL. The high school was organized to give advanced training for entrance into commercial life. To be admitted a pupil had to be of a certain age, usually from 9 to 12, and had to pass an entrance examination. The course ran for three or four years and was not preparatory for college.

ARTICULATION OF ELEMENTARY AND HIGH SCHOOL. Massachusetts led the way by basing the entrance examinations for high school upon subjects taught in elementary school. After the Civil War admission examinations were abandoned and children were admitted upon completion of the elementary school course. Gradually work of the two schools has been modified so as to form a unified and progressive system of education through the 17th year.

GROWTH OF COLLEGE PREPARATION. Early high schools were not college preparatory, this being cared for by the Latin Grammar School, the academies, or by private instruction. In 1830 and the years following high schools began to prepare for college. Many high schools offered the English Course for general education and the Classical Course for college preparation. Colleges held to entrance examinations so that gradually the high schools undertook to teach subjects upon which pupils would be examined. In 1870-1871 the University of Michigan established the policy of admitting students who had graduated from accredited high schools. This policy spread and became general. In some instances additional examinations are required. The professional schools became another step in the ladder and based their work upon that done in the colleges.

BIBLIOGRAPHY

I. Primary Sources:

Cubberley, Ellwood P., *Readings in Public Education in the United States*, pp. 129-263. New York, Houghton Mifflin Co., 1934.

Cubberley, Ellwood P., *Readings in the History of Education*, pp. 542-592. New York, Houghton Mifflin Co., 1920.

Eliot, Charles W., "Inaugural Address as President of Harvard College," in *Educational Forum*. New York, Century, 1898.

Porter, Noah, *The American College and the American Public*. New York, Chatfield & Co., 1870.

Tappan, Henry P., *University Education*. New York, Putnam, 1851.

Tappan, Henry P., "The 'New Education,'" in *The Atlantic Monthly*, February and March, 1869.

Wayland, Francis, *Thoughts on the Present Collegiate System in the United States*. Boston, Gould, Kendall & Lincoln, 1842.

2. Secondary Material

Brown, E.E., *The Making of Our Middle Schools*. New York, Longmans, Green and Company, 1905.

Brubacher, John S., *Henry Barnard on Education*. New York, McGraw-Hill Book Company, Inc., 1931.

Butts, R. Freeman, *A Cultural History of Education*, pp. 440-525. New York, McGraw-Hill Book Co., Inc., 1947.

Cubberley, Ellwood P., *A Brief History of Education*, pp. 352-393. New York, Houghton Mifflin Co., 1922.

Cubberley, Ellwood P., *The History of Education*, pp. 653-708. New York, Houghton Mifflin Co., 1920.

Cubberley, Ellwood P., *Public Education in the United States*, pp. 120-287. New York, Houghton Mifflin Co., 1934.

Eby, Frederick, and Arrowood, C.F., *The Development of Modern Education*, pp. 706-752. New York, Prentice-Hall, Inc., 1934.

Fitzpatrick, E.A., *The Educational Views and Influence of DeWitt Clinton*. New York, Teachers College, Columbia University Press, 1911.

Gifford, Walter J., *Historical Development of the New York State High School System*. Albany, J.B. Lyons Co., 1922.

Graves, Frank P., *A Student's History of Education*, pp. 317-371. New York, The Macmillan Co., 1936

Graves, Frank P., *A History of Education, In Modern Times*, pp. 165-189. New York, The Macmillan Co., 1927

Hinsdale, B.A., *Horace Mann and the Common School Revival.* New York, Charles Scribner's Sons, 1898.

Jackson, Sidney L., *America's Struggle for Free Schools.* Washington, American Council on Public Affairs, 1942.

Martin, George H., *The Evolution of the Massachusetts Public School System.* New York, D. Appleton-Century Co. , 1894.

Monroe, Paul, *Founding of the American Public School System,* pp. 222-507. New York, The Macmillan Co., 1940.

Mulhern, James, *A History of Education,* pp. 467-497. Ronald Press Co., New York, 1946.

Reisner, E.H., *The Evolution of the Common School.* New York, The Macmillan Co., 1930.

Thursfield, Richard, *Henry Barnard's Journal of Education.* Baltimore, The Johns Hopkins Press, 1946.

Thwing, C.F., *A History of Higher Education in America.* New York, D. Appleton-Century Co., 1906.

Williams, E.I.F., *Horace Mann.* New York, The Macmillan Co., 1936.

Woody, Thomas, *History of Education of Women in the United States.* Lancaster, Ps., Science Press, 1929.

CHAPTER XIX

Johann Friedrich Herbart (1776-1841)

His Life. Born in Oldenburg, Germany, of a brilliant mother and a father who attained success as a lawyer, Herbart was of delicate constitution because of an accident during his childhood. His mother devoted herself wholly to him and to his education. He received elementary schooling under Pastor Ulzen and secondary instruction at the Oldenburg gymnasium. He showed great ability at an early age and in his late teens was matching his talents with the best minds of Germany. He attended the University of Jena from 1794 to 1797 where he mixed with the finest minds and greatest creative geniuses of his day. In 1797 he became private tutor of the three sons of the Governor of Interlaken. This determined his educational theory and set him on the path of teaching. The periods of his university work and productive scholarship are: 1802-1809 - teaching at the University of Gottingen, lecturing on education and philosophy, and writing chiefly on education. 1809-1833 - occupied the chair of philosophy formerly held by Immanuel Kant at Konigsburg, lectured on philosophy, psychology, and education, conducted a pedagogical seminar, and wrote chiefly in the field of psychology. 1833-1841 - returned to Gottingen and wrote material which is relatively unimportant.

His Approach to a Science of Education. He held that one must first discover the aim of education, and then develop means for the realization of this aim.

THE AIM OF EDUCATION. "The one and the whole work of education may be summed up in the concept - Morality." By morality he meant a steady, dependable moral character. The moral man is one who is intelligently devoted to the highest ethical ideals, who wills the good freely and constantly because it is his nature to do so. Instruction must prepare the individual to desire and will the good and must develop in him the ability to attain it. This demands the broadest possible training, "many-sidedness of interest." This breadth of experience will make it possible for the individual to make the best choices throughout life. Thus, the complete aim of education is good moral character and many-sidedness of interest.

HOW THE AIM IS REALIZED. "Educative instruction" is the means of realizing the aim of education. Will and intellect develop by this process. Knowledge is the means for developing the will and the intellect. Thus, instruction is the only foundation of all education. "To instruct

181

the mind is to construct it." Knowledge builds the mind, creates the intellect.

His Educational Psychology

INTRODUCTION. The psychology of Herbart has ethical import. His contributions to the field include: 1. He built a psychology from a study of the facts of mental life rather than from mere speculative conclusions. 2. He taught that the mind is a unity and not a grouping of separate faculties. 3. He sought to make psychology mathematically certain and thus gave impetus to the development of experimental psychology. 4. He initiated physiological psychology.

ACTIVITIES OF THE MIND. Mental life has the basic activities of knowing, feeling, and willing. The soul is called mind when it knows and heart or disposition when it feels or wills.

THE DOCTRINE OF PRESENTATIONS. Presentations are the ingredients of mental life. These are the sensations and perceptions of objects. Objects are presented. Thus, presentations include all percepts, concepts, ideas, meanings - all objects of thought. Objects presented strive to remain in consciousness, but may be pushed aside by other presentations and forced into the subconscious. Thus, consciousness shifts constantly as new presentations enter and force others out. Those forced out strive to re-enter consciousness and depose other presentations.

THE NATURE OF MENTAL ACTIVITY. Feeling and willing result from presentations, they originate from the relations which presentations bear to each other. A feeling is consciousness of a helping or hindering of an idea which is trying to get control of consciousness. Pleasure results when one idea helps another and pain comes when one idea hinders another. Interest is an inner force holding ideas in consciousness or helping ideas to come into consciousness. The more often an idea is brought into consciousness, the easier it is to bring it to consciousness. The greater the number of ideas of similar nature in consciousness, the more easily a new idea will enter. Therefore, the teacher must continuously bring into consciousness those ideas which he wishes to dominate consciousness. In this way he builds a mass of ideas which attracts similar ideas and repels dissimilar ideas. This is the "apperceptive mass." The will is not a special faculty, but is the totality of ideas which make up experience and are expressed in action. Desire is a striving to bring some object into consciousness in a concrete way so that it will satisfy. If one is of the opinion that the object cannot be obtained, the desire remains a wish. If he is confident that it can be obtained, the desire may become a volition. Therefore, as the teacher presents ideas to the child he builds his mind and determines how the child wills and feels. Presentations are analyzed into parts and these parts are associated into masses of similar ideas or meanings. Experience begins with wholes and analysis follows. He calls these processes "analysis" and apperception.

His Educational Principles

THE PRINCIPLE OF APPERCEPTION. The teacher builds the "circle of thought" by manipulating presentations. There are three stages in the building of the mind: 1. The stage of sensations and perceptions. 2. The stage of imagination and memory. 3. The stage of conceptual thinking and judgment. The difference between an educated and an uneducated individual is one of association of ideas. The uneducated may have a mass of loosely associated ideas while the ideas of the other are closely related. New ideas are taken up by the "apperceptive mass" and united with it. This is the learning process.

CREATIVE ACTIVITY. The individual can never have an absolutely new experience since experience is an organic growth. When a new experience is contradictory of the old two things may happen: 1. One may be accepted and the other cast into the subconscious, or 2. The new concept may be formed to include both, a higher synthesis. This latter is creative mental activity.

THE CULTURAL-EPOCH THEORY. Our best guide for developing the mind of the child is the natural history of the human mind. This begins with the simplicity of primitive man and moves on to present-day social complexity. In this development are three stages: 1. The stage of sensations and perceptions when emotions are strong and the child's impulsiveness must be curbed. 2. The stage of memory and imagination when systematic training can be employed. 3. The stage of judgment when instruction has formed the will.

His Curriculum. The individual receives presentations from things, "empirical knowledge," and from social intercourse, "sympathy." Although the child gets many impressions before entering school, the teacher must fill in the picture and correct inaccuracies through the use of geography, mathematics, and natural history in the area of "empirical knowledge," and through history, literature, languages, religion, and art in the area of "sympathy." This leads to the principles of concentration and correlation.

His Methods of Teaching. All teaching must aim to build the mind into a compact body of knowledge and interests so that thought and ethical character are controlled from within. All knowledge must be properly assimilated and organized, apperceived. Thus, the "five formal steps" were developed by Herbart and his followers:

PREPARATION. Ideas already in consciousness or in the subconscious are recalled to attention. The proper apperceptive mass is made ready to receive the new presentations.

PRESENTATION. The new material is presented in concrete form and at the level of the child's development.

ASSOCIATION. The new material is assimilated with the old. Likenesses to and differences from the old are pointed out so that the new is properly related to the old.

GENERALIZATION. The experiences are analyzed and general conceptions formed so that the individual moves from the low level of perception and the concrete to the higher level of judgment.

APPLICATION. Use of knowledge as part of a living mind, as an aid in interpreting life.

The Spread and Influence of His Theory. In Germany Herbart's principles were almost universally adopted. In the United States they were spread and championed by several educational leaders (Charles De Garmo, Charles McMurray, and Frank McMurray) who studied in Germany and brought Herbart's ideas to America. These men published a great mass of literature dealing with the Herbartian principles. The National Herbartian Society was organized in 1892. The name of this society was changed in 1902 to the National Society for the Scientific Study of Education as American educators turned away from slavish adherence to Herbartianism.

BIBLIOGRAPHY

I. Primary Sources:

Cubberley, Ellwood P., *Readings in the History of Education,* pp. 639-645. New York, Houghton Mifflin Co., 1920.

Herbart, J.F., *ABC of Sense Perception.* New York, D. Appleton-Century Co., 1896.

Herbart, J.F., *The Application of Psychology to the Science of Education.* New York, B.C. Mullineer, 1898.

Herbart, J.F., *Outlines of Educational Doctrine.* New York, The Macmillan Co., 1901.

Herbart, J.F., *The Science of Education.* Boston, D.C. Heath and Co., 1908.

Herbart, J.F., *Textbook in Psychology.* New York, D. Appleton-Century Co., 1896.

2. Secondary Material:

Adams, John, *The Herbartian Psychology Applied to Education.* Boston, D.C. Heath and Co., 1897.

Cole, P.R., *Herbart and Froebel: An Attempt at Synthesis.* New York, Columbia University Press, 1907.

Compayre, Gabriel, *Herbart and Education by Instruction.* New York, Crowell, 1907.

Cubberley, Ellwood P., *A Brief History of Education,* pp. 419-424. New York, Houghton Mifflin Co., 1922.

Cubberley, Ellwood P., *The History of Education,* pp. 759-764. New York, Houghton Mifflin Co., 1920.

DeGarmo, Charles, *Herbart and the Herbartians.* New York, Charles Scribner's Sons, 1895

DeGarmo, Charles, *Outlines of Educational Doctrine.* New York, The Macmillan Co., 1901.

Duggan, Stephen, *A Student's Textbook in the History of Education,* pp. 243-255. New York, D. Appleton-Century Co., 1936.

Eby, Frederick, and Arrowood, Charles F., *The Development of Modern Education,* pp. 755-788. New York, Prentice-Hall, Inc., 1937.

Felkin, H.E., and E., *Herbart's Lectures and Letters on Education.* Syracuse, C.W. Bardeen, 1898.

Felkin, H.E., and E., *Herbart's Science of Education.* Boston, D.C. Heath and Co., 1902.

Graves, Frank P., *A History of Education, In Modern Times,* pp. 191-220. New York, The Macmillan Co., 1927.

Graves, Frank P. , *A Student's History of Education,* pp. 377-390. New York, The Macmillan Co. , 1936.

Graves, Frank P. , *Great Educators of Three Centuries,* Chapter X. New York, The Macmillan Co. , 1912.

Lange, Alexis F. , *Herbart's Outline of Educational Doctrine.* New York, The Macmillan Co. , 1901.

Lange, Karl, *Apperception.* Boston, D.C. Heath and Co. , 1893.

McMurry, Charles A. , *The Elements of General Method.* New York, The Macmillan Co. , 1914.

Melvin, A. Gordon, *Education, A History,* pp. 226-232. New York, The John Day Co. , 1946.

Monroe, Paul, *A Brief Course in the History of Education,* pp. 319-329. New York, The Macmillan Co. , 1909.

Monroe, Paul, *A Text-Book in the History of Education,* pp. 622-639. New York, The Macmillan Co. , 1907.

Mulhern, James, *A History of Education,* pp. 369-375. Ronald Press Co. , New York, 1946.

Randels, George B. , *The Doctrines of Herbart in the United States.* Philadelphia, University of Pennsylvania Press, 1909.

Smith, Margaret K. , *Herbart's Text-Book in Psychology.* New York, D. Appleton-Century Co. , 1891.

CHAPTER XX

Friedrich Froebel (1782-1852)

His Life. Born at Oberweisbach, in southern Germany, the son of a busy
pastor, Froebel, at nine months of age, lost his mother. After his
father remarried the boy was much of an outcast. His father was too busy
to pay much attention to him and his stepmother treated him with con-
tempt. Thus, the boy turned to nature and to a study of his own inner
impulses and feelings. After spending the years from 10 to 14 with his
uncle, Pastor Hoffman of Stadt Ilm, he was apprenticed to a forester who
failed to teach him as agreed. In 1799 Froebel entered the University of
Jena where he studied for a while. Then he tried several areas of work
with only slight success. An experience as teacher of drawing in Herr
Gruner's school at Frankfort convinced him that teaching was his career.
From 1807 to 1810 he worked with three boys, tutoring them and studying
with them at Pestalozzi's school at Yverdun. This experience laid the
foundation for his educational philosophy and method. Seeking a principle that would explain the basic laws of all phenomena, a principle of
unity, he turned to a study of the sciences - philosophy, chemistry,
physics, geology, mathematics, and minerology. He studied at Gottingen
and at Berlin. He opened a school for boys, similar to Pestalozzi's
school at Yverdun, at Keilhau in 1817. From 1831 to 1836 he worked with
several similar schools in Switzerland. In 1837 he opened the first
kindergarten at Blankenburg and continued with the kindergarten until
his death.

His Fundamental Philosophy

ROOTS OF HIS THEORY. Though influenced by many factors in his age,
Froebel was an original, creative thinker who used materials from many
sources to construct a unique system of thought. Influences upon Froebel's
thinking came from:

1. *The Post-Kantian Philosophic Thought of His Day:* He was especially
influenced by K.C.F. Krause who seemed to harmonize best the inner world
of man's soul and the outer world of phenomena. Krause held that everything is in and through God, an expression of his creative will.

2. *The Scientific Knowledge of His Time:* This was highly speculative
and seemed to Froebel to reveal laws of unity amid diversity.

3. *The Educational Writings of His Day and Earlier:* Those of Rousseau,
Pestalozzi, Arndt, Comenius, and Johann H.G. Heusinger (1766-1837).
Froebel added to these influences his own observations and the power of

187

his own creative mind.

THE ABSOLUTE. Education is part of the process of cosmic evolution. It includes the process by which mankind rises from nature to its present state and the process by which an individual develops into self-conscious adulthood. The Absolute, God, is the original active, energizing, creating, intelligent, and self-conscious source of all things. Both nature and mind come from this original unity. Both nature and man, force and thought, are this divine energy unfolding in diverse forms.

THE THEORY OF UNITY. Everything is both a unity in and of itself and is a member of a more inclusive unity. This is the theory of "part-whole" (Gliedganzes). The Absolute is the all-inclusive unity of which everything is a part. God does not lose his unity by unfolding himself in all the diversity of the universe. Each unity is best when all its parts function together, but in so functioning none of the parts loses its identity.

THE THEORY OF DEVELOPMENT. One law of development is found in every-thing, the inorganic, the organic, and the spiritual. This is the law of creative growth from unity to diversity in unity. This law is one of opposites, a law of action, reaction, and equilibrium. This is similar to the Hegelian dialectic, but it applies to all development in the universe, not merely to thought. Man is the latest product of development in which God becomes self-conscious. Thus, man attains freedom and is able to choose his ends. This enables him to know the correct method of education. It also means that the race will evolve to still higher forms and that there is unlimited progress.

THE PROBLEM OF EVIL. The child is naturally good and his essence is God. Thus, each vice is a virtue which has been perverted in its unfold-ing. Evil comes either through neglect of the development of a phase of the individual's native goodness, or through a distortion of that which was originally good.

THE RECAPITULATION THEORY. As the inner nature of the child unfolds, he repeats each stage of the development of the race. This applies to the physical and the mental. Recapitulation is not mere imitation of the past, but is the result of the inner urge of the individual. The growth of the individual is by stages: infancy, childhood, boyhood, youth, maturity. In these he repeats the development of the race.

THE THEORY OF CREATIVITY. God is creative. Man, as the unfolding of God, is creative and productive. This is not a utilitarian theory. Man creates because of his inner nature, not because of outer pressure.

THE THEORY OF FREEDOM. Man has attained self-consciousness. Thus, he is free to choose ends and evaluate outcomes. He is predetermined to become man, a free being.

EDUCATION. From his theory of development it follows that all education is a drawing out of the individual's inner potentialities. Learning should come when the child's inner nature demands it and reaches out for it. Thus, education must be passive, following.

His Theory of Education

AIMS OF EDUCATION. Education must bring man to a clear consciousness of himself, to peace with nature, and to unity with God. This necessitates knowledge of oneself, of nature, and of the laws of inner development. It also concerns development of the will. Thus, the highest aim of education is the development of character.

THEORY OF THE CURRICULUM. The purpose of the curriculum is not to transmit knowledge but to build habits, skills, and character. Learning must result in productive activity. Learning comes through doing. It must be a result of an inner craving to realize some objective.

THEORY OF "BUDDING-POINTS." Activities come from within and form a unity. Each new interest "buds" from an activity already there. The teacher must know when the child is ready for something new.

THEORY OF RELIGION. Religion is consciousness of one's unity with the Absolute, with God. This can be developed best in the normal home where the child is obedient to the father.

PERIODS OF DEVELOPMENT

1. *Infancy* (from birth to 3): The child is dependent upon his parents. His senses and motor activities develop in organic relation to each other. Hearing and vision are the most important senses.

2. *Childhood* (from 3 to 6 or 7): Here the "child begins self-actively to represent the internal outwardly." Forms of expression at this stage include language, play, drawing, rhythm. Education comes through "gifts and occupations."

3. *Boyhood* (from 6 or 7 to 9 or 10): This is the period when instruction predominates. Now the individual creates for a purpose, not merely for the sake of activity. He engages in constructive activities, play, reading of many stories of interest, and in the study of nature.

THE FUNCTION OF THE FAMILY. The family is the supreme human institution. It is a complete unity. In this unity the inner nature of the child unfolds completely and truly. The family is the source of the first religious consciousness.

SOCIAL EDUCATION. The child engages in group activities, thereby developing the sense of oneness with others. This counteracts extreme individualism and is a means of harmonizing the individual and the social group. As the individual becomes one with his fellows he develops the distinctly human qualities.

FROEBEL'S SYMBOLISM. Froebel used many objects (the ball, cube, cylinder, games, and apparatus) as symbols with inner meaning. He saw in the child's play a love of symbols and believed that this was the basis of education. Symbols contribute to the development of the child's intelligence.

Criticisms of Froebel's Theory. Froebel's educational theory and practice have been criticized vigorously. Some of the criticisms that have been put forth are: The Prussian government banned the kindergarten as too liberalizing and democratic; his emphasis upon play detracts from serious thinking and learning; his theory and methods disparage sound learning. Knowledge is necessary and must be secured by a hard road; his philosophy is mystical and pantheistic. Froebel denied this, but his writings are often confusing; he puts too much emphasis upon form and mathematical knowledge, and his law of evolution is meaningless.

Froebel's Contributions to Educational Theory: In education the natural sequence of the development of the child's activities must be followed; development is based upon the inner self-activity of the child; play is an important method of early education; the most important technique for the harmonious development of all powers of the individual is constructive activity; through creative activity the impulse for individual expression and social controls are harmonized; we must build the curriculum on the activities and interests peculiar to each stage of the child's development; the process of human development is continuous. Education is the means for future development, and knowledge is a means, not an end in itself, for the realization of the essential nature of the individual.

The Story of the Kindergarten. Froebel became interested in the kindergarten idea around 1828. In 1837 he opened the first kindergarten at Blankenburg. This failed, but another institution of similar nature was opened in 1840. This was successful and others followed. He also established a training school for women. Though Germany was opposed to the kindergarten, many German educators were enthusiastic about the program and plan. These included Diesterweg and the Baroness Bertha von Merenholz-Buelow. In the United States the kindergarten was introduced by Mrs. Carl Schurz who opened the first American kindergarten at Watertown, Wisconsin, in 1855; Caroline Frankenburg who opened a kindergarten at Columbus, Ohio, in 1858; Dr. William N. Hailman teaching at Louisville, Kentucky; and Elizabeth Palmer Peabody who opened the first English kindergarten in Boston in 1860. In 1873 William T. Harris made the kindergarten part of the school system at St. Louis, Missouri.

BIBLIOGRAPHY

I. Primary Sources:

Fletcher, S.S.F., and Walton, J., *Froebel's Chief Writings on Education*. New York, Longmans, Green and Co., 1912.

Froebel, F., *Autobiography*. Translated by E. Michaelis and H.K. Moore. Syracuse, C.W. Bardeen, 1889.

Froebel, F., *Education by Development*. New York, D. Appleton and Co., 1902.

Froebel, F., *The Education of Man*. New York, D. Appleton and Co., 1887.

Froebel, F., *Mother Play*. Translated by Eliot and Blow. New York, D. Appleton and Co., 1895.

Froebel, F., *Pedagogics of the Kindergarten*. New York, D. Appleton and Co., 1905.

2. Secondary Material:

Barnard, Henry, *Kindergarten and Child Culture Papers*. Hartford, American Journal of Education, 1884.

Blow, Susan E., *Letters to a Mother on the Philosophy of Froebel*. New York, D. Appleton and Co., 1899.

Bowen, H.C., *Froebel and Education Through Self-Activity*. New York, Charles Scribner's Sons, 1906.

Cubberley, Ellwood P., *A Brief History of Education,* pp. 424-428. New York, Houghton Mifflin Co., 1922.

Cubberley, Ellwood P., *The History of Education,* pp. 764-768. New York, Houghton Mifflin Co., 1920.

Duggan, Stephen, *A Student's Textbook in the History of Education,* pp. 255-268. New York, D. Appleton-Century Co., 1936.

Eby, Frederick, and Arrowood, Charles F., *The Development of Modern Education,* pp. 790-837. New York, Prentice-Hall, Inc., 1937.

Graves, Frank P., *Great Educators of Three Centuries,* Chapter XI. New York, The Macmillan Co., 1912.

Graves, Frank P., *A History of Education, In Modern Times,* pp. 220-251. New York, The Macmillan Co., 1927.

Graves, Frank P., *A Student's History of Education,* pp. 390-406. New York, The Macmillan Co., 1936.

Heinemann, A.H., *Froebel's Letters*. Boston, Lee and Shepard, 1893.

Herford, W.H., *The Student's Froebel*. Boston, D.C. Heath and Co., 1900

Hughes, J.L., *Froebel's Educational Laws For All Teachers*. New York, D. Appleton and Co., 1898.

International Kindergarten Union, *Pioneers of the Kindergarten in America.* New York, Century Co., 1924.

Kilpatrick, William H., *Froebel's Kindergarten Principles Critically Examined.* New York, The Macmillan Co., 1916.

Kraus-Bolte, Maria, and Kraus, J., *The Kindergarten Guide.* New York, Steiger and Co., 1906.

Lange, W., "Reminiscences of Froebel," in Barnard's *American Journal of Education,* Vol. XXX, pp. 833-845. Hartford, 1880.

MacVannel, J.A., *The Educational Theories of Herbart and Froebel.* New York, Columbia University Press, 1906.

Marenholz-Buelow, Baroness Bertha von, *Reminiscences of Friedrich Froebel.* Translated by Mrs. Horace Mann. Boston, Lee and Shepard, 1892.

Melvin, A. Gordon, *Education, A History,* pp. 234-247. New York, The John Day Co., 1946.

Michaelis, E., and Moore, H.K., *Froebel's Letters on the Kindergarten.* Syracuse, C.W. Bardeen, 1897.

Monroe, Paul, *A Brief Course in the History of Education,* pp. 329-348. New York, The Macmillan Co., 1909.

Monroe, Paul, *A Text-Book in the History of Education,* pp. 639-667. New York, The Macmillan Co., 1907.

Mulhern, James, *A History of Education,* pp. 375-383. Ronald Press Co., New York, 1946.

Shirreff, Emily, *A Short Sketch of the Life of Froebel.* London, Chapman and Hall, 1887.

Snider, Denton J., *The Life of Friedrich Froebel, Founder of the Kindergarten.* Chicago, Sigma Publishing Co., 1900.

Ulich, Robert, *Sequence of Educational Influences Traced through Unpublished Writings of Pestalozzi, Froebel, Diesterweg, Horace Mann, and Henry Barnard.* Cambridge, Mann., Harvard University Press, 1935.

Vanderwalker, Nine C., *The Kindergarten in American Education.* New York, The Macmillan Co., 1908.

CHAPTER XXI

The Scientific Movement

Introduction. The sciences and the scientific approach play a major role in modern education. The story of this movement has its theoretical phase in the educational theories of leaders like Herbert Spencer and its institutional phase in the gradual inclusion of the sciences and scientific method in schools.

Background Factors

SENSE REALISM. This movement was largely outside the schools of the 17th century and had only a slight influence upon the schools of the age. This influence is seen in the development of science at the University of Halle, the growth of the Realschule in Germany, and the development of the academy. The psychological import of the movement was developed by leading thinkers such as Descartes, Bacon, and Locke, and the educational implications were worked out to a degree by Rousseau, Basedow, and Pestalozzi.

SCIENCE IN THE 19TH CENTURY. During the 19th century pure science developed rapidly and its implications for the daily life of man were extended so that the Industrial Revolution was made inevitable. Applications of science to man's living included the cotton gin, the sewing machine, the steamboat, the locomotive, and many machines for the manufacture of goods.

EDUCATIONAL IMPLICATIONS. The pressure of scientific development and use upon education resulted in a new conception of a liberal education and a growing insistence that the sciences and scientific method be featured in the curriculum.

Herbert Spencer (1820-1903)

HIS LIFE. Born into a scholarly and prominent family, Spencer received a fine education. This was followed by work in the fields of architecture, engineering, and writing. From wide reading in many areas Spencer was familiar with the best thinking of his age and his essays on *Education* (1861), which contain a statement of his philosophy of education, reveal the influence of educational thinkers from Pestalozzi to his day.

HIS EDUCATIONAL POSITION. The aim of education is to prepare one for complete living. Complete living is analyzed into certain definite activities in which one must engage: 1. *Physical* - for this development physiology is necessary. 2. *Vocation* - here one must study mathematics, physics, chemistry, biology, and sociology. 3. *Parenthood* - the subjects necessary here are physiology, psychology, and ethics. 4. *Citizenship* - the subjects necessary here are political, social, and economic history. 5. *Enjoyment of the Finer Things of Life* - in this area the necessary subjects are physiology, mechanics, and psychology. The sciences, then, are necessary for complete living. This is the position developed in Spencer's *What Knowledge Is of Most Worth?*

Science in the Schools

IN THE UNITED STATES

1. *In the Elementary Schools:* Geography was first. Horace Mann introduced physiology. The Oswego movement stimulated the use of object lessons. William T. Harris introduced elementary science. The Froebelian influence stimulated nature study.

2. *In the Secondary Schools:* The academies introduced scientific subjects and these were carried over into the English High Schools. Later the laboratory method was introduced to supplement textbooks.

3. *In Higher Institutions:* The early course in "natural history" developed into courses in the various sciences. Experiments conducted by instructors gradually gave way to laboratory experimentation conducted by students. Many colleges and other institutions giving major emphasis to science were founded.

IN GERMANY

1. *In the Elementary Schools:* The Pestalozzian movement resulted in the addition of scientific material to the curriculum after the Napoleonic wars.

2. *In the Secondary Schools:* Science was featured in the Realschulen, Oberrealschulen, and in the Realgymnasien, challenged the monopoly over secondary education held for so long by the gymnasium and its classical curriculum. Vocational schools included considerable science in their curricula.

3. *In the Universities:* Many universities added the sciences to their curricula. The University of Halle was among the first. The laboratory method was introduced at Giessen in 1826. The Technische Hochschulen, higher schools of applied science, have been created with emphasis upon science as applied to industry.

IN FRANCE

1. *In the Elementary Schools:* Science came into the primary schools after 1870. In lower primary schools scientific material was developed around drawing, handwork, agriculture, and geography. In higher primary schools courses were introduced in the natural sciences, hygiene, and physical sciences.

2. *In the Secondary Schools:* Science courses were established at the close of the 18th century, during the Revolution of 1792-1799. Napoleon, in 1802, added a science course to the program of the lycees paralleling the classical course. Later an attempt was made to require science in the classical course, but this was vigorously opposed. This led to the establishment of four courses in the lycee, two of which emphasize science.

3. *In the Universities:* Higher technical schools were founded as early as 1747. After the Revolution many higher technical schools with major emphasis upon science were established.

IN ENGLAND

1. *In the Elementary Schools:* Subsidies were granted to schools teaching science at the close of the 19th century. After 1900 science was made compulsory.

2. *In the Secondary Schools:* The academies of the Dissenters included some science in their curricula. The English public and grammar schools were not influenced by the scientific movement until after 1868, after the government investigation of endowed schools. Then many introduced a "modern side." Subsidies for teaching of science stimulated many schools to introduce the subjects.

3. *In the Universities:* There was some science at Cambridge very early. Here Newton was working. Around 1850 biology and the laboratory method were introduced. Science has made its greatest advance in the municipal universities that have arisen at such centers as Sheffield, Leeds, Birmingham, Manchester, and London. Here practical applications of science are stressed.

BIBLIOGRAPHY

I. Primary Sources:

Cubberley, Ellwood P., *Readings in the History of Education*, pp. 655-661. New York, Houghton Mifflin Co., 1920.

Spencer, Herbert, *Education*. New York, D. Appleton and Co., 1860.

2. Secondary Material:

Compayre, Gabriel, *Herbert Spencer and Scientific Education*. New York, Thomas Y. Crowell and Co., 1907.

Cubberley, Ellwood P., *A Brief History of Education*, pp. 430-434. New York, Houghton Mifflin Co., 1922.

Cubberley, Ellwood P., *The History of Education*, pp. 772-779. New York, Houghton Mifflin Co., 1920.

Duggan, Stephen, *A Student's Textbook in the History of Education*, pp. 271-284. New York, D. Appleton-Century Co., 1936.

Graves, Frank P., *A History of Education, In Modern Times*, pp. 320-354. New York, The Macmillan Co., 1927.

Graves, Frank P., *A Student's History of Education*, pp. 495-513. New York, The Macmillan Co., 1936.

Melvin, A. Gordon, *Education, A History*, pp. 249-253. New York, The John Day Co., 1947.

Monroe, Paul, *A Text-Book in the History of Education*, pp. 677-703. New York, The Macmillan Co., 1907.

Mulhern, James, *A History of Education*, pp. 333-343, 413-426. Ronald Press Co., New York, 1946

Quick, R.H., *Educational Reformers*, Chapter XIX. New York, D. Appleton and Co., 1860.

CHAPTER XXII

Modern American Educational Leaders

Francis W. Parker (1837-1902)

HIS EARLY LIFE. Born at Piscataquog, New Hampshire, the son of a cabinetmaker and a school teacher, Parker lost his father when he was but six years old. At eight he was apprenticed to a farmer. During the period of his apprenticeship he received a meager education in the district school and a somewhat broader education through his contact with nature and through general reading. His study of nature lead him to a doctrine of unity similar to that of Froebel. This unity was interpreted in terms of "concentration," the idea of "the central subjects" which included geography, geology, mineralogy, astronomy, meteorology, botany, zoology, anthropology, ethnology, and history. At 13 he left the farm and worked at odd tasks while getting what education he could. At 16 he took his first position as a teacher with a salary of $15 per month and board. In 1859 he became teacher of the school at Carrolton, Illinois, and reformed the institution.

AT QUINCY, MASSACHUSETTS. After a period of service in the United States army, Parker spent two years in Germany studying the work of Pestalozzi, Herbart, and Froebel. Returning to the United States, he took charge of the schools of Quincy, Massachusetts. Here he introduced new methods and made the city a mecca for educators. Here he emphasized activity and concentration.

LATER ACCOMPLISHMENTS. As supervisor of the Boston schools and then as principal of the Cook County Normal School at Englewood, Illinois, Parker carried on his educational reforms. At the latter institution he became acquainted with John Dewey. Mrs. Emmons Blaine built and supported a private laboratory school for Parker. This became the School of Education of the University of Chicago. When Parker died, John Dewey, then head of the university's department of education, became director of the school.

G. Stanley Hall (1844-1924)

HIS LIFE. Born at Ashfield, Massachusetts, of an intelligent farm family, Hall graduated from Williams College in 1867. He attended Union Theological Seminary, preparing for the ministry. He then did graduate work at Bonn and at Berlin and later at Harvard where he studied under William James. After a period of teaching, first at Antioch College and then at Johns Hopkins University, he became president of Clark University

198   *History of Education*

in 1888. Here he developed one of the most famous graduate schools of the country and gathered about him a group of creative students.

HIS PSYCHOLOGY. Influenced by Charles Darwin's *The Origin of Species* and the theory of evolution, Hall sought to reconcile the development of mental life with the evolutionary hypothesis. He held that mental and physical life are always parallel. The child, in his development, repeats the evolution of the race. This is the recapitulation theory. Each stage is necessary for the higher. The stages are the prenatal, the primitive, the savage, and finally civilization.

CHILD STUDY. Hall was a leader in the study of child life. In 1880 he published *Contents of Children's Minds on Entering School*. In 1891 he began publication of the *Pedagogical Seminary*. He became the leader of the Child Study Movement in this country and throughout Europe. His book *Adolescence* is his masterpiece.

HIS EDUCATIONAL PRINCIPLES : 1. The central interest of education must be in those learnings which serve the continuation of the race. The individual is incidental. 2. Emotions are more significant and fundamental than intellect. 3. In human development we see the story of racial development repeated. This recapitulation must control the steps in education. 4. Education should be based upon the growth of the child's nature and lead to a well-balanced whole. 5. Basic to a science of education are all the sciences which throw light upon human nature.

John Dewey (1859-   )

HIS LIFE. Born at Burlington, Vermont, Dewey was educated in the public schools of the town, at the University of Vermont, and at Johns Hopkins University. After teaching for a time at the University of Michigan, in 1894 he became head of the department of philosophy at the University of Chicago. Here his interest in education lead to the establishment of the University Elementary School. In 1904 he became professor of philosophy at Columbia University. Here his influence both in philosophy and in education became world-wide.

THE UNIVERSITY ELEMENTARY SCHOOL. This was opened in 1896 as a laboratory school to supplement his course in education at the University of Chicago. There was no rigid grading, the work was informal, teachers sought to test new ideas, explore new methods, and criticize results. This experiment gave birth to Dewey's famous book, *School and Society*.

THE PHILOSOPHIC PRINCIPLES BASIC TO EDUCATION

1. *His Theory of Mind and Knowledge:* The mind evolves as the organism meets and solves problems. Thus, mind has developed as a tool for dealing with the environment. This is the "instrumental" theory of mind. On the basis of this, action precedes knowledge. Learning comes from acting

and experiencing results in action. This knowledge then changes, influencing action. As the race has developed knowledge it has given to the individual instincts, impulses, and interests. These are inherited urges. Knowledge is a social instrument.

2. *How the Individual Thinks:* Thinking comes through one's effort to solve a problem. The steps in the process are: a) A felt need. b) Analysis of the difficulty. c) Possible solutions are suggested. d) These are tried mentally until one is discovered which passes the mental test. e) The accepted solution is tried in overt action. This is the scientific method of experimenting.

DEWEY'S PHILOSOPHY OF EDUCATION. Education is "the process of the reconstruction or reconstitution of experience, giving it a more socialized value through the medium of increased individual efficiency." As one faces a changing environment and makes adjustments to it, he reconstructs experience and learns. The end or aim of education is more education. The aim of education is within the process of education, not a termination of education. Thus education is growth, actual living. The school is a social institution and must be real for the child.

DEWEY'S INFLUENCE. Modern education owes much to Dewey. Progressive education stems from his ideas, but in many instances has misrepresented his philosophy. The activity program reveals his influence. Dewey's influence is one of the major factors in the great mass of experimental education being undertaken throughout the world.

BIBLIOGRAPHY

I. Primary Sources:

Dewey, John, *Democracy and Education.* New York, The Macmillan Co., 1916.

Dewey, John, *Experience and Education.* New York, The Macmillan Co., 1938.

Dewey, John, *Human Nature and Conduct.* New York, Henry Holt and Co., 1922.

Dewey, John, *How We Think.* Boston, D.C. Heath and Co., 1933.

Dewey, John, *My Pedagogic Creed.* Chicago, A. Flanigan Co., 1910.

Dewey, John, *The School and Society.* Chicago, University of Chicago Press, 1915.

Dewey, John, and Dewey, Evelyn, *Schools of Tomorrow.* New York, E.P. Dutton and Co., 1915.

Hall, G. Stanley, *Adolescence; Its Psychology and Its Relation to Physiology, Anthropology, Sociology, Sex, Crime, Religion, and Education.* New York, D. Appleton and Co., 1904.

Hall, G. Stanley, *Contents of Children's Minds on Entering School.* New York, E.L. Kellogg and Co., 1893.

Hall, G. Stanley, *Morale, The Supreme Standard of Life and Conduct.* New York, D. Appleton and Co., 1920.

Hall, G. Stanley, *Youth; Its Education, Regimen, and Hygiene.* New York, D. Appleton and Co., 1906.

Hall, G. Stanley, and some of his pupils, *Aspects of Child Life and Education.* Boston, Ginn and Co., 1907.

Parker, Francis W., *Talks on Pedagogics.* New York, John Day Co., 1937.

2. Secondary Material

Ames, E.S., et al., *Essays in Honor of John Dewey, on the Occasion of His Seventieth Birthday.* New York, Henry Holt and Co., 1929.

Childs, John L., *Education and the Philosophy of Experimentalism.* New York, The Century Co., 1931.

Dangler, Edward, "The Consequences of Parker's Educational Philosophy," *Education,* June, 1942.

Dewey, John, "In Memoriam - Col. Parker" (address). *Elementary School Teacher,* June, 1902.

Heffron, Ida Casson, *Francis Wayland Parker, a Biography.* Los Angeles, Ivan Deach, Jr., 1934.

Hook, Sidney, *John Dewey: An Intellectual Portrait.* New York, John Day Co., 1939.

Horne, H.H., *The Democratic Philosophy of Education.* New York, The Macmillan Co., 1932.

Mulhern, James, *A History of Education,* pp. 383-392. Ronald Press Co., New York, 1946.

Patridge, Leila, *The "Quincy Method."* New York, E.L. Kellogg and Co., 1886.

Pruette, Loraine, *G. Stanley Hall; A Biography of a Mind.* New York, D. Appleton and Co., 1926.

Ratner, Joseph, *Philosophy of Dewey.* New York, Henry Holt and Co., 1928.

Thomas, M.H., and Schneider, H.W., *A Bibliography of John Dewey.* New York, Columbia University Press, 1929.

Wilds, Elmer H., *The Foundations of Modern Education,* pp. 547-589. New York, Rinehart and Co., 1942.

Wilson, Louis N., *Granville Stanley Hall.* New York, G.E. Stechert and Co., 1914.

Index